KV-638-196

Why Certification Insider Press Is Number 1...

I just finished writing and passing my Networking Essentials exam (70-058). I really couldn't have done it without the aid of the Exam Cram Networking Essentials book. I actually failed my first attempt at this exam about ten days ago, and based on the area where I did poorly (Implementation), I studied this area in the book. Not only did I pass that part of the test on the second exam, **I got 100%!!!!!** I studied two other manuals (from cover to cover) that are approved Study Guides for the MCSE, and the Exam Cram was really the one that did the trick. It let me know the key points to know cold and gave excellent reference material if I wanted to know more. Also, the thing that was key, between the other two manuals and the exam cram book, all the standards and terminology, etc., were completely up to date, so you weren't second guessing yourself when it came to the exam. I will definitely be purchasing the whole line of books for my future MCSE exams.

—*Ken Campbell*
   Consultant

My boss came to me and told me that I needed to pass my NT Server 4 test within a month. Although I had been planning to take the test, I was only studying when I had extra time. Suddenly, I needed to pass it NOW! **I bought the Exam Cram** and really focused on what I needed to study. **In less than a week, I took the test and PASSED.** This was the **first time I passed a Microsoft test on my first try**! I'm ready to cram for the NT Server in the Enterprise with another Exam Cram!

—*Catherine Bostic*

Yes, **this was the best book I have ever purchased**. That is the NT Server in the Enterprise. I self-studied the materials for that test and found the test to be very difficult. I scored 675—not enough to pass. After going through your manual from cover to cover and reviewing some material, I took the test again with a **score of 895**. Thanks— your study guide helped very much and **saved me many hours of study time**!!!!

—*Darrel Corazalla*

I bought the 4-pack at a reasonable rate and am very happy with the information I am getting. I have definitely gotten much **more information than I expected** or paid for.

—*Shams Mohammad*
   LAN Administrator

These are very good books, and I have ordered several of the other books in the series based on what I have read so far. I haven't finished the book yet, but it **has a lot of information and explanations that are missing from my other study guides**.

—*Michael Towers*
   Systems Administrator

What a great idea—Cliffs Notes for NT. As a study tool, to **better focus on the exam strategy**, I think it's great. I especially like your approach of asking the question, answering the question, and most importantly explaining how the other choices were wrong, totally made-up, or not as completely correct. I feel that this is where **your books have it over any of the others**. Keep up the GREAT work.

—*Jerry Nagano*
   Systems Administrator

After reading this book **over the space of a week, I passed this Exam** (Windows NT Workstation) **with 960/1000**. I've been raving about the book so much at work, that the trainer here is looking into buying the books in bulk to stock her library.

—*Simon Pengelly*

GET ON THE ROAD TO CERTIFICATION SUCCESS

We recognize that studying for an MCSE certification exam is a monumental task. Most people fail an exam the first time around because of the enormous complexity of the MCSE program. That's why we've created our new publishing and training program, *Certification Insider Press,* to help you accomplish one important goal: to ace an MCSE exam without having to spend the rest of your life studying for it.

You've probably read, seen, or heard about one of our very popular *Exam Cram* guides. We initially published these guides to help busy people like you zero in and focus on passing an exam. Because of the overwhelming success of the *Exam Cram* guides and all the great feedback we've received, we expanded our study guide product line and now we are happy to bring you one of our new *Exam Prep* guides.

The book you have in your hands is especially designed to complement our highly successful *Exam Cram* guides. As with our *Exam Cram* series, each *Prep* book is designed not only to help you study for an exam but also to help you understand the important concepts and techniques that all MCSE professionals need to know. Inside these covers you'll find hundreds of tips, insights, and strategies that simply cannot be found anyplace else. In creating our guides, we've assembled the very best team of certified trainers, MCSE professionals, and networking course developers.

Our commitment is to ensure that the *Exam Prep* guides offer proven training and active-learning techniques not found in other study guides. We provide unique study tips and techniques, custom quizzes, techniques on understanding and applying Microsoft technologies, sample tests, and much more. In a nutshell, each *Exam Prep* guide is designed to help dig in and gain a real mastery of Microsoft networking technology. In addition to the in-depth study materials we've provided inside these pages, each *Exam Prep* comes with an interactive CD-ROM that provides high-quality practice tests that will help you prepare for an exam.

To help us continue to provide the very best certification study materials, we'd like to hear from you. Write or email us (craminfo@coriolis.com) and let us know how our *Exam Prep* guides have helped you study, or tell us about new features you'd like us to add. If you send us a story about how an *Exam Prep* guide has helped you ace an exam and we use it in one of our guides, we'll send you an official *Certification Insider Press* shirt for your efforts.

Good luck with your certification exam, and thanks for allowing us to help you achieve your goals.

Keith Weiskamp
Keith Weiskamp
Publisher, Certification Insider Press

EXAM PREP™

TCP/IP

MICROSOFT CERTIFIED SYSTEMS ENGINEER

Certification Insider™ Press

CORIOLIS

Richard Burke

The Coriolis Group, Inc.
An International Thomson Publishing Company
14455 N. Hayden Road, Suite 220
Scottsdale, Arizona 85260
602/483-0192
FAX 602/483-0193
http://www.coriolis.com

Printed in the United States of America
ISBN: 1-57610-239-4
10 9 8 7 6 5 4 3 2 1

Certification Insider Press Team

Publisher
Keith Weiskamp

Acquisitions Editor
Shari Jo Hehr

Managing Editors
Kristen Duerr
Paula Kmetz

Product Managers
Jennifer Normandin
Ann Waggoner Aken

Production Editors
Nancy Shea
Kim Eoff

Development Editor
Deb Kaufmann

Technical Editing
Gate City Consulting, Inc.

Composition and Text Design
GEX, Inc.

Cover Design
Anthony Stock

Marketing Specialist
Josh Mills

CD-ROM Developer
Robert Clarfield

Certification Insider™ Press
International Thomson Publishing I(T)P®

Published by

Albany, NY • Belmont, CA • Bonn • Boston • Cincinnati • Detroit
Johannesburg • London • Madrid • Melbourne • Mexico City • New York • Paris
Singapore • Tokyo • Toronto • Washington

ABOUT THE AUTHOR

Richard Burke is the president of a firm that specializes in computer network consulting and development of training materials related to computer networks. He has a Ph.D. in Physics and a M.S. in Computer Engineering. Prior to starting his own business, Richard was in charge of the Networking Technologies Department at Wake Technical Community College in North Carolina, where he taught a wide range of computer networking courses. He was also the director and instructor for the "Networking Fundamentals" course at the American Research Group, Inc., a commercial training organization.

Acknowledgments

In order to implement the network required for the development of this book and to do the exercises at the end of each chapter, a significant amount of hardware and software was required. The author is grateful to the publisher, Course Technology, which purchased the Windows NT 4.0 Server operating system. The help of Joanie Miller, Eldrice Murphy and Keith Snyder of the IBM PC Product Review Division in the Research Triangle Park of North Carolina was also needed to make the book possible. The Product Review Division loaned me an Intellistation Z Pro workstation and the Windows NT Workstation operating system and provided free technical support on an as-needed basis. This support included delivery of the product and a house call on one occasion. I wish doctors still did that. The second workstation used on the development network was loaned by the Multimedia Laboratory at North Carolina State University. This was the result of time and effort by Professor Mladen Vouk who provided other valuable support when asked.

There were a number of occasions when a colleague, Duane Reaugh of DTS Software, Inc. of Raleigh provided networking insight. Pin Point Software Corporation and Peter Halliday of Network World were kind enough to donate copies of Click Net and Net Draw, respectively. These software applications provide excellent network device clip art. Invaluable discussions were had with Scott Anderson and Lori Bush of Cisco Systems. Lori provided us with a copy of Ciscoworks, an excellent router management tool. John Feldmeier of Technically Elite, Inc. (formerly Network Applications Technology, Inc. [NAT]) provided a Beta2 copy of MeterWare for Windows95/NT. This is an excellent generic network management utility based on the TCP/IP protocol SNMP. The staff at Black Box Corporation, particularly Patricia Race, was helpful on a number of occasions. Black Box donated a Quick Test Plus device which, as its name implies, provides a quick test that cables are correctly connecting device interfaces.

As anyone who has ever written a book knows, the cooperation and patience of several people over a long time period are critical to success of the project. The author wishes to thank the Managing Editor, Kristen Duerr, and the Project Manager, Jennifer Normandin, of Course Technology, and the Development Editor, Mary Terese Cozzola of Writing and Editing Services, Inc. for their support in making this book possible. Finally, the willingness of a spouse to sacrifice a lot of companionship during an effort such as this cannot be overvalued. Arlene Burke contributed peace of mind throughout the process.

TABLE OF CONTENTS

FOREWORD

The big technology question for the '90s and beyond is, "Are you certified?" Certification is rapidly becoming the key to professional career enhancement for network engineers, technicians, software developers, web designers, and even professional office workers.

WHY BECOME A MICROSOFT CERTIFIED PROFESSIONAL?

Becoming a Microsoft Certified Professional can open many doors for you. Obtaining the appropriate Microsoft Certified Professional credentials can provide a formal record of your skills to potential employers. Certification can be equally effective in helping you secure a raise or promotion.

The Microsoft Certified System Engineer (MCSE) program is made up of a series of required and elective exams in several different tracks. Combinations of individual courses can lead to certification in a specific track. Most tracks require a combination of required and elective courses. (Internetworking with Microsoft TCP/IP on Microsoft Windows NT 4.0 Exam #70-059 is among the required course offerings.) Your MCSE credentials tell a potential employer that you are an expert in TCP/IP.

WANT TO KNOW MORE ABOUT MICROSOFT CERTIFICATION?

There are many additional benefits to achieving Microsoft Certified status. These benefits apply to you as well as to your potential employer. As a Microsoft Certified Professional (MCP), you will be recognized as an expert on Microsoft products, have access to ongoing technical information from Microsoft, and receive special invitations to Microsoft conferences and events. You can obtain a comprehensive, interactive tool that provides full details about the Microsoft Certified Professional Program online at **www.microsoft.com/train_cert/cert/cert.htm**. For more information on texts from Certification Insider Press that will help prepare you for certification exams, visit our site at **www.certificationinsider.com**.

When you become a Microsoft Certified Professional, Microsoft sends you a Welcome Kit that contains the following:

1. Microsoft Certified Professional wall certificate. Also, within a few weeks after you have passed any exam, Microsoft sends you a Microsoft Certified Professional Transcript that shows which exams you have passed.

2. License to use the Microsoft Certified Professional logo. You are licensed to use the logo in your advertisements, promotions, proposals, and other materials, including business cards, letterheads, advertising circulars, brochures, yellow page advertisements, mailings, banners, resumes, and invitations.

3. Microsoft Certified Professional logo sheet. Before using the camera-ready logo, you must agree to the terms of the licensing agreement.

4. Access to technical and product information directly from Microsoft through a secured area of the MCP Web site. Dedicated forums on CompuServe (GO MECFORUM) and The Microsoft Network, which enable Microsoft Certified Professionals to communicate directly with Microsoft and one another.

5. One-year subscription to *Microsoft Certified Professional Magazine*, a career and professional development magazine created especially for Microsoft Certified Professionals.

6. Invitations to Microsoft conferences, technical training sessions, and special events.

A Microsoft Certified Systems Engineer receives all the benefits mentioned above and the following additional benefits:

1. Microsoft Certified Systems Engineer logos and other materials to help you identify yourself as a Microsoft Certified Systems Engineer to colleagues or clients.

2. One-year subscription to the Microsoft TechNet Technical Information Network.

3. One-year subscription to the Microsoft Beta Evaluation program. This benefit provides you with up to 12 free monthly beta software CDs for many of Microsoft's newest software products. This enables you to become familiar with new versions of Microsoft products before they are generally available. This benefit also includes access to a private CompuServe forum where you can exchange information with other program members and find information from Microsoft on current beta issues and product information.

CERTIFY ME!

So you are ready to become a Microsoft Certified Professional. The examinations are administered through Sylvan Prometric (formerly Drake Prometric) and are offered at more than 700 authorized testing centers around the world. Microsoft evaluates certification status based on current exam records. Your current exam record is the set of exams you have passed. To maintain Microsoft Certified Professional status, you must remain current on all the requirements for your certification.

Registering for an exam is easy. To register, contact Sylvan Prometric, 2601 West 88th Street, Bloomington, MN, 55431, at (800) 755-EXAM (3926). Dial (612) 896-7000 or (612) 820-5707 if you cannot place a call to an 800 number from your location. You must call to schedule the exam at least one day before the day you want to take the exam. Taking the exam automatically enrolls you in the Microsoft Certified Professional program; you do not need to submit an application to Microsoft Corporation.

When you call Sylvan Prometric, have the following information ready:

1. Your name, organization (if any), mailing address, and phone number.

2. A unique ID number (e.g., your Social Security number).

3. The number of the exam you wish to take (#70-059 for the TCP/IP exam).

4. A method of payment (e.g., credit card number). If you pay by check, payment is due before the examination can be scheduled. The fee to take each exam is currently $100.

ADDITIONAL RESOURCES

One of the best sources of information about Microsoft certification tests comes from Microsoft itself. Because its products and technologies—and the tests that go with them—change frequently, the best place to go for exam-related information is online.

If you haven't already visited the Microsoft Training and Certification pages, do so right now. As of this writing, the Training and Certification home page resides at **www.microsoft.com/Train_Cert/default.htm**. Note that it may not be there by the time you read this, or it may have been replaced by something new, because the Microsoft site changes regularly. Should this happen, please read the next section, titled "Coping with Change on the Web."

The menu options in the home page's left-hand column point to important sources of information in the Training and Certification pages. Here's what to check out:

- **Train_Cert Summaries/By Product and Technology** Use this to jump to product-based summaries of all classroom education, training materials, study guides, and other information for specific products. Under the heading "TCP/IP," you'll find an entire page of information about TCP/IP training and certification. This tells you a lot about your training and preparation options, and mentions all the tests that relate to TCP/IP.
- **Technical Certification/Find an Exam** Pulls up a search tool that lets you list all Microsoft exams and locate all exams pertinent to any Microsoft certification (MCP, MCSD, MCSE, MCT, and so on), or those exams that cover a particular product. This tool is quite useful not only to examine the options, but also to obtain specific test preparation information, because each exam has its own associated preparation guide.
- **Site Tools/Downloads** Here, you'll find a list of the files and practice tests that Microsoft makes available to the public. These include several items worth downloading, especially the Certification Update, the Personal Exam Prep (PEP) tests, various assessment exams, and a general Exam Study Guide. Try to peruse these materials before taking your first test.

Of course, these are just the high points of what's available in the Microsoft Training and Certification pages. As you browse through them—and I strongly recommend that you do—you'll probably find other information we didn't mention here that is every bit as interesting and compelling.

COPING WITH CHANGE ON THE WEB

Sooner or later, all the specifics I've shared with you about the Microsoft Training and Certification pages, and all the other Web-based resources I mention throughout the rest of this book, will go stale or be replaced by newer information. In some cases, the URLs you find here may lead you to their replacements; in other cases, the URLs will go nowhere, leaving you with the dreaded 404 error message, "File not found."

When that happens, please don't give up! There's always a way to find what you want on the Web, if you're willing to invest some time and energy. To begin with, most large or complex Web sites—and Microsoft's qualifies on both counts—offer a search engine. As long as you can get to the site itself, you can use this tool to help you find what you need.

The more particular or focused you can make a search request, the more likely it is that the results will include information you can use. For instance, you can search the string "Training and Certification" to produce a lot of data about the subject in general, but if you're specifically looking for, for example, the Preparation Guide for Exam 70-059, Internetworking with Microsoft TCP/IP on Microsoft Windows NT 4.0, you'll be more likely to get there quickly if you use a search string such as: **"Exam 70-059" AND "Preparation Guide."** Likewise, if you want to find the Training and Certification downloads, try a search string such as: **"Training and Certification" AND "download page."**

Finally, don't be afraid to use general search tools like www.search.com, www.altavista.com, or www.excite.com to find related information. Although Microsoft offers the best information about its certification exams online, there are plenty of third-party sources of information, training, and assistance in this area that do not have to follow a party line like Microsoft does. The bottom line is: if you can't find something where the book says it lives, start looking around.

INTRODUCTION

Welcome to *MCSE TCP/IP Exam Prep!* This new book from Certification Insider Press offers you real-world examples, interactive activities, and dozens of hands-on projects that reinforce key concepts and help you prepare for the exam. This book also features troubleshooting tips for solutions to common problems that you will encounter.

An interactive CD-ROM with two complete practice exams that allow you to test your skills and knowledge makes this the perfect study guide for the Microsoft certification exam. These materials have been specifically designed to help individuals prepare for Microsoft Certification Exam #70-059, "TCP/IP." Answers to end-of-chapter review questions and projects are also found on the CD-ROM.

ABOUT THE BOOK

To aid you in fully understanding TCP/IP concepts, there are many features in this book that have been designed to help you logically work through and confidently prepare for the exam.

- **Chapter Objectives** Each chapter in this book begins with a detailed list of the concepts to be mastered within that chapter. This list provides you with a quick reference to the contents of that chapter, as well as a useful study aid.

- **Illustrations and Tables** Numerous illustrations aid you in the visualization of common setups, theories, and architectures. In addition, many tables provide details and comparisons of both practical and theoretical information.

- **Chapter Summaries** Each chapter's text is followed by a summary of the concepts it has introduced. These summaries provide a helpful way to recap and revisit the ideas covered in each chapter.

- **Key Terms** Following the Chapter Summary, a list of new TCP/IP terms and their definitions encourages proper understanding of the chapter's key concepts and provides a useful reference.

- **Review Questions** End-of-chapter assessment begins with a set of review questions that reinforce the ideas introduced in each chapter. These questions not only ensure that you have mastered the concepts, but are written to help prepare you for the Microsoft certification examination.

- **Hands-on Projects** Although it is important to understand the theory behind this technology, nothing can improve upon real-world experience. With the exception of those chapters that are purely theoretical, each chapter provides a series of exercises aimed at providing you with hands-on implementation experience.

- **Case Projects** Finally, each chapter closes with a section that proposes a real-world situation. You are asked to evaluate the situation and decide upon the course of action to be taken to remedy the problems described. This valuable tool helps the reader sharpen decision-making and troubleshooting skills.

TEXT AND GRAPHIC CONVENTIONS USED IN THIS BOOK

Wherever appropriate, additional information and activities have been added to this book to help the reader better understand what is being discussed in the chapter. Icons throughout the text alert readers to additional materials. The icons used in this book are described below.

Note icons present additional helpful material related to the subject.

Tip icons highlight suggestions on ways to attack problems you may encounter in a real-world situation. The author has practical experience with how TCP/IP works in real business situations.

Caution icons appear in the margin next to concepts or steps that often cause difficulty. Each caution anticipates a potential mistake and provides methods for avoiding the same problem in the future.

Hands-on project icons precede each hands-on activity in this book.

Case project icons are located at the end of each chapter. They mark a more involved, scenario-based project. In this extensive case example, readers are asked to independently implement what they have learned.

WHERE SHOULD YOU START?

This book is intended to be read in sequence, from beginning to end. Each chapter builds upon those that precede it, to provide a solid understanding of internetworking with TCP/IP. After completing the chapters, you may find it useful to go back through the book, and use the review questions and projects to prepare for the Microsoft certification test for TCP/IP (#70-059). Readers are also encouraged to investigate the many pointers to online and printed sources of additional information that are cited throughout this book.

DON'T MISS IT! VALUABLE INFORMATION AT THE END OF THE BOOK

In addition to its core materials, this book includes information that is worthy of further investigation.

- **Appendix: Useful Windows NT TCP/IP Diagnostic Utilities** The diagnostic utilities provided by Windows NT that were found to be most useful in demonstrating the concepts that are covered and to analyze the results are described.
- **Glossary** This is a complete compendium of all of the acronyms and technical terms used in this book, with definitions.

HARDWARE AND SOFTWARE REQUIREMENTS

Before You Begin

Individuals who wish to get the most from these materials should have access to a networked PC that is running Microsoft Windows 95, Windows NT Workstation 4.0, or Windows NT Server 4.0. If you have access to a Web browser, you will be able to complete all of the exercises in this book. The following table summarizes the requirements and recommendations (in parentheses) for each of these operating systems:

Item	Windows 95	NT Workstation 4.0	NT Server 4.0
MB RAM	16 (32)	12 (64)	16 (64)
MB Disk space	90 (200)	116 (400)	124 (1,000)
CPU	386/16 (486+)	486/33 (Pentium)	486/33 (Pentium)
Display type	VGA(SVGA)	VGA(SVGA)	VGA(SVGA)
Network	Yes	Yes	Yes

When it comes to any of these operating systems, it's wise to meet the recommended configurations, rather than the minimum configurations. While each of them will work at the minimum configurations, such systems will be slow and sometimes painful to use. In fact, it's nearly impossible to give any of these operating systems too much memory, disk space, or CPU power. These various Windows environments almost exemplify the notion that "more is better" when it comes to such things.

SYSTEM REQUIREMENTS FOR TEST PREP SOFTWARE:

- 8 MB RAM (16 MB recommended)
- VGA/256 Color display or better
- 4X CD-ROM Drive
- Windows NT 4.0 or Windows 95

ABOUT THE CD-ROM

To become a Microsoft Certified Professional, you must pass rigorous certification exams that provide a valid and reliable measure of technical proficiency and expertise. The CD-ROM that comes with this book can be used in conjunction with the book to help you assess your progress in the event you choose to pursue Microsoft Professional Certification. The CD-ROM contains specially designed test simulation software that features two 58-question practice exams. The questions were expertly prepared to test your readiness for the official Microsoft certification examination on TCP/IP (Exam #70-059). The practice exam questions simulate the interface and format of the actual certification exams.

PRACTICE EXAM FEATURES:

- 58 questions, just like the actual exam
- 90-minute timed test to ensure exam readiness
- Questions can be marked and answered later
- Graphical representation of your test grade

SOLUTIONS TO END-OF-CHAPTER QUESTIONS AND PROJECTS

For further help in making sure you are prepared for the TCP/IP certification exam, we have included solutions for the end-of-chapter Review Questions, Hands-on Projects, and Case Projects on the CD.

COMMUNICATIONS ARCHITECTURES

This chapter provides you with a review of communications architecture concepts. This book examines one communications architecture: the **Transmission Control Protocol/Internet Protocol (TCP/IP)** and its implementation with Microsoft Windows NT 4.0. The purpose of this chapter is to highlight concepts that form the basis of network communications in general and are fundamental to the topics covered in this book.

IN THIS CHAPTER YOU WILL:

LEARN ABOUT PEER-TO-PEER COMMUNICATIONS ARCHITECTURE

LEARN ABOUT CLIENT/SERVER COMMUNICATIONS ARCHITECTURE

LEARN ABOUT THE OSI REFERENCE MODEL

LEARN ABOUT LOCAL AREA NETWORK (LAN) COMMUNICATIONS

LEARN ABOUT FRAMES

LEARN ABOUT WIDE AREA NETWORK (WAN) COMMUNICATIONS

LEARN ABOUT THE CASE PROJECT

COMMUNICATIONS ARCHITECTURES

Architecture is the art and science of designing and building structures. In a **communications architecture**, the structure is not a tangible object, such as a house or school, but rather a system of rules and practices that enable computers to share information over a network. The architectural structure of a house precedes any other step in its completion, such as installing electrical wiring or putting up drywall. Similarly, in a computer network, the communications architecture underlies all other processes involved in connectivity, including hardware (such as cables connecting the computers) or software (such as the network operating system or application programs). Just as a building is constructed of many integrated parts, a working communications architecture requires the integration of many **protocols** (rules). Both a building and a communications architecture are too complex to be constructed from only one element. Therefore, as you will see, several protocols are combined to construct a communications architecture. Finally, the roof of a building depends on the building for support. Application programs, such as word processing, spreadsheet, or database software, are the "roof" of a communications architecture in that they require network resources and so are supported by the communications architecture.

There is no one communications architecture—many are in use today. These include IBM's System Network Architecture (SNA), Digital Equipment Corporation's DECnet, Banyan's Vines, Apple's AppleTalk, the Microsoft and IBM NetBIOS Extended User Interface (NetBEUI), Novell's IPX/SPX, TCP/IP, and the Open System Interconnection (OSI) Model. Each of these architectures was developed according to a slightly different approach. Some architectures are designed with a particular operating system in mind—for example, TCP/IP and the UNIX operating system, and AppleTalk and the Macintosh operating system. However, if the appropriate software interface module is provided, most communications architectures can be made to work with any operating system. This interoperability is common in today's networking environment. For example, even though NetBEUI is the communications architecture native to Microsoft Windows Networking, the emphasis of this book is on the use of the TCP/IP architecture with Windows NT 4.0.

The application programs that you run on your computer have been designed to work with a particular operating system, such as DOS or Windows. The function of operating systems is to manage the resources on your computer and, in so doing, to satisfy your request for service. However, when your application program makes a request for service that requires the request to be passed across the network to a server, the **Network Operating System** (**NOS**) in the server will handle that request. A network operating system is one that is designed to handle many simultaneous requests for service and to provide secure file sharing. The NOS must have access to the same communications architecture as the computer that sent the request. In the networking environment that is explored in this book, workstations using the Windows NT 4.0 Workstation operating system and servers using the Windows NT 4.0 Server operating system use the same communication architectures. Thus communication is not a problem. If you were to add a computer to the network that is running a different operating system, such as DOS or Macintosh System 7.x, your server would need an additional software module that would translate the request from the "foreign" operating system into one that could be understood by Windows NT 4.0 Server. In the next section, two categories of communications architectures that are used in Local Area Networks (LANs) today are examined. A **LAN** is a network of limited size. Information is broadcast by one computer attached to the LAN and every other machine on the network reads the destination address included with the information. The machine to which the information is addressed processes the information.

PEER-TO-PEER COMMUNICATIONS ARCHITECTURE

A peer is one who is in equal standing to others in some respect. Your peers might be your coworkers at a company or your fellow students in school. A **peer–to–peer communications architecture** is an architecture in which every machine on the network has the same resources. In the context of communications architecture, **peer–to–peer communication** means that the PCs that are communicating with one another have the same hardware and software capabilities and the same level of responsibility. In a peer-to-peer network, every machine can talk directly to every other machine without the help of any other computer or device on the network. The primary purpose of a peer-to-peer network is to share resources such as a printer, hard drive, application program, or database. Every peer is in total control of all of its resources and has to manage those resources. Access privileges to those resources are determined by that machine. Peer-to-peer communication is an important capability of Microsoft Windows Networks.

In a peer-to-peer network, the operating system of each networked computer needs to perform more tasks than it performs when it is used as a standalone computer. In addition to supporting the programs that run on the local computer, it must provide occasional service to other computers on the network, and it will use network resources to do so. In order to provide such service, the operating system must be enhanced with communications architecture software such as one of the types described previously. Microsoft Windows NT 4.0 Workstation provides this enhancement. Other operating systems that support peer-to-peer LANs include UNIX, Macintosh System 7.x, Windows for Workgroups, and Windows 95. Figure 1-1 shows Peers 1 and 2 sharing application programs, Peers 2 and 3 sharing data files, and Peer 4 using a shared network printer.

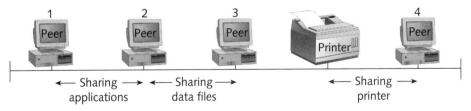

Figure 1-1   Typical peer-to-peer architecture

The obvious *advantage* to the peer-to-peer communications architecture is that everyone can share everyone else's resources to the degree allowed by each peer. If one peer lacks a resource—a printer, for example—it may be able to use that of another peer. The obvious *disadvantage* to this communications architecture is that everyone has some control over everyone else's resources. That can lead to problems with privacy and productivity. If other computers on the network have complete access to your computer, other users can access all of your files. Also, your PC's processing power decreases whenever too many other PCs are reading files from your hard drive or using your processor to do some of their work. Thus, peer-to-peer architectures are typically best used for small networks where these potential problems can be more easily managed.

CLIENT/SERVER COMMUNICATIONS ARCHITECTURE

In contrast to peer-to-peer architecture, in a client/server architecture there is central control of network resources. The server stores application programs and data files, manages access to them, and sends them over the network to a client when requested. Thus it is even possible for a client computer not to have nonvolatile storage resources such as a floppy disk, CD-ROM, or hard drive. In a **client/server communications architecture**, one or more server computers are designated to serve several other computers by providing resources. These resources often include attached printers, network printers, hard drives, application programs, and databases, and may also include remote services such as e-mail over the Internet. The primary *advantage* of this architecture is that the burden of supplying the resources is carried by the server computer, so that each client computer is free to support only the individual using it. In addition to freeing up individual computer resources, the client/server communications architecture facilitates software installation because programs can be installed and upgraded on the server instead of on every individual computer. As the central point of network control, the server effectively implements privacy and security.

Figure 1-2 shows a simple client/server network containing one server.

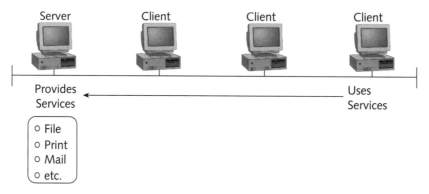

Figure 1-2   Typical client/server architecture

More specifically, the advantages of the client/server architecture derive from the following:

- The client's primary function is to service the local user.
- The server's primary function is to provide service to clients.

- The server hardware and software are optimized to provide fast, reliable, and secure service to simultaneous requests from clients. This can be accomplished because:

1. Only one PC, which is equipped with the best hardware, has to be utilized to provide service to many users.

2. Only the server needs to be provided with a large amount of primary storage, **dynamic random access memory** (**DRAM**). After a file is requested the first time by a client, it is kept in DRAM. On a large network, many clients may make a request for the same file. Because the server does not have to resort to accessing the slower hard drive, network throughput is significantly enhanced.

3. With a large DRAM, buffer storage to handle many simultaneous requests can be increased.

4. Cache memory, the most expensive form of RAM, provides the fastest access to information, by using static random access memory (SRAM) technology. **SRAM** is used to store items that are most often used by the operating system, and to keep track of the location of specific files that are stored on the hard drive. It is a temporary holding place for data being written to or retrieved from system devices such as the hard drive. With only one computer, the server, requiring large amounts of SRAM, the price is affordable.

5. In a NOS, the server's instruction set and the server's file system are optimized to serve clients. This results in a "lean" operating system that executes quickly. Novell and Banyon Vines have been the major providers of such NOSs, and now Windows NT 4.0 Server is doing so as well.

6. In any network where multiple users access the same file or program, security is a very important issue. Security is built into a server NOS. This approach minimizes, the number of extra program instructions that are required to implement security when security is an add-on, and maximizes the number of security mechanisms.

7. The reliability of the network can be significantly enhanced by providing the server with a number of hard drives that contain the same information. If one drive fails, the server automatically switches to another.

8. Because of its comprehensive resources, a server can perform additional client services, such as mail and print services, and a connection to a wide area network. A **wide area network** (**WAN**) is a network of unlimited size that is composed of a network of switches that route messages between computers or networks attached to those switches. The telephone network is an example of a WAN.

In view of the server functionality just described, the client can concentrate on providing:

- A user-friendly environment with a **graphical user interface** (**GUI**) such as Windows 3.1, Windows 95, or Windows NT

- Execution of programs that are stored on the client or that are obtained from the server over the network

The client requires a software module that is not always needed by the server. This module is usually referred to as a **redirector**. The redirector intercepts application program requests for service and directs them to the local operating system if the resources needed are local, or to the communications architecture if the resources are on the server.

The diagram on the right of Figure 1-3, labeled General Environment, shows the typical software environment of a client.

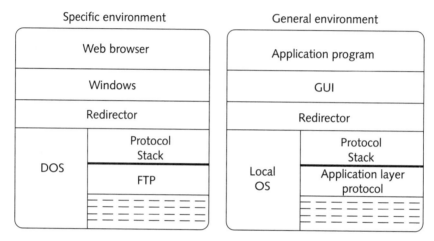

Figure 1-3   Typical client software environment

This software environment consists of an application program, a GUI, the redirector, the local operating system, and the **protocol stack** (the term *protocol* is defined in detail in the next section). The *Protocol stack* is the name that is commonly used to refer to a communications architecture. The term *protocol stack* is appropriate because a communications architecture is implemented by chaining together a set of software modules, each of which implements one of the protocols in the stack. The *application layer* is the top layer in the protocol stack. The diagram on the left of Figure 1-3 is specific to the title of this book. It shows a Windows GUI and implies that the TCP/IP protocol stack is being used because FTP is a TCP/IP application layer protocol. In the next section, you will examine the details of a protocol stack.

THE OSI REFERENCE MODEL

In this section you will examine the nature of protocol stacks in more detail. This examination is necessary because you need to understand the functions of the different layers of the TCP/IP protocol stack in order to use it with Windows NT 4.0.

In diplomatic circles, a protocol is a set of procedures that are followed to simplify the meetings of heads of state. These procedures, or rules, make it possible for each participant to anticipate the behavior of their counterparts. Thus these rules expedite personal communication. In the context of data communications, a **protocol** is the set of rules that *must* be followed in order for two devices to communicate. In this context, these rules do expedite communication, but they must be followed exactly in order for any communication to take place.

You could construct one large, integrated set of rules that implement network communications. However, such a large set would be difficult to check for correctness, manage, and later modify if new features were to be added. For example, if you later found a more efficient or useful way to rewrite part of the software implementation of the protocol, you would have to check the influence of the change on every line of code in the program. You might even have to rewrite the entire program.

Because there are so many functions that a communications architecture must provide, it is designed according to the "divide and conquer" approach. This approach leads naturally to the protocol stack. Vendors can develop software implementation of protocols for one layer that are independent of implementations for any other layer. Standardized interfaces are then used to integrate these protocols into a working architecture. Each protocol implementation can be independently improved, as long as the interfacing implementations are not changed. No protocol implementation needs to take into account the details of the implementation of another protocol in the stack.

An expanded view of a protocol stack is shown in Figure 1-4.

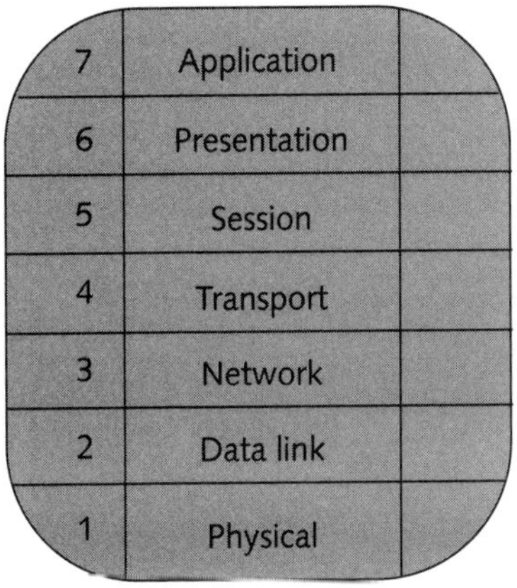

7	Application
6	Presentation
5	Session
4	Transport
3	Network
2	Data link
1	Physical

Figure 1-4 The OSI Reference Model

This seven-layer stack of protocols is called the **Open Systems Interconnection (OSI) Reference Model.** This reference model was established by the International Organization for Standardization (**ISO**) in 1983 in order to provide a target for the future development of interoperable communication standards. The ISO charter is to encourage, facilitate, and document the cooperative development of standards that meet with international approval. Although most protocol stacks in use today do not map exactly to the OSI Reference Model, the model is almost universally referenced when explaining protocol stack concepts. Protocols have been developed that do conform exactly to the OSI model, and the long-term goal of the standards organizations has been to have all developers convert to this model. The TCP/IP protocol stack consists of four layers, rather than the seven layers of the

OSI model. Nevertheless, the functions performed are essentially the same. The TCP/IP stack was conceptualized and developed in 1974 by an agency of the U.S. Department of Defense (DOD), the **Advanced Research Projects Agency** (**ARPA**). It is the most popular stack in use today. TCP/IP was originally tested on a network that included only a few academic institutions. This network became known as the **ARPANET**. Soon other networks attached themselves to the ARPANET, and the Internet was born. The **Internet** is an interconnected set of networks that uses the TCP/IP suite to provide seamless communication, as if the Internet were one homogeneous network.

The OSI model will be discussed first, and then a comparison to other models in use today will be presented.

Each of the seven layers in the OSI model is labeled in Figure 1-4. The function of each layer is described in the following.

 The ISO/IEC 8802-3 standard is an international standard that incorporates the ANSI/IEEE 802-3 standard.

PHYSICAL LAYER

This layer defines the electrical, mechanical, functional, and procedural specifications for the hardware that connects a device to the network. For example, a standard that is developed for the Physical layer would specify a connector's size and shape, the exact number of pins it should have, the signals that can be used on the circuits attached to those pins, and the functions performed by each circuit. This is the layer where bits are transformed into voltages. The Electronic Industries Association/Telecommunications Industries Association (**EIA/TIA**) standard 232-E is a good example of a Physical layer specification. It defines precisely the connectors and cable that connect a computer and a modem. Two other examples of Physical layer devices are the network interface card (NIC) and the repeater. The **ISO/IEC standard 8802-3** specifies the interfaces of these devices to a LAN. The NIC and repeater contain a **medium access unit** (**MAU**) that receives signals from the network and transmits signals onto the network. A **NIC** provides the physical interface between a network device, such as a computer, and the network. A **repeater** connects LAN segments, amplifies the signal received from one segment, and transmits it onto the other segment.

DATA LINK LAYER

This layer specifies the procedures that are followed in order to achieve reliable point-to-point transfer of information between two devices on a network. The ISO/IEC standard 8802-3 specifies an implementation of the OSI Data Link layer protocols. In this implementation, the Data Link layer is divided into two sublayers: the Logical Link Control (**LLC**) sublayer and the Medium Access Control (**MAC**) sublayer. This division provides a convenient distribution of labor between functions that ensure reliable transmission and functions that ensure orderly access to the network medium, respectively. For a computer attached to a LAN, the MAC sublayer implements the Carrier Sense Multiple Access with Collision Detection (CSMA/CD) access method. **CSMA** means that a computer waits until there is no signal from any other computer on the LAN before it sends a message. **CD** means that this approach does not always work—collisions of signals occur, and the two or more computers wanting to send messages wait different amounts of time before trying to send their messages again. The MAC sublayer constructs the frame, the basic unit of information transferred from one device to another on the network. The best example of a Data Link device is the bridge. A **bridge** connects two segments of a LAN. It receives frames from one segment and forwards them to the next segment. Unlike the repeater, the bridge implements the MAC sublayer as well as the Physical layer. Using the hardware destination address in the MAC header of the frame, the bridge decides if the frame should be forwarded to the next network.

 You will be examining the format of TCP/IP addressing in detail in Chapter 5 "IP Addressing."

NETWORK LAYER

In contrast to the point-to-point information transfer function of the Data Link layer, the Network layer provides the mechanisms for transporting a packet from the source network to the destination network. A **packet** is the message that is processed by the Network and higher layers of the protocol stack. A packet is encapsulated by the header and trailer constructed by the MAC sublayer of the Data Link layer to form a frame. In a multinetwork system, such as the Internet, networks are connected by routers. It is the **router**'s job to pass the packet to another network that will get the packet closer to its destination. The Network layer provides the IP addresses of the source and the destination networks. The format of a network address varies depending on the protocol stack that is being used.

TRANSPORT LAYER

This layer provides both "reliable" and "unreliable" transport protocols. The reliable protocol, which is called the **Transport Control Protocol** (**TCP**) in the TCP/IP stack, provides the mechanisms that ensure that the packet sent by an application program in the source computer is the same packet received by an application program in the destination computer. In essence, TCP provides end-to-end error detection and recovery. TCP is also responsible for inserting information that requests a specific type of service in the packet. For example, the requested service could (1) use the fastest networks, or (2) use the least expensive networks. The unreliable transport protocol, which is called the **User Datagram Protocol** (**UDP**) in the TCP/IP stack, places no constraints on the network. Best-effort delivery from the application program in the source machine to the application program in the destination machine is all that is requested. UDP is used when speed is of the essence, and the effort spent on ensuring reliability is not cost-effective. Whether it is TCP or UDP that is used, application-to-application communication is requested by specifying the source and destination ports of the communicating programs. A **port** is a number that serves as an ID for a process that is either sending or receiving a packet. A port ID is mapped to an address in memory by the operating system.

SESSION LAYER

The Session layer provides the mechanisms necessary to "open" and "close" multiple logical connections between processes on different PCs. It is a software-implemented switch. A logical connection exists when two processes in different computers are able to send packets to one another. Many logical connections can use the same physical connection. The Session layer also makes it possible to have many-to-many process connections. Figure 1-5 is a schematic diagram of the Session layer implementing multiple sessions between a process in the client computer and a process in the server computer.

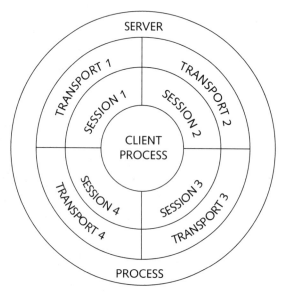

Figure 1-5   The function of the Session layer

To better understand this figure, let's use a specific example. Assume that you are using a Web browser client application program. The Web browser is represented by the client process in the circle at the center of the diagram. This Web browser can obtain a variety of services from a single remote Web server process when you click on different links in the browser window. Each service requested by the browser is considered a session. Different sessions between the browser and the remote server process require different support from the Transport layer. The Session layer protocol opens these different logical connections when you click on links, and closes them after the requested data is transferred to the client.

PRESENTATION LAYER

The Presentation layer provides an interface between the Application layer and the layers below the Presentation layer. The layers below the Presentation layer use information in a format that is useful for transmission across the network. This format is called **transfer syntax**. It is basically a byte stream formatted according to **Basic Encoding Rules** (**BER**), which are designed to be used for representing packets sent across a network. The Application layer encodes information in a generic, language-independent format that is more useful for the management of information. This generic format is called **abstract syntax notation.1** (**ASN.1**). ASN.1 represents information in a hierarchical structure. The Presentation layer translates between these two formats. The Presentation layer also translates transfer syntax into machine language used by the local machine. The Presentation layer is responsible for compression and encryption of information, and the reverse processes. A familiar protocol in the Presentation layer is the **Virtual Terminal Protocol**, which allows a PC to emulate a terminal of a remote computer.

APPLICATION LAYER

The Application layer contains software that provides common services needed by application programs such as word processors, spreadsheets, and e-mail. This approach not only minimizes the amount of "network awareness" that application programs need to have, but also increases efficiency by eliminating the need to include common services in each application program. One of the most prominent examples of an Application layer protocol (although not one used by the Application layer of the OSI stack) is the TCP/IP **File Transfer Protocol** (**FTP**). In Figure 1-3, you first saw that FTP was an Application layer protocol in the TCP/IP stack. As its name implies, a request for a file is passed from the client application program to the FTP process in the Application layer of the TCP/IP protocol stack. This request is formed into an IP packet by the Transport layers of the stack and transmitted in a frame to the server. The protocol stack in the server transports the request to the FTP server process in the Application layer, which finds the requested file and returns it to the client application program.

Figure 1-6 summarizes the communication services between PCs that are provided by the OSI protocol stack.

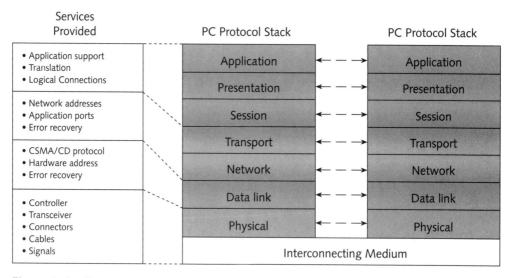

Figure 1-6 Communication services provided by the OSI protocol stack

In Figure 1-6, the diagram on the far left is a brief list of the services provided by the different layers of the protocol stack. The dashed lines with arrows between the protocol stacks of the two PCs represent the logical connections between peer layers in each PC. The lines are dashed because they represent logical connections, not physical connections.

Figure 1-7 presents a comparison of DOD TCP/IP, NetWare, and OSI stacks to the Windows NT 4.0 Server environment.

7	Application	Process/Application	Processes				NetWare Core Protocols
6	Presentation		File System Servers				
5	Session		Redirectors				
			TDI				
4	Transport	Host to Host	Net BEUI Transport	TCP/IP Transport	NW Link Transport	Apple Talk Transport	SPX
3	Network	Internet					IPX
2	Data link	Network Interface					
1	Physical						

OSI stack   DOD TCP/IP stack   Windows NT 4.0 Server Environment   Netware stack

Figure 1-7 Comparison of DOD TCP/IP, NetWare, and OSI stacks to the Windows NT Server networking environment

The Process/Application layer of the TCP/IP stack and the NetWare Core Protocols layer of the NetWare stack perform approximately the functions of the OSI Application, Presentation, and Session layers. There is also good functional overlap of these three stacks at the Transport and Network layers. Below these layers, different approaches are taken to the interface with the network.

The Windows NT Server environment integrates the protocol stacks shown. NetBEUI is the default stack used on Microsoft networks. NW Link is a stack that provides compatibility with NetWare networks. AppleTalk is used to provide connectivity to networks of Macintosh computers. Although not shown, the Data Link Control (DLC) stack, used for connection to IBM mainframes, is also provided. Above the Transport layer, the correspondence of the Windows NT 4.0 environment with the OSI stack is more difficult to perceive. The Transfer Device Interface (TDI) and the Redirectors' layers are "Session" layer entities, and as such serve as software switches that make connections between the Transport layers below and the processes above. The **redirectors** are application programming interfaces (APIs) called by application programs depending on which transport stack the application program wants to use. The redirector makes a call to the **TDI**, which provides the connection to the stack indicated in the call. **File system servers** perform a "Presentation layer" function. They translate between the NTFS file system, which is used to manage storage in the server, and the file systems understood by clients on the network. **NTFS** is the Windows NT file system that is typically used on Windows NT 4.0 Servers because it provides faster access to large volumes, compared to the FAT system, and because it contains enhanced security features. The **Processes** layer contains the many server processes, which include most of the DOD TCP/IP processes as well as others unique to the Windows NT 4.0 environment.

Now that the communications architecture concepts have been examined, the next step is to see how they are used on a network. Let's start with communication on a LAN.

Twisted pairs will be discussed later in this chapter.

LAN COMMUNICATION

LANs can be implemented with coaxial cable, optical fiber cable, or twisted pairs of wires, which are commonly used in existing telephone connections, or they can be wireless. Figure 1-8 shows conceptually what a LAN looks like when the interconnecting medium is coaxial cable or optical fiber, or when it is wireless.

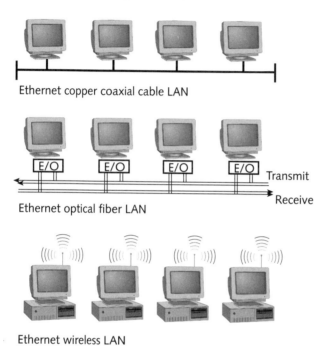

Ethernet copper coaxial cable LAN

Ethernet optical fiber LAN

Ethernet wireless LAN

Figure 1-8 Three types of Ethernet LANs

Figure 1-9 shows examples of interconnecting media in more detail.

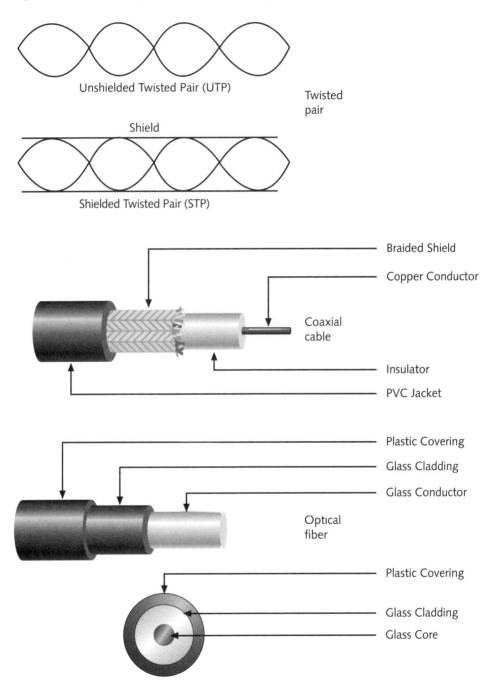

Figure 1-9   Types of Ethernet media

The coaxial cable was the dominant LAN interconnecting medium for many years because of its large bandwidth and immunity to electrical interference. The ISO/IEC standard 8802-3 imposes the constraints indicated in Figure 1–10 on "thinnet" coaxial cable LANs.

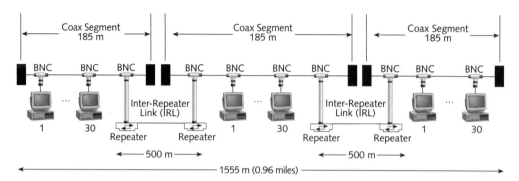

Figure 1-10   10BASE2 Ethernet specifications

Thinnet is a term used to distinguish the thinner, 0.25-inch-diameter, more flexible coaxial cable from the thicker, 0.50-inch-diameter, more rigid coaxial cable first used, which is called **"thicknet."**

The ISO/IEC standard 8802-3 specifies that a single thinnet LAN segment should be no longer than 185 meters and that no more than 30 devices should be attached to it. Thinnet is called **10BASE2** cable, a shorthand for saying that the cable operates at a transmission rate of 10 Mbs, that it uses baseband (meaning that the complete frequency spectrum of the cable is available to the transmitter), and that the maximum length of a segment without repeaters is 185 meters (185 has been rounded off to 200 meters in this shorthand). No more than five segments are allowed in a single LAN, and at most three of these can have devices attached. The other two segments are "inter-repeater" segments. Thus a single thinnet LAN is limited to 90 devices if the standard is followed. Segments are connected by repeaters, which amplify the signal and then transmit it to the adjacent segment. The combined length of all segments cannot exceed 1555 meters. All of these constraints are imposed to ensure that the CSMA/CD medium access method will work properly.

Figure 1–11 shows how a LAN is constructed using twisted pairs of wires. This configuration is called a **10BASET** Ethernet. **T** stands for twisted pair.

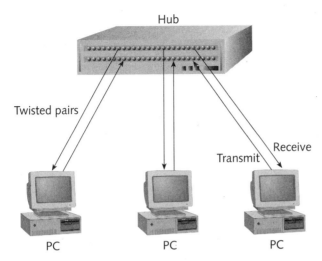

Figure 1-11   10BASET Ethernet configuration

Each PC is connected to a hub. The **hub** is a multiport repeater. Every transmission received by the hub on one port is amplified and retransmitted out all other ports. This arrangement forms a LAN in which there are only two devices in a segment: the transceiver in the PC and the transceiver in the hub. The maximum length of any segment is 100 meters. Each segment contains two twisted pairs of wires. One pair is used to transmit a signal to the hub, and the other is used to receive a signal from the hub. Hubs and twisted pairs of wires dominate Ethernet installations today. One reason for this is the convenience of having a single location for access to connections to all PCs on the LAN. Another reason is that new installations of twisted pair wiring in buildings using Category 5 cable achieve the same signal quality that once required coaxial cable. The EIA/TIA has specified twisted pair wiring according to category. The thickness of the wire, the number of twists per foot, and other parameters determine the **category** number. Category 5 is the category of wiring used today for data rates up to 100 MHz. Large LANs can be constructed by cascading hubs in a tree-like structure. Hubs can also be attached to coaxial cable segments to form a hybrid media LAN.

In a company environment, everyone would like to be able to communicate with everyone else. However, it is typical that people in different departments don't do this all the time, because different departments focus on different types of work. In order to eliminate unnecessary traffic and increase useful network throughput, it is desirable to have different departments on different LAN segments and to allow intersegment traffic only when necessary. To accomplish this the bridge is used. As was mentioned in an earlier section of this chapter, the function of a bridge is to pass only those frames that are destined for a PC on another segment. Like a PC, a bridge has a protocol stack. It consists of two layers, the Physical and Data Link layers. The bridge uses the MAC sublayer of the Data Link layer to read the destination field in the frame's MAC header. If the frame is for a PC on the LAN from which the frame was received, the bridge discards the frame. Otherwise the Bridge retransmits the frame onto the adjacent LAN segment. Figure 1-12 shows a Bridge connecting two LAN segments.

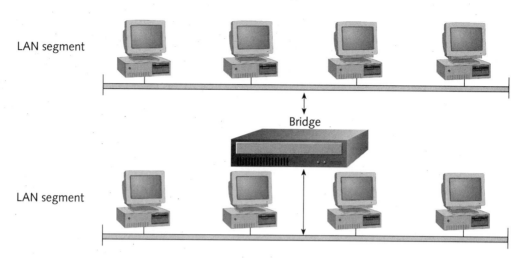

Figure 1-12   Bridge connecting two LAN segments

FRAMES

PCs communicate by sending messages to one another over the interconnecting medium. These messages are called **frames**, the smallest unit of information that is sent. Frames consist of bits, which are either a one (1) or a zero (0). Electronics on your NIC convert the bits into voltage pulses that are sent over the interconnecting medium. On the typical Ethernet LAN, bits are transmitted at the rate of 10 million per second. When an application program makes a request for service from another computer on the network, this request consists of a packet of bits that is passed to the top of the protocol stack. Each layer of the stack adds its bits to the packet received from the layer above, to form a larger packet. These added bits are called a **header**. A header tells the peer layer in the destination computer how to process the packet it receives. In the OSI Reference Model, after the Data Link layer has added its header, the frame is complete and is transmitted.

To better understand this cooperative effort between peer layers, let's compare it to the Postal Service communication process. The steps that occur in each process are compared in Table 1-1 and diagrammed in Figures 1-13 and 1-14.

Table 1-1 Steps in the Postal Service and Network Communication Processes

Steps	Postal Service	Network
1	Raleigh division director	Application program
2	Document	Application program data
3	Cover letter	Protocol stack headers
4	Destination address	Destination address
5	Return address	Source address
6	Envelope	MAC header and trailer
7	Postal Service bag	Source computer transmit buffer
8	Regional post office	LAN default router
9	Boston division	Destination computer receive buffer
10	Intradivision mail process	Protocol stack
11	Boston division director	Application program

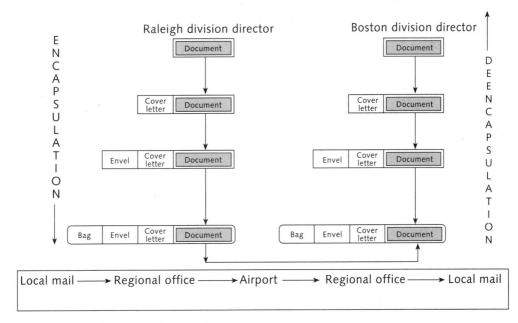

Figure 1-13 The Post Office mail process

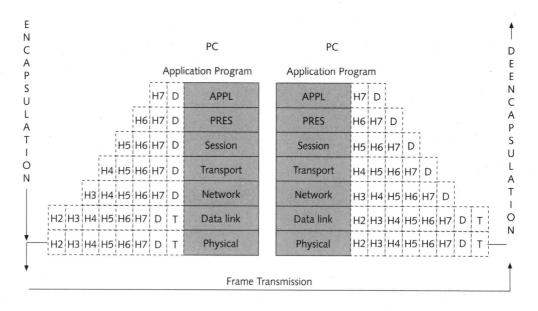

D= Data;   H= Header;   T=Trailer

Figure 1-14   Communication of a frame between PCs

The great similarity between these two structures suggests that human beings tend to follow the same organizational patterns no matter what process we are organizing. In both diagrams we see that there are processes of encapsulation and de-encapsulation taking place. **Encapsulation** refers to enclosing one layer inside another, like the layers of an onion. **De-encapsulation** means removing the layers of the "onion." In the Postal Service diagram, the document is encapsulated in a cover letter, then an envelope, and then a bag. In the network communication diagram, the data being sent by the application program is encapsulated in six headers. At the destination, each step of de-encapsulation reads the header provided by the peer encapsulation step, and then it discards that header, resulting in information that is delivered to the Boston division director (in the case of the Postal Service process) and to the application program (in the case of the network communication process). An important point to be made is that both processes require a lot of overhead to work. **Overhead** is defined as the nonproductive part of a process. In these two cases, the overhead is incurred because of the distance between the communicating entities. For example, in a direct asynchronous communication between two computers, the frame contains a message that consists of 8 bits, 1 start bit, and 1 stop bit. The overhead is therefore 2 bits out of 10 bits, or 20%.

Now let's look more closely at the network communication process shown in Figure 1-14. This figure shows the protocol stacks of two PCs communicating. The frame is constructed in the PC on the left of the figure. The data (D) from the application program is passed to the Application layer of the protocol stack. The Application layer adds its header (H7) and passes H7 and D to the Presentation layer. The Presentation layer adds its header (H6) and passes H7, H6, and D to the Session layer. Passing continues until D and H7–H3 reach the Data Link layer. The Data Link layer adds H2, and also a Trailer (T). No information is added by the Physical layer, so there is no header H1. The frame is now complete. The data has been encapsulated within all the headers necessary for it to be transported to and processed by the destination PC, where de-encapsulation takes place.

The bits in the frame are converted by the transceiver on the NIC in the source PC into voltage pulses, and these pulses are transmitted across the network to the destination PC. The frame is received by the Physical layer, which is represented by the transceiver of the destination NIC, and is passed to a DRAM buffer on the NIC. The transceiver controller signals the PC's interrupt controller that a frame has been received. An **interrupt** is a signal that indicates to the operating system which device needs its attention. The operating system calls the process that gets the frame and passes it to the MAC sublayer of the Data Link layer. At each step of the de-encapsulation process, a header is read and discarded and the part of the frame that remains is passed to the next higher layer in the protocol stack. Finally, only the data remains and is passed to the designated application program.

 You will examine the Ethernet II frame in much more detail in Chapter 4: "The TCP/IP Protocol Suite."

To conclude the present discussion about frames, let's consider a well-known frame format, the Ethernet II frame, which is shown in Figure 1-15. This is the frame primarily used by TCP/IP.

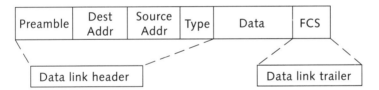

Figure 1-15   Ethernet II frame

The smallest units of information in the frame are bits. Frames are always constructed of an integral number of 8-bit units called **bytes**. The frame is subdivided into a number of fields, each of which has a specific function necessary for the communication process. These fields are constructed as the information passed down the protocol stack. Table 1-2 describes each of these fields.

Table 1-2   Description of the Fields in the Ethernet II Frame

Field	Bytes	Description
Preamble	8	Used by the destination PC to synchronize with the bit rate of the source PC
Destination address	6	Hardware address of the NIC in the destination PC in hexadecimal digits. An example of a hardware address for a card made by 3COM is 00-60-8c-5a-17-2f. Each pair of hexadecimal digits is one byte.
Source address	6	Hardware address of the NIC in the source PC in hexadecimal digits
Type	2	The hexadecimal ID of the network layer protocol. When using the IP network layer, the ID = 0800.
Data	46-1500	Includes data from the application program and all headers created by the source protocol stack
FCS	4	Frame Check Sequence, created by the source PC and used by the destination PC to check the accuracy of the frame received

WIDE AREA NETWORK COMMUNICATIONS

This chapter's discussion has thus far centered on communications architectures used by PCs to broadcast information over a LAN to other PCs on that LAN. This type of communication requires only that the PCs be linked by a single medium, such as a cable. However, networks often incorporate many LANs, including LANs that are separated by large distances. LANs separated by large distances are connected by serial links, such as the link provided by a modem and the public telephone network. As mentioned earlier in this chapter, such networks are called wide area networks (WANs).

Enterprise networks, or **intranets**, are networks that provide global connectivity for a company. Intranets can be part of or independent of the Internet. In addition to connection by modem, remote or global connectivity can be provided directly by private or leased networks such as T1 lines, optical fiber lines, and microwave. **T1** lines provide a serial service at 1.544 megabits per second. Optical fiber and microwave links provide much greater data rates. Additional devices and protocols are needed to make connections to WANs. One device, the modem, has been mentioned.

In a company environment, a connection to the company's intranet or to the Internet will make use of a router. **Routers** are multiport computers that are designed to connect networks and, when necessary, to isolate networks from one another. As its name implies, a router routes frames. A router, like a bridge, has a protocol stack. The router stack contains the Physical layer, the Data Link layer, and the Network layer. The Network layer allows the router to examine the destination network address. The router maintains a routing table in which it can find the interface needed to retransmit the frame and minimize the distance that the frame has to travel to reach its final destination.

Figure 1-16 shows a simplified view of how routers and modems might be used to provide intranet connectivity for a company.

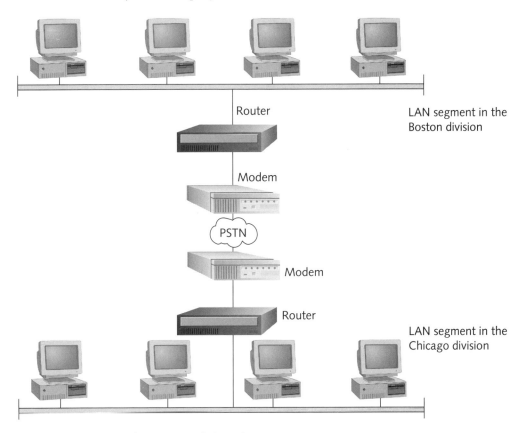

Figure 1-16   A simple company intranet

In Figure 1-16, we are connecting a LAN segment in the Boston division of the company to a LAN segment in the Chicago division of the company. The router becomes another device connected to the LAN segments. A serial port on the router is connected to a modem, and the modem is connected to the telephone system PSTN. The remote link formed in this way is another network with a router at each end. The modems are considered to be end points of the PSTN.

CHAPTER SUMMARY

- Peer-to-peer and client/server network communications architectures were examined.

- The peer-to-peer architecture, of which Microsoft Windows for Workgroups is an example, is a good choice for small networks on which the users want to share files and programs.

- A primary advantage of the client/server architecture is that it provides centralized storage, management, and security for files that can be accessed by clients over the network. This architecture also allows the client computer to focus on doing work for only one client and on providing a user-friendly environment for that client.

- You saw how a computer communications architecture is constructed by examining the functions of the layers in the protocol stack of the OSI Reference Model. This stack was compared to others that are used today, and to the Windows NT 4.0 environment, which you will use in this book.

- Typical topologies of Ethernet LANs, LAN communications media, the CSMA/CD medium access method, and the structure of frames were discussed.

- You learned that a LAN constructed using a twisted pair medium requires a hub to connect the computers.

- A bridge is used to connect segments of a LAN, in order to filter traffic between LANs. A router is used to connect a LAN to a WAN.

REVIEW QUESTIONS

1. For which of the following reasons would you choose to install a peer-to-peer network instead of a client/server network?

   a. In a client/server network, users cannot control who accesses their files.

   b. You do not want one department to communicate with another department.

   c. There are only a few network users, and you want them to be able to share files directly.

2. Which of the following is the correct reason for installing a client/server network instead of a peer-to-peer network?

   a. The client/server architecture provides better control and management of network resources.

   b. The client/server architecture is less expensive to install.

   c. Data transfer rate (bits/sec) is greater in the client/server architecture.

3. Which layer in the OSI protocol stack is responsible for reliable point-to-point communication on a LAN?

   a. The Network layer

   b. The Physical layer

   c. The Data Link layer

4. Which layer in the OSI protocol stack is responsible for reliable end-to-end communication between application programs?

   a. The Data Link layer

   b. The Transport layer

   c. The Session layer

5. Which layer in the OSI protocol stack is responsible for managing communications between client and server processes on different PCs?

   a. The Application layer

   b. The Presentation layer

   c. The Session layer

6. Which layer in the OSI protocol stack is responsible for providing services that are needed by most application programs?

   a. The Physical layer

   b. The Session layer

   c. The Application layer

7. What is the primary disadvantage of client/server computing compared to standalone computing?

   a. Client/server computing requires a network.

   b. Client/server computing is subject to transmission errors.

   c. The inherent overhead required for client/server computing.

8. What is a hardware address?

   a. The address of a network

   b. An IP address

   c. The address of a network device

9. How many bits does an Ethernet hardware address contain?

   a. 16

   b. 32

   c. 48

10. What number system is used to express the hardware address?

   a. The decimal number system

   b. The hexadecimal number system

   c. The binary number system

11. What is the maximum number of PCs that you can attach to a 10BASE2 LAN segment?

   a. 90

   b. 48

   c. 30

12. How long is a 10BASE2 LAN segment allowed to be?

   a. 100 feet

   b. 185 meters

   c. 500 meters

13. How many devices are attached to a twisted pair segment of a hub?

   a. 2

   b. 16

   c. 5

14. What does a PC do with a frame when the PC is not the intended recipient?

   a. Forwards it to the intended destination

   b. Stores it in RAM on the NIC

   c. Discards it

15. What does a bridge do when it receives a frame that has a destination address that is on the network from which it was received?

   a. Returns it to the sender

   b. Discards it

   c. Forwards it to the other network to which it is attached

16. Why does a router need a protocol stack that contains a Network layer?

   a. To determine whether the frame is destined for this router

   b. To know what PC should receive the frame

   c. To determine the destination network of the Network layer packet

17. How many circuits are there in an RJ-45 cable? (See the Case Project in the next section.)

   a. 2

   b. 4

   c. 8

18. How many circuits in the RJ-45 cable are used in a twisted pair network? (See the Case Project in the next section.)

    a. 2

    b. 4

    c. 8

19. How many circuits does a coaxial cable contain?

    a. 1

    b. 2

    c. 3

20. What is the purpose of the Type field in the Ethernet II frame?

    a. To specify the type of medium that is being used

    b. To specify the type of frame that is being used

    c. To specify the type of protocol header that starts the Data field

CASE PROJECT

A Case Project will serve as the focus of the exercises throughout this book. This project follows the steps that you would take to produce a working communications architecture for a small company that consists of three divisions that are geographically separated. By completing the hands-on exercises in each chapter, you will have installed the complete company architecture when you reach the end of this book. Depending on your school or work environment, you may not be able to actually implement all or any of the steps. However, the steps and the results they generate are described in the detail necessary for you to think your way through the steps, if you are not able to put them into practice.

An overview of the desired company connectivity is shown in Figure 1-17.

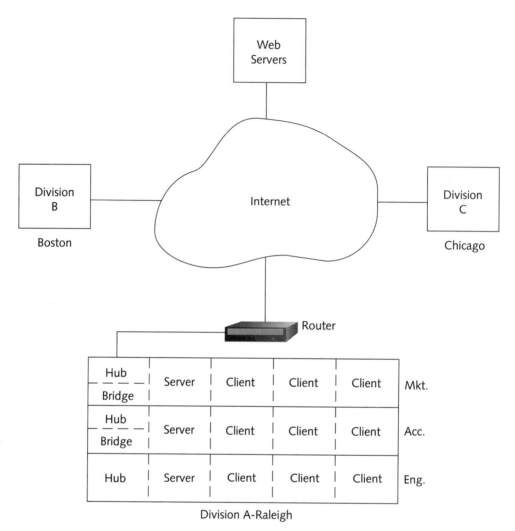

Figure 1-17   Case Project environment

The company consists of three divisions that need to be interconnected. Each division has a building that is identical to the building in Raleigh. The Raleigh building has three floors with three employees working on each floor. All employees want to be able to communicate with all other employees in the company. The machines on each floor are attached to a twisted pair LAN. Bridges connect the floors. Employees on the first floor work in the Engineering Department. Those on the second floor work in the Accounting Department, and those on the third floor work in the Marketing Department. Most of the time, it is only necessary for employees in the same department to share information. Occasionally, employees in different departments and in different divisions need to communicate. You will also want to provide employees access to Web servers on the Internet. Windows NT 4.0

Workstation will be installed on the client computers, and Windows NT 4.0 Server will be installed on the server computers. The building is wired with Category 5 twisted pair.

Figure 1-18 provides a closer look at the layout of the network in the Raleigh division.

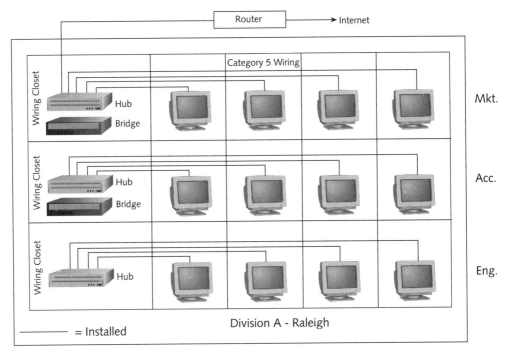

Figure 1-18   Raleigh division network environment

The layout of the Boston and Chicago divisions will be the same as shown for the Raleigh division. Although the company is small, the communications architecture required will contain many of the components used by a contemporary company. Let's further examine the communications architecture requirements, using Figure 1-18.

The building is wired with Category 5 **unshielded twisted pair (UTP)** cable. **Twisted pair** means that each circuit in the cable consists of two copper wires that are twisted around one another, each covered with an insulating material. This twist helps to eliminate electromagnetic pickup from other equipment in the area that produces electrical noise in the wires. Category 5 UTP cable contains four twisted pairs, in which the copper wires are either solid or braided, and are American Wire Gauge #24 (AWG 24). **Unshielded** means that there is no metallic covering surrounding the group of pairs. Cable that meets the Category 5 standard can be used in a LAN at data rates up to 100 megabits per second, if the cable lengths are no longer than 100 meters. Category 5 wiring is being installed in new buildings today. You can assume that Category 5 wiring has been installed in all buildings owned by your company.

The lower the AWG #, the thicker the wire.

The networks in each division will be established by connecting the Category 5 building wiring to the hubs that are housed in **wiring closets**. This term is derived from telephone wiring closets. Telephone wiring closets typically exist on each floor of a building. From these closets, telephone repairmen can access all the telephone circuits on one floor and the connections to other floors. There are also bridges in the wiring closets. The bridges will be used to control traffic between floors. The router will be used to connect the Raleigh network to a WAN.

As was mentioned earlier in this chapter, hubs are multiport repeaters. A frame received from a network device attached to one interface of the hub is amplified to a standard voltage level and retransmitted out of all the other interfaces. All other network devices attached to the hub receive the retransmitted frame. However, only the device whose hardware address is in the destination address field of the transmitted Ethernet frame will process the frame. The other devices will discard it. In order to connect to the hub, each device must have a NIC installed. The NIC plugs into one of the bus slots on the motherboard of a device and is the hardware that transmits and receives frames. The NIC has a connector on it, which, for a twisted pair network, is named **RJ-45** and is similar in appearance to the telephone connector named **RJ-11**. An RJ-45 connector contains eight pins, while an RJ-11 connector has four pins. Computers are connected to the hub by a twisted pair cable that has an RJ-45 connector on each end. One end plugs into the NIC and the other into a wall jack having an RJ-45 connector. From the wall jack, twisted pair cable runs within the wall or ceiling of the building to the wiring closet.

Figure 1-18 shows the current status of the network environment in the Raleigh building. In the next chapter, you will install the Windows NT 4.0 Server operating system on a computer that you want to be one of the servers in the Raleigh building.

WINDOWS NT 4.0 INSTALLATION

You can install utilities using the Control Panel window after the installation of Windows NT 4.0.

The installation of Windows NT 4.0 Server can take from one to four hours, depending on CPU speed, amount of RAM, and the number of resources installed.

Because of the highly interactive nature of the installation process, the exercises for this chapter, which would normally be done in the Case Project section, will consist of the installation steps within the chapter. If you are unable to install Windows NT 4.0 at this time, read through the steps to learn what the process involves. If you plan to do an installation now, read through the installation steps described in this chapter before proceeding.

The installation steps and their descriptions were generated by an actual installation of Windows NT 4.0 Server. The installation of Windows NT 4.0 Workstation is similar but simpler. By reading through the steps, you will be able to decide in advance which components of the system you want to install and what information you need to gather. These steps also provide you with a record of the installation process, which can be referred to later. Such a record can be useful because you can only return to any particular step in the installation process by starting the installation from the beginning.

IN THIS CHAPTER YOU WILL:

IDENTIFY SYSTEM REQUIREMENTS FOR WINDOWS NT 4.0 INSTALLATION

GATHER SYSTEM INFORMATION THAT YOU WILL NEED DURING THE INSTALLATION

STEP THROUGH THE WINDOWS NT 4.0 SERVER INSTALLATION

SYSTEM REQUIREMENTS

Table 2-1 lists the system requirements for installation of Windows NT 4.0 Server and Windows NT 4.0 Workstation operating systems that are specified in the manuals distributed with these products. Also distributed with operating system software is the *Windows NT Hardware Compatibility List* booklet. This booklet lists all hardware that had tested successfully with Windows NT 4.0 at the time the *List* was compiled.

Table 2-1   System Requirements for Installing Windows NT 4.0
Server and Workstation

Row	Windows NT 4.0 Server	Windows NT 4.0 Workstation
1	486DX/33 or higher, DEC Alpha, Power PC, or MIPS R4x00	Same as server requirements
2	Hard disk with 124 MB minimum free space on the partition that will contain the server system files	Hard disk with 117 MB minimum free space on the partition that will contain the workstation system files
3	High-density 3.5 in. disk drive	High-density 3.5 in. disk drive
4	CD-ROM drive unless installing over a network	CD-ROM drive unless installing over a network
5	16 MB	12 MB
6	Network interface card (NIC) with the appropriate connector for your network	Same as server requirement
7	Driver for your NIC	Same as server requirement
8	Driver for your CD-ROM	Same as server requirement
9	VGA or higher resolution monitor	Same as server requirement

If you want to be able to *dual boot* Windows NT 4.0 with any other operating system, you should create a separate partition on the hard disk for the other operating system. If the other operating system is MS-DOS, you will need to install the driver that came with your CD-ROM and include its path in the CONFIG.SYS file. You will also need the file MSCDEX.EXE (Microsoft CD-ROM extensions), which comes with MS-DOS 6.22 or can be found in the Windows 95 "Windows" subdirectory. MSCDEX.EXE translates between the CD-ROM file format and the MS-DOS file format (FAT). The path to MSCDEX.EXE should be placed in your AUTOEXEC.BAT file. Windows NT operating systems provide many drivers for CD-ROMs and NICs. A **driver** is a software extension of the operating system, and controls the operation of devices such as NICs. However, you should have the drivers that came with the devices for your system handy. The installation process gives you opportunities to install those drivers if necessary.

INSTALLATION PREPARATION

You may be able to start the Setup program directly from the CD-ROM if your (basic input/output system) (**BIOS**) allows it. Setup disks would then not be required. The BIOS is a set of files, installed in ROM (read-only memory) on the motherboard, that initializes the startup process when you turn on the computer and provides input/output functions for the operating system.

Both Windows NT 4.0 Server and Windows NT 4.0 Workstation installation media consist of three setup disks and one CD-ROM. The setup disks contain the program that installs the Windows operating system executive and other files that guide you through interactive configuration of your system. The setup disks also contain the program that installs the Windows NT 4.0 files from the CD-ROM onto your hard drive.

The Windows NT manuals provide World Wide Web (WWW) addresses that can be used to get updates on hardware that is now known to be compatible with the NT operating systems. The addresses are: **http://www.microsoft.com/hwtest**, **http://www.microsoft.com/ntserver/hcl/hclintro.htm**, and **ftp://microsoft.com/bussys/winnt/winnt_docs/hcl**. There is also the **Microsoft Download Service** (**MSDL**), which is direct modem access to a variety of technical information. Dial (206) 936-6735; connect using 1200, 2400, 9600, or 14,400 baud, no parity, and 8 data bits and 1 stop bit. Then there is the **Microsoft Fast Tips** service, an automated service that provides answers to common technical questions. The number for Personal Systems Products is (800) 936-4200. The Business Systems number is (800) 936-4400.

Windows NT 4.0 provides a comprehensive set of system files and utilities. Thus, getting Windows NT 4.0 to work correctly with your hardware can be a challenging experience. If you just turn on your machine and start the installation process without doing the homework suggested in the introduction to this chapter, you may not have a successful installation. If you can do so, obtain a copy of the *Windows NT 4.0 Hardware Compatibility List* and check the WWW information before you buy a system on which you will be running Windows NT 4.0.

If you will be installing onto an existing computer, make a table of vendor names, models, versions, and identifying numbers of hardware devices such as disk drives, modems, video cards, sound cards, NICs, and Small Computer Systems Interface (**SCSI**) adapters in your machine. Also note the configuration parameters recommended in the original instruction manuals. Some examples of devices, and parameters that you may need to specify for these devices during installation, are listed in Table 2-2.

Table 2-2   Typical Configuration Parameters of Computer System Devices

NIC	CD-ROM	Modem	Mouse	Audio	Printer
Driver (e.g., Etherjet ISA)	Driver (e.g., Mitsumi FX)	Driver (e.g., Harmony)		Driver (e.g., OPL3-Sax)	Driver (e.g., HP 690C)
Bus type (e.g., ISA or PCI)				Bus type (e.g., ISA)	
	Controller (e.g., IDE or SCSI)				
		COM port ID (e.g., COM 2)	COM port ID (e.g., COM 1)		LPT ID (e.g., LPT1)
IRQ setting (e.g., 9)	IRQ setting (e.g., 15)	IRQ setting (e.g., 3)	IRQ setting (e.g., 5)	IRQ setting (e.g., 10)	IRQ setting (e.g., 7)
DMA setting (e.g., 3)				DMA setting (e.g., 1)	
Memory, (e.g., DC000)				CD-ROM interface (e.g., IDE)	
Port address (e.g., 300h)		Port address (e.g., 03E8h)	Port address (e.g., 03F8)	Port address (e.g., 530h)	Port address (e.g., 0378h)

As Table 2-2 shows, there are many parameters that must be correctly specified for a system to work properly on a network. Some of these parameters are set automatically by the BIOS. The parameters in Table 2-2 that cause the most problems when you are configuring a system are the IRQ settings and the COM port IDs. Most computers have only two COM ports, and the number of available IRQ settings is very limited.

Trouble Shooting

If you are unable to find an IRQ number that will work with one of your legacy adapters, disable a plug-and-play adapter using the Network utility of Control Panel. This may release an IRQ number that can be used. Then reenable the plug-and-play adapter. The plug-and-play adapter may be able to use an available IRQ number.

Windows NT parallel ports, such as a printer port, do not use IRQs. This frees up one IRQ, such as IRQ 7 or 5.

IRQ settings range from 0 to 15, and many of these are used by the operating system. Each hardware component must have a unique IRQ setting. When a device wants to make data available, for example when an NIC receives a frame from the network, it signals the IRQ controller, using the bus line that corresponds to its assigned IRQ. From this IRQ setting, the IRQ controller computes a number that maps to the location in RAM of the driver for the device, and then sends that information to the CPU. The CPU calls the operating system, which then starts the execution of the device driver. Thus, if two devices have the same IRQ setting, one of them will not get the right driver, and typically neither device will function.

Of the IRQ settings that are available, some may not be usable by a device. Plug-and-play adapters are often used today. Their parameters are automatically configured by the operating system from the pool provided by the adapter. Using plug-and-play adapters is convenient, but if a legacy adapter is installed later, there may not be an IRQ available that it can use. A **legacy adapter** is one that uses the ISA bus and must be configured by setting jumpers on the NIC or by using software to set the parameters. The **ISA bus** is the Industry Standard Architecture bus that was first used in the IBM PC computer design. It is the basic 8-bit or 16-bit bus that connects computer system devices. Today's plug-and-play adapters often use the PCI bus. The **PCI bus** is the Peripheral Component Interface bus, the local bus that connects the processor and RAM. The data rate on the PCI bus is much higher than that on the ISA bus. Collect the disks that contain drivers for all the devices on your system. If Windows NT 4.0 does not include these drivers, you will install them from the disk that came with the device.

There are three files that you *must* read, and another that is helpful to read. SETUP, README.WRI, and NETWORK.WRI are the must-read files, and PRINTER.WRI is helpful. SETUP is a text file on the CD-ROM. It contains information about known difficulties that can occur during installation, depending on the devices that you have installed in your computer. The README.WRI file is found in the C:\WINNT\SYSTEM32 directory after installation. It contains important information about all aspects of installing and using Windows NT 4.0. The NETWORK.WRI file is found in C:\WINNT after installation. This file contains network-related information in addition to that found in README.WRI. The PRINTER.WRI file contains tips about printer drivers for Windows NT 4.0 and about using drivers designed for Windows 95 and earlier Windows NT versions.

THE INSTALLATION STEPS

Before you read the installation steps that follow, you can get a "real-time" feel for some of the screens you will encounter during an actual installation by looking at the Windows NT Server Installation Simulator that is on the disk provided with this book. (Some of the installation steps also include actual screens.) Insert this disk into drive A:. From Windows, click the drive icon. You will see two files: README.TXT and WINNTSIM.EXE. Click **readme.txt** to see how to use the simulation WINNTSIM.EXE. Click **winntsim.exe** to start the simulation, and then follow the instructions on the screens.

Step 1: Setup Disk 1

If your system does not start from drive A:, press the **Delete** key during the startup of your computer and check the CMOS database to see if the start sequence is A, C, as it should be.

The standard installation begins with your system turned off and Setup Disk 1 inserted into the A: drive. You see the following on the screen when you turn on your computer:

    A. Setup is loading files

    B. Loading Windows NT Executive

    C. Loading Hardware Abstraction Layer

    D. Insert Disk 2 and press Enter

Step 2: Setup Disk 2

You see the following on the screen:

    A. Loading Windows NT configuration

    B. Loading Windows NT setup

    C. Loading PCMCIA support. (**PCMCIA** is the PC Memory Card International Association. It was established in 1989 to standardize a method for connecting peripherals to PCs. PCMCIA support includes drivers for, and software configuration of, PCMCIA cards in laptop computers.)

    D. Loading Video driver

    E. Loading Floppy driver

    F. Loading Keyboard driver

    G. Loading FAT file system. (**FAT** stands for File Allocation Table. It has long been the standard method for managing the distribution of file clusters on hard disks.)

Step 3

You see the following at the top of the next screen, all by itself: Microsoft Windows NT 4.0 Build 1381 xxx MB RAM. **Build 1381** means that modules of this operating system were assembled and tested 1381 times. **xxx MB RAM** is the amount of RAM in this particular machine. After a few moments you are presented with a screen that reads, "Welcome to Setup."

Step 4

After the Welcome screen appears, you can choose from one of four options:

    A. Learn more

    B. Setup now

    C. Repair a previous installation

    D. Quit setup

Click **Learn more** first. It will provide you with some additional guidance about installation. After reading Learn more, click **Setup now**.

2

Step 5

You see the following on the screen:

    A. Setup automatically detects floppy disk controllers and standard ESDI/IDE hard disks without user intervention. (**ESDI/IDE** stands for Enhanced Small Device Interface/Integrated Drive Electronics. It specifies a drive that has a high data transfer rate and a controller that is integrated with the drive.)

    B. Detection of SCSI and CD-ROM drives can cause computers to malfunction. Therefore you can skip mass storage device detection and manually select SCSI, CD-ROM, and Disk Array Controllers . (A daisy chain of many devices of any type can be attached to a SCSI adapter on a computer bus.) Press the S key to skip mass storage detection.

Click **Enter** to allow Setup to detect mass storage devices. You are asked to insert **Setup Disk 3**.

Step 6: Setup Disk 3

The following are examples of what you might see on the next screen, depending on what devices are installed in your computer:

    A. Loading device drivers

    B. Found IDE CD-ROM <ATAPI 1.2> PCI IDE Controller

    C. Found Adaptec AHA - 294x/AHA - 394x/AIC - 78xx SCSI controller

    D. Press S to install other drivers from disk. Otherwise press ENTER.

Pressing Enter produces the following for this particular computer:

    A. Loading NT File System (NTFS) (NTFS is a file system that is provided by Windows NT. It provides more file security than the FAT file system and faster access to large files or files in large partitions.)

    B. Loading IDE Device driver

    C. Loading SCSI CD-ROM driver

    D. Loading SCSI driver

    E. Loading CD-ROM file (This is the file that translates between the FAT file system and the CD-ROM file system.)

Items B through E in the above list are the drivers that must be in RAM to control the devices that allow installation to continue.

Step 7

The next screen reads, "Insert CD-ROM." After inserting the CD-ROM, you see the Microsoft Licensing Agreement. This agreement is several pages of information governing use of Windows NT 4.0 Server and Windows NT 4.0 client software. Be sure to read about choosing whether to use the server software in Per Server mode or Per Seat mode. These terms are also described in Step 17, where this choice must be made. You must accept all terms of the Agreement by pressing F8 before you can continue with the installation.

Step 8

You are now provided with the first Setup screen, which displays:

A. Install a fresh copy of Windows NT?

B. Upgrade current copy in C:\WINNT? (This statement appears if you have a current copy in that directory.)

Click **Install a fresh copy of Windows NT**.

Step 9

You are next presented with a screen that says that Setup has determined that your computer has particular hardware and software components. In the case of the IBM Intellistation Z Pro computer, on which this installation is being performed, you see:

A. Computer: MPS Uniprocessor PC

B. Display: Auto Detect

C. Keyboard: XT, AT or Enhanced (83–104 keys)

D. Keyboard layout: US

E. Pointing Device: Logitech mouse port mouse

If the content of the list you see is not correct for your computer, you can change the list at this time. If the list is correct, press **Enter**.

Step 10: Partitioning the Hard Drive

 You will need more than 124 MB for the Windows NT 4.0 Server partition if files other than system files will be in this partition. 500 MB is a good choice, if you have it available.

A hard drive usually contains more than one disk. Each disk has tracks on both sides. Tracks with the same diameter on all disks constitute a "cylinder." The information on the hard drive is therefore stored on a set of cylinders. One or more cylinders form a partition. Partitions are totally independent and can be treated as if they were different physical drives.

Partitioning allows multiple operating systems to reside on the same hard drive. The next screen shows the partition information in the case of this IBM computer.

2

    A. C:\WINNT (FAT)   512 MB (Contains Windows NT 4.0 Workstation)

    B. Unpartitioned space   3781 MB

The options are to:

    A. Delete the current partition (C:) and reuse

    B. Create a new partition in the unpartitioned space

If creating a new partition on the unpartitioned space is chosen, you are presented with a screen which, for this IBM computer, says:

    Create New Partition on 4299 MB disk 0 at ID 0 on bus 0 on aic 78xx

    Create partition of size _____

You type in the desired partition size in MB. As you saw in Table 2-1, a minimum of 124 MB is required for the Windows NT 4.0 Server operating system.

You are then presented with a screen that shows the status of the disk partitions after your choice is made. For this computer, which has a 4.29 GB hard drive and 800 MB selected for the new partition, you would see:

    C: FAT <WINNT>   518 MB

    D: New <unformatted>   800 MB

    Unpartitioned   2981 MB

To install Windows NT on the new partition and to see the next screen, press **Enter**.

Step 11: Formatting the New Partition

You can format for the FAT file system now and convert to NTFS later without having to repartition and lose all data on the partition.
Formatting took about three minutes on this machine but will vary, depending upon the size of the partition and your hardware.

On this screen you are asked the following questions:

    Format using the FAT file system?

    Format using the NTFS file system?

You can use either, depending on the following considerations:

    A. If you want operating systems other than Windows NT 4.0 to have access to the files, click Format using the FAT file system.

    B. If you want the advantages of Windows NT file security and fault-tolerance mechanisms, click **Format using the NTFS file system**.

Step 12: Location for Windows NT files

On this screen, you choose where to have the Setup program install the Windows NT files. The default directory is:

\WINNT

You can type in another location if you like, or press **Enter** to accept the default directory.

Step 13: Examination of Hard Disk(s) for Corruption

On this screen, you can choose either:

A. Exhaustive exam

B. Basic exam

The exhaustive exam only took two minutes on this machine, which has one 4.29 GB disk. After the exam and pressing **Enter**, some files are copied from the CD-ROM to the new partition. At this point, you are asked to **Remove the diskettes and CD-ROM** from the computer and to press **Enter** to restart the computer. This is the end of the Text mode of the Setup program.

Step 14: Choices of Operating Systems

When the system restarts, you are presented with the possible choices of operating systems from which a choice will be made later. In the case of this computer, one sees:

A. Windows NT 4.0 Server

B. Windows NT 4.0 Workstation

C. Windows NT 4.0 [VGA]

When Windows NT is started by selecting item C, the default VGA driver is loaded, and other drivers that are being loaded are shown. You do *not* make a selection here. The Windows NT 4.0 Server operating system loads, and you are provided with the next screen.

Step 15

This screen asks you to **Insert the CD-ROM** and to press **Enter**. When you do, files are loaded. You are then presented with the first of the screens that make up the Graphics mode part of the installation.

Step 16: Windows NT Setup Wizard

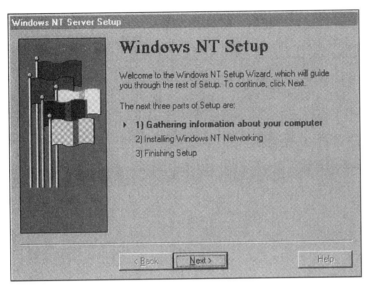

Figure 2-1   Windows NT Setup: Gathering information about your computer

The next three parts of Windows Setup are:

A. Gathering information about your computer

B. Installing Windows NT Networking

C. Finishing Setup

Click the **Next** button on this screen to begin using the Gathering information dialog boxes.

Step 17: Preparation of the Windows NT Directory

A. Name of Owner: _____

B. Organization: _____

Click the **Next** button

C. Registration CD key: _____ _____ (This key is on the back of the CD-ROM) box. You must type it in to proceed.

Click the **Next** button.

Selection of Per Seat mode is permanent. You cannot change back to Per Server mode.

D. Licensing Mode: Check one of the following:

- Per Server Mode: Number of concurrent sessions for which you have Client Licenses for the Windows NT 4.0 Server operating system: _____.

    (You can change to Per Seat Mode at any time.)

- Per Seat Mode: (Microsoft describes this mode as follows: "The Per Seat licensing mode requires a client access license for each computer that will access a particular BackOffice product on any server. Once a computer is licensed for a particular product, it can be used to access that product on any computer running Windows NT Server.")

Click the **Next** button

E. Computer Name: _____ (This is a name that must be unique on the Windows NT domain and is the name of this server.)

Click the **NEXT** button.

Domain controllers will be discussed in detail in Chapter 8: "Windows NT Domains."

F. Server Type: Check one of the following:

- Primary Domain Controller

- Backup Domain Controller

- Stand-Alone Server

You must check **primary domain controller (PDC)** if there is no other PDC on your domain. The PDC maintains a database of domain computer and user accounts. A **backup domain controller** maintains a copy of this database that is synchronized with that on the primary domain controller. **A standalone (member) server** is a server that does not store a copy of the domain's database. It maintains its own database of users and does not participate in authenticating domain user logon information.

Click the **Next** button

A password is not required to continue. You can log on to a domain as Administrator after installation without a password. However, since an Administrator has full access to domain resources, it is recommended that you set the password now. Be sure to store it in a safe place because you will need it in order to log on and create accounts for other users. The password is case-sensitive.

2

G. Administrator Account

Fill in the password for the domain Administrator account and confirm it.

Password: _____

Confirm Password: _____.

Click the **Next** button.

Step 18: Emergency Repair Disk

 An emergency repair disk can be created at any time after installation with the RDISK utility. The RDISK utility is accessed by clicking **Run** in the Start menu, typing **Rdisk** in the text box, and then clicking **OK**.

Check one of the following:

- Yes, create an emergency repair disk (recommended). Provide a 3.5 inch diskette and follow the instructions that will appear if you choose this option.
- No, do not create an emergency repair disk.

Click the **Next** button to obtain the screen shown in Figure 2-2 on which you can select optional software to install.

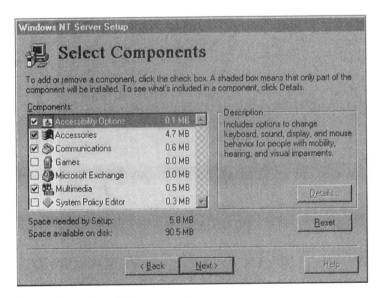

Figure 2-2   Select Components

Step 19: Selecting Software Components for Installation

Components selected will be installed from the CD-ROM onto the hard drive. Table 2-3 describes some of the options that can be selected from the Figure 2-2 screen.

 You can add options after installation from the Control Panel window.

Table 2-3   Software Options That Can Be Selected for Installation

Options Groups	Options
Accessibility	Options that provide other types of computer access for people with disabilities
Accessories	Calculator, clock, etc.
Communications	Chat, Hyperterminal, and Phone Dialer
Games	Solitaire, pinball, etc.
Multimedia	MIDI (Musical Instrument Digital Interface), etc.
Windows Messaging	Internet Mail, Microsoft Mail, Windows Messaging

You highlight a group and click the **Details** button on the screen to see the options for that group. You then select the desired options in that group and click the **OK** button on the Details screen. This action returns you to the screen in Figure 2-2. If you selected any options in a group when you were in the Details dialog box, you will see that the check box is checked. If you did not select all of the options in a group, the box will be checked and will also be gray. Continue this process for the other options groups. After selecting all options desired, click the **Next** button to install the selected options and to go to the next Wizard Setup screen, which is shown in Figure 2-3.

Step 20: Windows NT Setup Wizard

> **A.** Gathering Information
>
> **B. Installing Windows NT Networking**
>
> **C.** Finishing Setup

This is the start of the networking installation phase. Click the **Next** button to go to the next screen, which is shown in Figure 2-4.

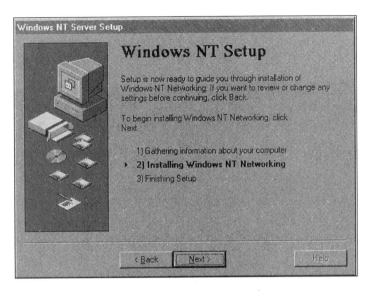

Figure 2-3   Installing Windows NT Networking

Step 21: Network Access Selection

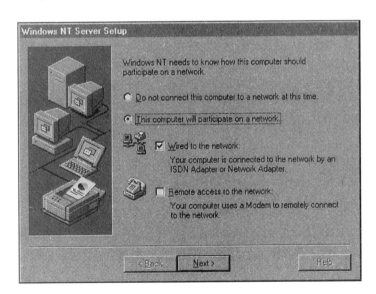

Figure 2-4   Network access selection

At, this screen, you specify how the current computer should participate on a network. You can choose:

- Do not connect the computer to a network at this time.
- This computer will participate on a network.
  - Wired to the network. Your computer is connected to the network by an ISDN Adapter or Network Adapter.

    (**ISDN** is the Integrated Services Digital Network. It is the standard that provides full digital service that can be bought from a telephone company rather than the standard analog service. The basic ISDN service is two 64-Kbits-per-second channels or one 128-Kbits-per-second channel.)
  - Remote access to a network. Your computer uses a Modem to remotely connect to the network.

    (Windows NT Remote Access Service (**RAS**) provides the client and server software that allows computers to dial in or use a WAN option to establish access to computers on a remote Windows NT network.)

If you want to configure RAS now for a modem or a WAN connection to a network, check the second box and follow the procedures given in the resulting dialog boxes. For this installation, let's assume that the connection is wired only. You can set up RAS from Control Panel at any time after the installation. Thus, check the first check box, and then click **Next** to go to the next screen shown in Figure 2-5.

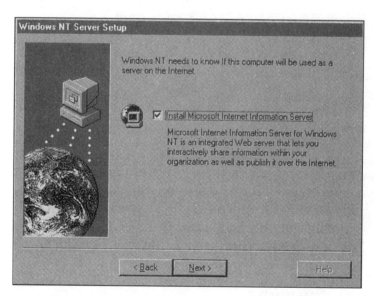

Figure 2-5   Microsoft Internet Information Server (IIS) selection

This screen provides the opportunity to install Internet Servers.

Microsoft Internet Information Server (IIS) is an Internet server service. It uses the protocols HTTP, FTP, and GOPHER to share information with remote web browsers. **HTTP**, **FTP**, and **Gopher** are TCP/IP Application layer protocols.

2

Check the box, and then click **Next** to go to the next screen.

Step 22: Installing a Network Adapter

 If your NIC is plug and play, IRQ and Port settings will have been configured by the operating system.

The screen you are shown suggests one of the following actions:

   A. Have Setup search for a network adapter and install the appropriate driver. To do this, click **Start Search**. After the search, you will be presented with a screen like the one shown in Figure 2-6.

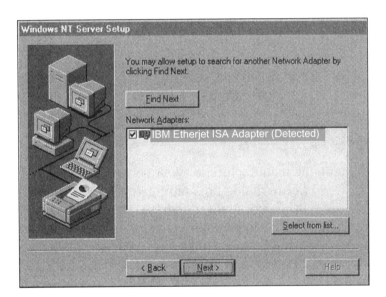

Figure 2-6   Adapter Driver selections

This is the first adapter that Setup found for this server and Setup installed its driver. If there are more adapters, click **Find Next** to have setup install their drivers. If Setup did not find one of your adapters, click **Select from list** to see if you can find the right adapter on the list that is presented. Also, after you click Select from list you have the opportunity to install a driver from a disk that you have. Then click **Next** to go to the screen where you select the network protocols to install. (See Figure 2-7), or,

   B. Click **Have disk**. You are presented with a text box in which you type the drive containing the disk with your network adapter driver. Click **OK** to have Setup install the adapter driver from the disk. Then click **OK** to go to the screen where you select the network protocols to install. (See Figure 2-7.)

Step 23: Install Network Protocols

After you have completed either item A or B in Step 22, you are presented with the screen shown in Figure 2-7 where you select network protocols for installation.

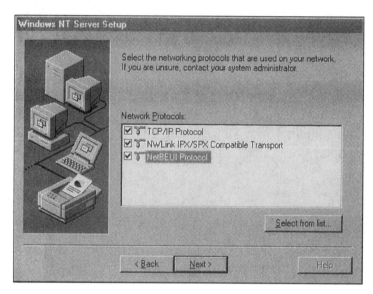

Figure 2-7   Network Protocols

These protocols are described in Table 2-4.

Table 2-4   Network Protocols

Protocol	Description
TCP/IP	The protocol suite used on the Internet and the focus of this book
NW Link IPX/SPX Compatible Transport	The protocol suite that makes it possible for Netware clients to communicate with the server
NetBEUI	The default protocol suite for Microsoft Networks. This is a non-routable protocol

Click all three boxes in Figure 2-7 so that all three protocols will be installed. You can select other network protocols for installation if you click **Select from list**. Then click **Next** to go to a screen where you can configure IRQ and Port settings, if necessary. Otherwise you are presented with the screen that is used to install network services.

Step 24: Install Network Services

Do not check Remote Access Service (RAS) in the Network Services list because a serial interface was not configured in Step 21. You will install and configure RAS in Chapter 10: "Internetworking".

Table 2-5 shows and describes the Network Services list that was generated by selections you have made up to this point in the installation process.

Table 2-5   Default Network Services to be Installed

Service	Description
Microsoft Internet Information Server (IIS) 2.0	Provides information to remote web browsers from databases installed on the server
Remote Access Service (RAS)	Provides access to remote Windows NT networks
Remote Procedure Call (RPC)	Provides access to procedures on remote computers
NetBIOS Interface	The interface to which many application programs have been written for the DOS environment. Using this interface, these applications can run on Windows NT.
Workstation	Installs the Microsoft networking client Service Message Block (SMB) protocol
Server	Installs the Microsoft networking server SMB protocol

You need to install additional network services to use with the exercises in this book. Therefore, click **Select from list** on the Network Services installation screen (see Figure 2-7). The additional network services that you should add are described in Table 2-6.

Table 2-6   Additional Network Services

Service	Description
Microsoft DHCP server	The service that leases IP addresses from the pool of addresses that it maintains
Microsoft DNS server	DNS is Domain Name System. The DNS server translates between Internet domain names and IP addresses
Network Monitor and Agent	The agent process captures frames on the network from or to the server computer and the monitor process analyzes the frame content
RIP for Internet Protocol (IP)	RIP is Routing Information Protocol. RIP generates messages between routers that provide updates to routing tables
Simple TCP/IP services	Includes processes such as Daytime, Echo, Quote of the day etc.
Windows Internet Name Server (WINS)	WINS provides translation between NetBIOS names used on a Microsoft Network and IP addresses

Highlight a service, and click **OK**. You are returned to the screen that showed the original list of network services. You should see the service that you just added at the top of the original list and the adjacent check box should be checked. Click **Select from list** again, highlight another service in Table 2-6, and click **OK**. Keep doing this until you have selected all the services listed in Table 2-6. When you have added all the services, click **Next** on the original screen (Figure 2-7) to install the services, then go to a screen where you click **Next** again to install the selected components.

Step 25: Network Hardware

 The screens that you see in this section depend on the network hardware installed on your computer.

This screen for the IBM computer used for this installation shows:

A. Network Address: _____.

If you do not want to use the manufacturer's Universally Administered Address (UAA), which is stored in the ROM on the NIC, you can enter a twelve-digit locally administered address. Using UAA is strongly recommended. The UAA is a twelve-digit hexadecimal number. The first six digits are the ID of the company that manufactured the NIC, and the second six digits are the unique ID of the NIC.

Click the **Continue** button to move to the next screen, which shows:

B. Cable Type: _____ Auto Detect _____

Auto Detect is the default setting. With this setting, the driver detects the cable type (e.g., coaxial, twisted pair) and uses the adapter hardware accordingly.

C. Duplex mode: _____ Auto Negotiate _____

Auto Negotiate is the default setting. The driver will determine the mode in which the network should operate, depending on the medium access protocol used. Click **Continue** to accept these selections and go to the next screen.

Step 26: TCP/IP Setup

This screen asks the question: Use DHCP server to dynamically configure the IP address?

Click **No**, because you will configure IP. Network-related files are then installed and the next screen is presented.

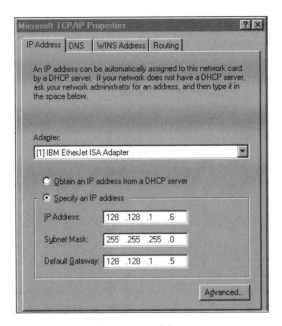

Figure 2-8   Adapter IP addresses

Step 27: Microsoft TCP/IP Properties

 IP addressing is the subject of Chapter 5: "IP Addressing." However, the values
you see in Figure 2-8 are typical IP addresses.

This screen shows a dialog box with five tabs at the top. The IP Address tab is active.

The IP information on this screen was provided for the IBM computer used for this installation. It is described as follows:

> The IP Address 128.128.1.6 is the IP address of the IBM machine.

> The Subnet Mask 255.255.255.0 is the set of numbers that specifies which part of
> the IP address is the address of the subnetwork to which the computer is attached.

> The Default Gateway 128.128.1.5 is the address of the router that will be used to
> route a frame to a destination on another network, if necessary.

Click **OK** to store the IP configuration and go to the next screen. On the next screen click
Next to "start the network."

Step 28: Computer and Domain Name

The name of a primary domain controller (PDC) cannot be changed except during installation of Windows NT 4.0 Server.

A. Computer Name: _____ This is the name of a PDC, BDC (Backup Domain Controller), or member server.

B. Domain: _____ This is the name of the Microsoft Network domain to which the server belongs. You must install a PDC if there is no other PDC on the domain.

Click the **Next** button to store this information and go to the screen where you see the following information.

Step 29: Windows NT Setup

A. Gathering Information

B. Installing Windows NT Networking

C. Finishing Setup

Click the **Finish** button on this screen to begin the steps that will finish the installation.

Step 30: Microsoft Internet Information Server (IIS) 2.0 Setup

The items described in Table 2-7 are the topics discussed in Chapter 10: "Networking Services."

Check each box shown in Figure 2-9. The services provided by IIS are described in Table 2-7. The default installation directory for these options is:

D:\WINNT\SYSTEM32\inetsrv

Click the **OK** button on this screen to install the options in the default installation directory and go to the next screen.

Table 2-7   IIS Services

Service	Description
Internet Service Manager	The utility that manages access to services such as FTP, Gopher, and WWW that are available in Microsoft Windows Internet Explorer
WWW Service	The process that services WWW clients
WWW Service Samples	Example HTML files
Internet Service Manager (HTML)	**HTML** is Hypertext Markup Language, the language used to write scripts that are interpreted by Web browsers. This utility provides for remote administration of the Microsoft Internet Information server using Internet Explorer.
Gopher Service	Provides a graphical access to files on a home Gopher server and the ability to link to other Gopher servers
FTP Service	**FTP** is File Transfer Protocol. It is the TCP/IP protocol in which the command line is used to type in FTP and an IP address to obtain access to a server from which a specific file can be transferred.
ODBC Drivers and Administration	**ODBC** is Open Database Connectivity. It provides and manages the drivers that interface with databases stored on the server—for example, a SQL database.

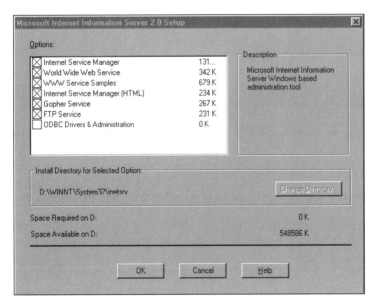

Figure 2-9   Microsoft Internet Information Server (IIS) setup

Step 31: Publishing Directories

The following are default directories where files that are to be shared over the Internet will be stored for access by remote clients.

> D:\inetpub\wwwroot
>
> D:\inetpub\ftproot
>
> D:\inetpub\gophroot

For example, wwwroot is the directory where files to be accessed by a WWW browser are stored.

Click the **OK** button to create the default directories and go to the next screen.

Step 32: ODBC Drivers

You are presented with a list of drivers from which to choose. The SQL (Structured Query Language) driver is the only driver that is shipped with Windows NT 4.0. Check this driver and click **OK** to install it and move to the next screen.

Step 33: The Finishing Screens

A. The Date and Time screen lets you specify your time zone relative to Universal Time. Universal Time is the time in Greenwich, England. It was originally called Greenwich Mean Time.

B. The Video Adapter screen allows you to choose the number of colors, resolution, and total number of pixels on your screen.

After these screens are configured, the remaining CD-ROM files are copied to the directory you chose in Step 12 of the installation. In the case of this installation, the directory was: D:\WINNT

C. The Windows Messages screen appears. You see related files being installed.

D. The Security on Files screen appears. You see related files being installed.

E. You are asked to remove disks from the floppy and CD-ROM drives and to press the Restart Computer button.

F. The first Windows NT 4.0 Server Logon screen appears.

- This first logon screen asks you to press the **CTRL+ALT+DEL** keys at the same time.

- The next logon screen asks for your User ID and Password. You must type the Password *using the same case* in which you first entered the Administrator password in installation Step 17.

- Click **OK** to obtain the desktop screen of Windows NT 4.0 Server shown in Figure 2-10. This screen provides your entry into the world of Windows NT 4.0.

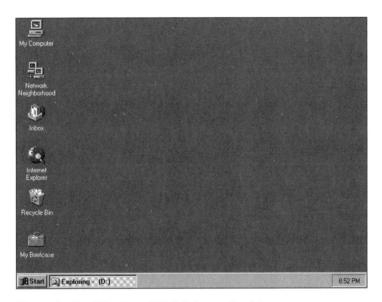

Figure 2-10   Windows NT 4.0 Server Desktop

The installation of Windows NT 4.0 Server is now complete. In the next chapter, you will examine the Windows NT 4.0 Server menus and explore some of the utilities that are accessed from these menus. You will be using these utilities to do exercises in later chapters of this book.

CHAPTER SUMMARY

This chapter covered:

- The hardware and software required to install Windows NT 4.0 Server and Windows NT 4.0 Workstation operating systems and the associated utilities
- Other sources of information about Windows NT hardware requirements
- Sources of Windows NT technical information
- Configuration of the devices in a modern computer
- A step-by-step installation of the Windows NT 4.0 Server operating system
- Descriptions of the resources provided by each installation step

REVIEW QUESTIONS

1. What is the minimum disk storage required to install Windows NT 4.0 Server, according to the Windows NT 4.0 Server manual?
   a. 100 MB
   b. 206 MB
   c. 124 MB
2. How many IRQ numbers are available in a computer with the AT architecture?
   a. 8
   b. 16
   c. 24
3. How is the IRQ number of a plug-and-play adapter selected?
   a. By using a DIP switch on the adapter
   b. By configuration software that comes with the adapter
   c. By the operating system
4. What is a device driver?
   a. A software module that controls the device
   b. The RAM located on the device
   c. The controller on the device
5. How do you access the CMOS database on a computer using an Intel processor?
   a. By typing CTRL+ALT+DEL
   b. By pressing the ESC key while the computer is starting up
   c. By pressing the DEL key when you see the related message on the screen during the startup process

2

6. What is a device port?

    a. A connector on the device

    b. The address in RAM where the device driver is stored

    c. A range of addresses in RAM that is used to store information that the operating system uses to communicate with the device

7. Which of the following distinguishes the FAT file system from the NTFS file system?

    a. Windows NT must use the FAT file system

    b. NTFS provides more file security mechanisms

    c. FAT provides faster access to large files

8. When you partition a hard drive into a FAT partition and an NTFS partition, which of the following is true?

    a. The FAT partition can be converted to an NTFS partition without having to back up the FAT partition and reinstall the files.

    b. Windows NT cannot access files in the FAT partition.

    c. You cannot dual boot if the Windows NT operating system is on the FAT partition.

9. Can you have Windows NT 4.0 Server and Windows NT 4.0 Workstation operating systems on the same hard disk?

    a. Yes

    b. No

    c. Yes, if Windows NT 4.0 Server is installed first

10. What is the minimum amount of RAM that is needed by Windows NT 4.0 Server?

    a. 16 MB

    b. 12 MB

    c. 32 MB

11. What is the default order in which the BIOS checks disk drives to find an operating system from which to start up?

    a. D then C

    b. A then C

    c. C then A

12. If you want to change the order in which the BIOS on computers with Intel processors checks disk drives, how do you do it?

    a. Obtain a modified BIOS

    b. Select the order from on-screen choices provided during the computer's Power On Self Test (POST)

    c. Enter the CMOS database by pressing the Delete key during POST and selecting BIOS Features Setup from the main menu

13. What is the advantage of an IDE hard drive?

  a. It has the largest storage capacity of all drive types.

  b. It has the fastest access time of all drive types.

  c. Its adapter is integrated with the drive itself.

14. Which of the following server types can you *not* rename after installation?

  a. Primary domain controller

  b. Back-up domain controller

  c. Standalone server

15. During the installation of Windows NT 4.0 Server, an Administrator account was created, and you set a password for the account. An Administrator account has privileges that User accounts do not. Which of the following is one of these privileges?

  a. An Administrator can change the name of a primary domain controller after installation.

  b. An Administrator can browse directories on workstations.

  c. An Administrator has access to all domain resources.

16. What is NetBEUI?

  a. A network layer protocol

  b. A routable protocol stack

  c. The default protocol stack for the Microsoft Network

17. What is a Universally Administered Address?

  a. An arbitrary network address assigned at the discretion of the network administrator

  b. A-six digit hexadecimal address that is stored in the ROM of a NIC

  c. A twelve-digit hexadecimal address that is stored in the ROM of a NIC

18. What is Universal Time?

  a. An arbitrary time that is set by the primary domain controller for synchronization with other servers on the domain

  b. The time kept by a DOD satellite

  c. The time in Greenwich, England

19. In Step 24 of the installation, two of the network services installed were server and workstation. Because you were installing a server, what does it mean to provide a workstation service?

  a. The server can function as the client of another server.

  b. When the user selects workstation mode, no services are provided to other computers on the network.

  c. Full access to all files on the server is allowed.

20. During installation you selected a name for the server. How is this name used?

   a. It is the address of a server on a Microsoft Network.

   b. It is the address of the server on the Internet.

   c. It is only a mnemonic.

CASE PROJECT

The status of the Case Project after Chapter 1, "Communications Architectures," is shown in Figure 2-11.

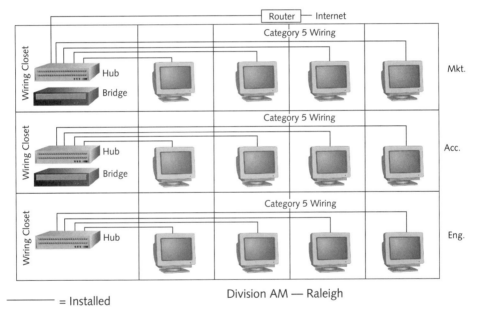

Figure 2-11   The Case Project environment prior to Chapter 2

In this chapter the Case Project exercises included the thirty-three server installation steps you took to install Windows NT 4.0 Server on one computer. The Case Project for this chapter assumes that you then proceeded to install the server operating system on the other two servers in the Raleigh building, and then installed Windows NT 4.0 Workstation on the other computers in the building. The status of the Case Project is now as shown in Figure 2-12.

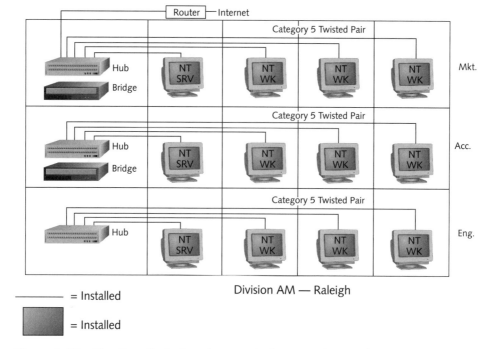

Figure 2-12 The Case Project environment after completing Chapter 2

WINDOWS NT 4.0 UTILITIES

Now that you have installed Windows NT 4.0, this chapter provides you with an overview of the utilities that we have included in the installation, and enables you to practice using those that you will need most often. You will see these and other utilities when you complete exercises in later chapters.

IN THIS CHAPTER YOU WILL:

EXAMINE THE DESKTOP UTILITY

EXAMINE THE SHUT DOWN UTILITY

EXAMINE THE HELP UTILITY

EXAMINE THE FIND UTILITY

EXAMINE THE CONTROL PANEL UTILITY

EXAMINE THE WINDOWS NT EXPLORER UTILITY

EXAMINE THE DISK ADMINISTRATOR UTILITY

EXAMINE THE SERVER MANAGER UTILITY

EXAMINE THE NETWORK MONITOR UTILITY

THE DESKTOP

The starting point for the journey through the Windows NT 4.0 utilities is the Desktop. Windows NT 4.0 uses the Windows 95 graphical user interface (GUI). A typical Desktop is shown in Figure 3-1.

Figure 3-1   Desktop

At the bottom left of the figure you see the Start button. The Start button is part of the taskbar. The **taskbar** shows buttons that are labeled with the names of tasks that are open. You make a task active by clicking its button. The button becomes indented, and the task uses the full-screen display.

Clicking the Start button would produce the Start menu as shown in Figure 3-2.

On the left of this menu are the words "Windows NT Server," indicating that you are looking at the main menu for the server operating system and its utilities. The Start menu contains items that you will access continuously. Those you will probably use most often are Programs, Settings, Find, Help, and Shut Down.

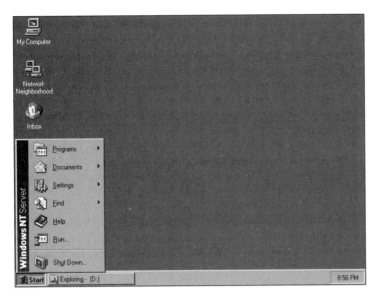

Figure 3-2 Main menu

SHUT DOWN

Clicking Shut Down on the Start menu will produce the menu shown in Figure 3-3.

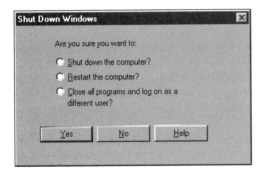

Figure 3-3 Shut Down menu

The first option is "Shut down the computer." This is a shutdown that is controlled by the computer. It is important to shut down your computer by selecting this option because it allows all the open files to be saved to the hard drive in an orderly fashion. After this controlled shutdown, you are presented with a screen that tells you, "It's now safe to turn off your computer." The second menu item, "Restart the computer," causes the computer to do a controlled shutdown and then restart itself. You will find this very convenient whenever you have changed a device configuration and want the change to take effect. You will use this option often during the early stages of your use of Windows NT 4.0. The last option, "Close all programs and log on as a different user," allows another user with a different ID and password to have access to the system.

HELP

The next important Start menu item is Help. The source of most help for Windows NT 4.0 is online. For this reason, you will find Help to be indispensable. Figure 3-4 shows the window that opens when you click Help.

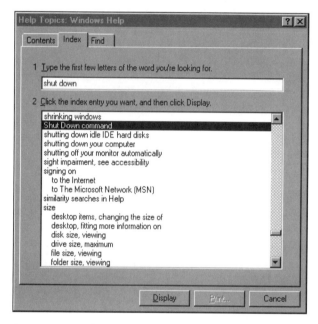

Figure 3-4   The Help utility

The **Contents** tab opens a list of Help topics. The **Index** tab opens the window you see in Figure 3-4. The **Find** tab lets you type in the words or phrases you are looking for. In the Index window, in text box 1, you can see that "shut down" has been typed in. Index found and displayed the highlighted "Shut Down command." You would click on "Shut Down command" to have information displayed about that command.

You can return to the Help Topics window from any other window, type in a subject you need to know more about, and a text window will open that either provides the information you need or leads you to other information. Help often displays a button that brings up a configuration screen that lets you change device parameters.

Windows NT 4.0 has so many folders (directories) and files that it is often difficult to find a file by searching through drives and folders. Let Find, on the Start menu, do it for you.

FIND

Figure 3-5 shows the screen that appears when you click Find. The dialog box allows you to specify the file you are looking for and select the drive that should be searched.

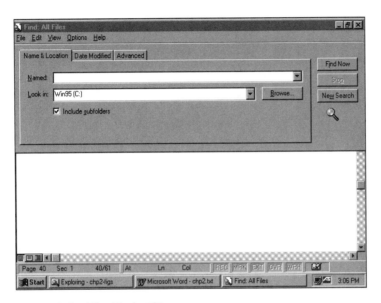

Figure 3-5   The Find utility

You can also tell Find which folder to look in. Type in the name of the file to look for, using wildcard characters if you cannot remember the name exactly, and then click the Find Now button. A window opens at the bottom of the Find dialog box listing the files found. Double-click on the filename to open the file.

Now you will look at items on the Start menu that provide more detail about the components in your system and the system utilities. The Settings item points ▶ to a submenu that contains two items of special importance: Control Panel and Printers. Only Control Panel will be considered at this point.

CONTROL PANEL

Dragging the mouse pointer from Settings to the right and clicking Control Panel once on the submenu opens the Control Panel window shown in Figure 3-6.

Figure 3-6   Control Panel

Control Panel takes on special significance in Windows NT 4.0. The richness of Windows NT 4.0 makes it necessary to return to Control Panel often, in order to check out device configurations, examine the status of devices, check network services, install hardware and software, and Start services.

The Programs option on the Start menu item also points to ▶ a submenu. Dragging the pointer from Programs to the right opens this submenu, which is shown in Figure 3-7.

3

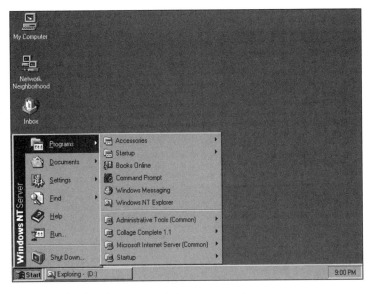

Figure 3-7   Start menu and Programs submenu

WINDOWS NT EXPLORER

Like Windows 95 Explorer and an enhanced version of Windows 3.1 Program Manager, Windows NT Explorer is the place to start to look for drives, folders, and files. Clicking Windows NT Explorer opens a window like the one shown in Figure 3-8.

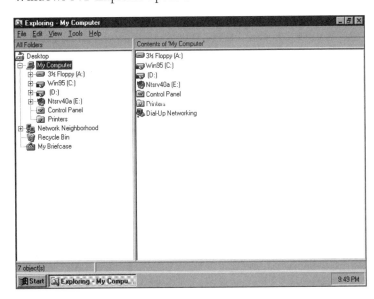

Figure 3-8   Windows NT Explorer

In the left panel of this window you see the hierarchy of Windows NT 4.0 resources. At the top of this hierarchy is the Desktop, which we have been exploring. A box with a plus (+) sign next to a device or folder means that the device or folder has subfolders that can be seen in the left panel by clicking on the (+). Below Desktop is "My Computer." My Computer has been clicked once, to show its contents in the right panel. You can see that this computer has four drives: A:, C:, D:, and E:.

The Windows NT 4.0 system files (Winnt) have been installed on the D: drive. Clicking (+) next to the D: drive in Figure 3-8 will generate a list of folders on the D: drive. One of these folders is Winnt. Clicking on Winnt will produce the window shown in Figure 3-9.

Figure 3-9   The Winnt folder

Double-clicking any of these folders or files in the right panel of the window opens them, or directs you to an application program that can open them. Most of the Winnt files are in the System32 folder.

There is only one hard drive and one CD-ROM drive on this computer. Drive E: is the CD-ROM drive, so you may wonder why two hard drives, C: and D:, are listed in the Windows NT Explorer panels in Figure 3-8. The reason is that the hard drive has two partitions—C: and D:. Windows NT 4.0 provides a utility that shows how a hard disk is partitioned. Figure 3-10, in the next section, shows how to access this utility.

DISK ADMINISTRATOR

The Programs menu in Figure 3-10 contains the menu item Administrative Tools (Common), which points ▶ to a menu containing the menu item Disk Administrator. Clicking Disk Administrator will produce the window shown in Figure 3-11.

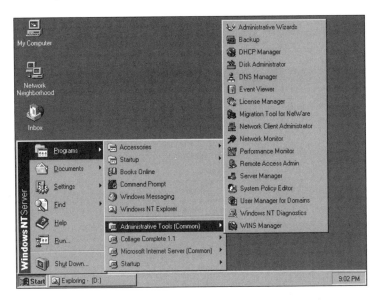

Figure 3-10   Start, Programs, and Administrative Tools (Common) menus

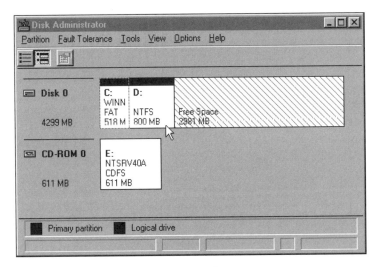

Figure 3-11   Disk Administrator utility

Here you see that drives C: and D: are the partitions of one hard drive labeled Disk 0. In the case of the computer on which this utility resides, the Windows NT 4.0 Workstation operating system is stored on the C: partition (drive), and the Windows NT 4.0 Server operating system is stored on the D: partition (drive). Using the Partition Menu on the menu bar of Disk Administrator, you could change or delete partitions just as you did during the installation of Windows NT 4.0 Server. Notice also that the file system for drive C: is the FAT (File Allocation Table) system, while that for drive D: is NTFS (NT File System). Windows NT can use either the FAT system or NTFS. The FAT system was chosen for the workstation so that all workstation application programs could read the files.

Now let's take a quick look at the Server Manager item on the Administrative Tools (Common) menu.

 You will be using Server Manager and domains in much more detail in Chapter 8: "Windows NT Domains." Don't be concerned about the names that are given to servers and workstations in this section on Server Manager. They are only examples.

Clicking Server Manager will produce a window like the one shown in Figure 3-12.

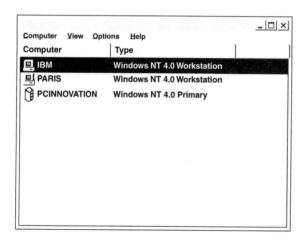

Figure 3-12   Server Manager utility

Server Manager is the utility that Windows NT 4.0 Server uses to set up a domain on a Microsoft Windows Network. A Microsoft Windows network **domain** consists of at least one computer that is using the Windows NT Server operating system and other computers that could be using, for example, the Windows NT Workstation operating system, the Windows 95 operating system, or Windows for Workgroups and DOS, NetWare, or Macintosh client software. If there is more than one server in the domain, one server has to be the primary domain controller, one might be a back-up domain controller, and one might be a standalone member server. A **primary domain controller** is the server on the domain that maintains the master list of authenticated domain accounts, files identified as sharable, and user permissions for file access. A user of a computer that has an account on a domain can access the resources of any computer on the domain. Domains can be any size. The company can be a domain, or you might want to have divisions in your company be domains. All computers on the domain can be managed from the primary domain controller.

The Server Manager window, shown in Figure 3-12, is what a domain administrator uses to create accounts so that other computers can join the domain. As you can see in that figure, accounts have been created for three computers: a server that is a primary domain controller, which has the name PCINNOVATION; and two computers with the names PARIS and IBM, which are using the Windows NT 4.0 Workstation operating system. These are the names by which these computers will be known to all other computers in the domain, and by which the server will be accessed for service. The domain administrator determines which computers will be in the domain by using the Computer Menu on the Server Manager menu bar to create accounts for other computers. When an account has been created, the name of the computer will appear in the Server Manager window.

Once a computer account is created, a user with the appropriate logon authority, such as Administrator, must use the Network utility in the Control Panel of that computer to confirm the workstation name to which Server Manager assigned the account.

 The Microsoft Windows Network domain name BURKE.COM has the format of a domain name used on the Internet. This is not necessary, but is convenient if you would like your computer to have the same name on both networks.

Double-clicking Network in the Control Panel of the computer running Windows NT Workstation will result in the window shown in Figure 3-13.

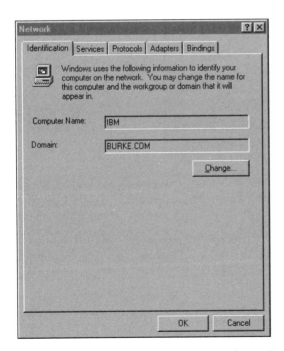

Figure 3-13   Network utility in Control Panel

The Identification tab of the Network utility is active. The dialog boxes say that the computer name is IBM, and the domain name is BURKE.COM. You can accept these names or change them by clicking the Change button. Clicking the Change button takes you to another window, where you make the name changes and save them. In this example, you want to keep the name IBM, because this is a name that was assigned when the account was created in Server Manager. The other computer running Windows NT Workstation has the name PARIS. You want to keep this name too, because it is also a name assigned to an account by Server Manager. When you click OK, you establish a domain with one server, PCINNOVATION, and two workstations, IBM and PARIS.

The Help menu for Server Manager is excellent. Figure 3-14 shows the list of Help Topics that is produced by selecting Help on the Server Manager menu bar and then clicking Contents.

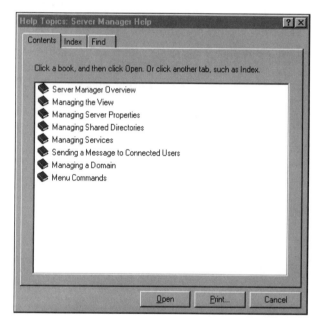

Figure 3-14   Server Manager Help

This list of topics will provide you with all the information you need to manage domains. Let's look at a few examples.

Clicking Server Manager Overview in Figure 3-14 and then clicking What Is Server Manager? in the next screen produces Figure 3-15.

3

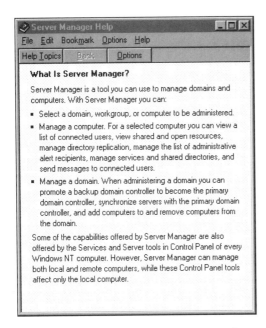

Figure 3-15   What Is Server Manager?

To see how to manage server properties, you would click Managing Server Properties in Figure 3-14 to obtain the list shown in Figure 3-16.

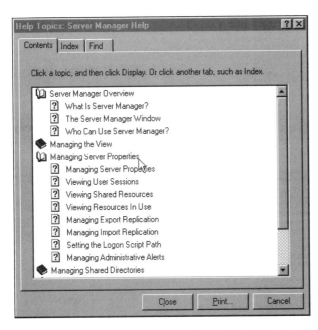

Figure 3-16   Managing Server Properties Help topics

As you can see, this list provides access to much more detail about what you can do with the Server Manager utility. We will explore some of these details in Chapter 8. In the next section, the Administrative Tools (Common) menu item Network Monitor is examined.

NETWORK MONITOR

The last Administrative Tools (Common) menu item that will be examined in this chapter is Network Monitor. Network Monitor is a valuable utility, and you will use it often for the exercises in this book. Network Monitor gives you the ability to capture and look inside the frames that are being transmitted on the network. Windows NT 4.0 Network Monitor is an example of the network monitors that are on the market today. Perhaps the best-known network monitor is the Network General Sniffer. The Sniffer, a separate device attached to the network, combines hardware and software to do its job. The Windows NT 4.0 Network Monitor is an example of a monitor that is implemented by software alone. Some monitors operate in promiscuous mode; that is, they capture and read all frames that are on the network. Novell LANalyzer is of this type. The Windows NT 4.0 monitor runs only on the server, and captures and displays only frames for which the server is either the source or the destination. Clicking Network Monitor in the Administrative Tools (Common) menu will present you with the window shown in Figure 3-17.

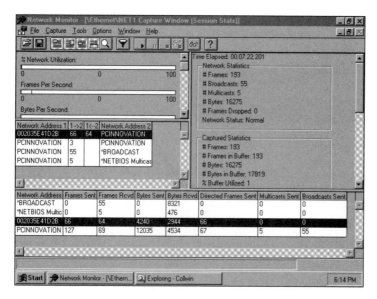

Figure 3-17   Network Monitor

There are four panels in the Network Monitor window. The one on the upper left gives dynamic information about the traffic on the network, for example, the number of frames per second at any given time. The panel on the upper right lists a variety of frame statistics, such as the total number of frames on the network during the time that is shown at the top of the panel. The panel in the middle left gives the name of the server (PCINNOVATION), the hardware address (002035E41D2B) of the computer named IBM, and the number of frames sent and received by them. The panel at the very bottom of the window shows more statistics about frames on the network. The ones headed with a star (★) are either broadcast frames or multicast frames.

You capture frames on the network by clicking Capture on the Network Monitor menu bar and then clicking Start. To view the content of the frames you have captured, you click Stop And View on the Capture menu. You are then presented with a numbered list of the frames captured, and you can scroll through them to find the one you want to examine. The panel at the top of the window in Figure 3-18 shows a partial list of frames captured.

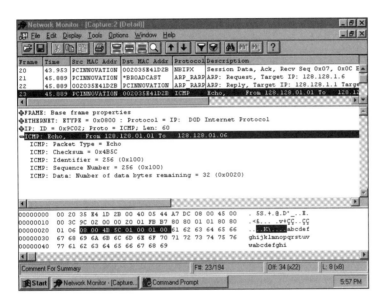

Figure 3-18 Network Monitor Capture

Frame 23 is highlighted. The protocol headers in frame 23 are analyzed in the middle panel of the window. The bottom panel shows the data in the frame (headers and application program data) in hexadecimal notation.

 The details of the protocols shown in Figure 3-18 are discussed in Chapter 4: "The TCP/IP Protocol Suite."

From the user's perspective, the power of Network Monitor resides in the middle panel. This panel is the result of decoding the hexadecimal notation. In this example, the following is some of the information that is visible:

1. ETHERNET:ETYPE = 0x0800 means that this is an Ethernet II frame in which the Type field had the value 0x0800. A Type field with the value ID = 0x0800 means that the network layer protocol is IP.

2. Proto = ICMP is the Internet Control Message Protocol. This protocol header and application program data are encapsulated in the IP datagram.

3. ICMP: Packet Type = Echo is one of the packets created by ICMP. For example, an Echo Request is a packet that asks the designated receiver to send an Echo Reply packet to test the connection between sender and receiver.

4. Checksum is an error-checking number that will be read by the receiver to check for transmission errors in the received message.

5. Identifier and Sequence Number will be included in the Echo Reply to check that the reply is a response to the specific request sent.

6. Data: is optional data that can be sent in the Echo Request packet, and is to be returned in the Echo Reply packet. More information appears when you click the (+) at the left of the line.

CHAPTER SUMMARY

- You saw that the Windows NT 4.0 GUI is very similar to that of Windows 95.

- You obtained an overview of the menus of utilities that are provided by Windows NT 4.0 Server and explored in more detail some of the utilities that you will use most often in the course of this book.

- The utilities explored were Desktop, Shut Down, Help, Find, Control Panel, Windows NT Explorer, Disk Administrator, Server Manager, and Network Monitor. You will practice using some of what you have learned about these utilities in the exercises that follow.

REVIEW QUESTIONS

1. Where is the Shut Down utility in the Windows NT 4.0 Desktop?
   a. On the Start menu
   b. On the Desktop
   c. In Windows NT Explorer

2. Why *should* you use the Shut Down utility to turn off your computer?
   a. The hard drive may be damaged otherwise
   b. This utility saves open files to the hard drive before turning off the computer
   c. To restart the computer automatically

3. What is the main reason that you need to use online Help in Windows NT 4.0?

   a. It is the primary source of help that comes with the system

   b. It is easier to read than the manual

   c. It is easier to make use of Help when you are online

4. How do you add hardware and software to your computer system after installation?

   a. You have to reinstall the operating system

   b. Using the Programs menu

   c. In Control Panel

5. What utility do you use to add a partition to the free space on your hard drive?

   a. Disk Administrator

   b. Partition Manager

   c. Windows NT Explorer

6. What utility do you use to add computers to an existing domain?

   a. The Network utility in Control Panel

   b. The Devices utility in Control Panel

   c. The Server Manager utility

7. The Help utility on the Start menu is help for Windows NT 4.0. How do you get help specific to utilities and application programs?

   a. From the Programs menu

   b. From the Find utility

   c. From the Help menu on the menu bar of the specific utility or application program

8. How do you access the MS-DOS prompt?

   a. From Control Panel

   b. From the Command Prompt icon on the Programs menu

   c. By using StartUp on the Programs menu

9. How can you tell whether the driver for a device has been started or not?

   a. Use Windows NT Explorer to see if the driver file is in the Drivers folder of the System32 folder.

   b. Use the Windows NT Diagnostic utility in the Administrative Tools (Common) menu.

   c. Use the Devices utility in Control Panel.

10. How do you change the characteristics of your monitor display?

   a. Tune the monitor from the controls on its front

   b. From the System utility in Control Panel

   c. From the Display utility in Control Panel

11. What is the most direct way to find out what devices are installed on your computer system?

    a. Clicking Desktop in Windows NT Explorer

    b. Clicking My Computer in Windows NT Explorer

    c. From the Devices utility in Control Panel

12. What menu on the menu bar of Server Manager do you use to create an account for a computer in the server's domain?

    a. View

    b. Options

    c. Computer

13. What utility in Control Panel do you use to add a computer to the domain in which the computer account was created?

    a. Network

    b. Services

    c. Add/Remove Programs

14. How do you access help for Server Manager?

    a. From the Help item on the Start menu

    b. From the Help menu in the Network utility

    c. From the Help menu on the Server Manager menu bar

15. How do you manage server properties?

    a. By selecting View from the Server Manager menu bar

    b. By selecting Options from the Server Manager menu bar

    c. By selecting Computer from the Server Manager menu bar

16. What is the name of the utility that lets you capture frames?

    a. Server Manager

    b. Network Monitor

    c. Network utility in Control Panel

17. Does the Windows NT 4.0 utility that captures frames operate in promiscuous mode?

    a. Yes, always

    b. No, never

    c. It can be configured to do so

18. What is the hexidecimal value of the IP protocol ID?

    a. 0x0800

    b. 0x0805

    c. 0x0806

19. What does ICMP stand for?

a. Interface Computer Memory Profile

b. Internet Control Message Protocol

c. Internet Computer Message Protocol

20. What is the ICMP Echo Request message used for?

a. To obtain the IP address of a computer on the network

b. To test connectivity between two computers on the network

c. To check for transmission errors on the network

CASE PROJECT

The current status of the networking environment in the Raleigh division is shown in Figure 3-19.

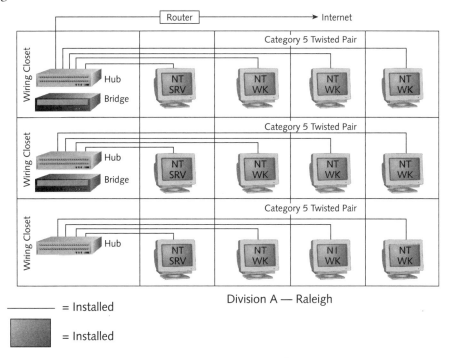

———— = Installed

▮ = Installed

Figure 3-19   Case Project environment prior to Chapter 3

In the exercises that follow, you will not make any changes to this networking environment. However, you will make use of the utilities discussed in this chapter and thus become more familiar with these utilities. The exercises may seem very basic. Further practice will, however, make it more likely that you will remember how to access these utilities when you need them.

EXERCISE 1—EXPLORING WINDOWS NT 4.0 SERVER MENUS

1. Click the **Start** button on the taskbar to open the Start menu.
2. Fill in Table 3-1 with the data requested after the table.

Table 3-1   Description of Start menu items

Start Menu Item	Description

   a. In the first column, write the names of the items on the Start menu.

   b. In the second column, write a brief explanation of the service provided by each item. Click **Help** on the Start menu to look up explanations of the services, if you are unsure.

EXERCISE 2—EXPLORING CONTROL PANEL ON THE SETTINGS MENU

1. Click the **Start** button on the taskbar.
2. Highlight **Settings**.
3. Drag the mouse pointer right to **Control Panel** on the Settings menu.
4. Click **Control Panel** to open the Control Panel window.

   The Control Panel window is typically the place to start when you want to make a change in the computer system configuration. Double-clicking an icon opens a program that presents a dialog box in which you can make changes. Possibilities include:

   a. Adding a printer driver to your system

b. Adding and configuring the network interface card (NIC)

c. Adding an application program such as a word processor

d. Changing Interrupt Request Numbers and/or I/O addresses of your communication (COM) ports

e. Reviewing the status of system devices such as a disk drive

5. Fill in Table 3-2 with the following data:

a. In the first column write down the following names: PRINTER, NETWORK, DEVICES, DISPLAY, and SERVICES.

b. In the second column, describe two of the properties of these utilities that can be controlled by using the dialog box that opens when you double-click on the utility icon. Use Help on the Start menu to look up information about these names, if necessary.

Table 3-2   Properties of Control Panel Utilities

Control Panel devices	Properties

EXERCISE 3—EXAMINING WINDOWS NT EXPLORER

1. Click **Start** on the taskbar.

2. Highlight **Programs**.

3. Drag the mouse pointer right to **Windows NT Explorer** on the Programs menu and click.

Table 3-3   Steps to Access the etc Folder

Step	Description

In Table 3-3, describe the steps you would take to access a file that is in the etc folder, which is in the drivers folder in the System32 folder, which is in the Winnt folder, which is in the root of the C: drive.

EXERCISE 4—FINDING FILES

As you saw in Exercise 3, Windows NT 4.0 Server has many folders and many files in each folder. It is almost a certainty that sooner or later you will forget where a particular file is located. It can be very frustrating trying to find it with a manual search. Perhaps more than in previous versions of Windows, Find is an important friend.

In step 4 of this exercise, you may not see any files with the extension .sys. If that is the case, in step 8 click "Show all files" instead of "Hide all files of these types." The result of step 11 will be that files with the extension .sys (as well as other files) will be listed.

1. Click the **Start** button.
2. Highlight **Find**, drag the mouse pointer right to Files or Folders and click **Files** or **Folders**.
3. Type **C:** in the Look in: text box.
4. Type in the names of files to be found in Named:. Use wildcards (* and ?) if desired. For this exercise, search for all files with the extension **.sys**.
5. Click **Find now**. A window opens that list all files with extension .sys found.
6. Close the Find: dialog box.
7. Open **Windows NT Explorer**. From the View menu on the menu bar, select **Options**. The dialog box that opens provides two options: "Show all files" and "Hide files of these types."
8. Click **Hide files of these types** and select .sys from the list provided.
9. Click **OK**.
10. Click Start, highlight **Find**, and click **Files or Folders**.
11. Look in the C: drive for files with the extension **.sys** again. No such files should be listed.

The two choices that you can make in the View/Options selection in Windows NT Explorer both have an advantage and a disadvantage. The *advantage* of "showing all files" is that you will always be able to use Find to determine the existence of a file on your system; the *disadvantage* is that a user could accidentally delete a critical system file. The *disadvantage* of "hiding files" is that although you won't accidentally delete any critical files, you may forget that you hid them and wonder what happened to them.

EXERCISE 5—EXAMINING THE SERVER MANAGER UTILITY

In this exercise you will use Server Manager on the PDC to create a backup domain controller (BDC) on the network in the Engineering Department and then enable its membership in the domain from that computer.

CREATE A BACKUP DOMAIN CONTROLLER

1. Click **Start**.
2. Highlight **Programs**.
3. Drag the mouse pointer right to **Administrative Tools (common)** on the Programs menu.
4. Continue to drag the mouse pointer right from **Administrative Tools (common)** to **Server Manager** in the Administrative Tools (common) menu.
5. Click **Server Manager** to open the Server Manager utility.
6. Use the **Computer** menu to **Add to Domain**.

ENABLE BDC DOMAIN MEMBERSHIP

1. In Control Panel on the BDC computer, double-click **Network**
2. On the **Identification Tab** you are given the opportunity to name the BDC that has been assigned an account in Server Manager and the domain to which it has been assigned. Click the **Change** button to do this
3. Type the name Engineering in the box labeled **Computer Name**
4. Type the domain name in the **Domain Name** box
5. Click **OK** to return to the Network window
6. Click **OK** in the Network window. You have just established membership for the Engineering Department BDC in the domain.
7. Highlight the BDC computer on Server Manager.
8. Select Properties from the Computer Menu and you will see a screen that allows you to manage the properties of the BDC from the PDC.

THE TCP/IP PROTOCOL SUITE

The Internet is a network of heterogeneous networks. Internet users depend on the TCP/IP protocols to provide an end-to-end service that is independent of network implementation. This chapter explains the TCP/IP protocols and how they are implemented.

IN THIS CHAPTER YOU WILL:

REVIEW THE DEVELOPMENT OF TCP/IP AND PACKET SWITCHING

EXAMINE CLIENT/SERVER MODEL CONCEPTS AND METHODS

REVIEW THE OPERATIONS OF THE PROTOCOLS IN THE TCP/IP PROTOCOL STACK

EXAMINE THE TCP, UDP, IP, AND ICMP PACKET HEADERS

HISTORY OF TCP/IP AND PACKET SWITCHING

The suite of protocols that is called TCP/IP, after the names of the two major protocols in the suite, was developed in the early 1970s under funding provided by the Department of Defense (DOD) Advanced Research Projects Agency (**ARPA**). ARPA also supported the incorporation of TCP/IP into the Berkeley Software Distribution (**BSD**) version of the **UNIX** operating system. To encourage the use of TCP/IP, ARPA distributed it widely to the academic community. Subsequently, agencies of the federal government used TCP/IP to establish a communications network among major computer facilities such as the National Science Foundation (**NSF**) Supercomputer Centers. This activity formed the foundation for the **Internet** as we know it today. In the late 1980s, commercial organizations began to connect their component suborganizations with TCP/IP. This activity was the beginning of the **intranet**.

The evolution of TCP/IP was driven by de facto standards. Standards were proposed in Requests for Comments (**RFCs**) that were widely distributed to workers in the field. These comments evolved to a standard that was accepted by the community because its implementation provided a specific solution to a network communications requirement. This RFC practice still exists and is today coordinated by the Internet Activities Board (**IAB**). Because of this practice and widespread distribution during early stages of development, the TCP/IP suite of protocols is the dominant suite used to provide network communication.

Another reason for the success of TCP/IP is that its developers provided interprocess communication mechanisms that form a logical link between processes on different machines. An **interprocess communication** is one in which two processes (active programs) send information to one another. A **logical link** is a conceptual communication link between two processes, rather than a physical communication link. It is independent of the way the link is physically constructed, the operating systems used by the communicating computers, and the network devices that connect networks between the source and destination computers. As intended by the developers, the TCP/IP protocol suite makes it unnecessary for the communicating processes to have any knowledge of the physical mechanisms that make up the communications network. This transparency makes the Internet or an intranet appear to be one network rather than a set of connected dissimilar networks.

At about the same time as the development of TCP/IP was taking place, ARPA was funding research on packet switching to connect the academic networks that were to use TCP/IP. Prior to packet switching, circuit switching was used. **Circuit switching** is typified by telephone networks. A permanent physical circuit between the caller and receiver is established. Talking can begin after this circuit setup is complete. The total bandwidth of the circuit is reserved for this one conversation until one person hangs up. The **bandwidth** of a telephone circuit is 3000 cycles per second, or 3000 hertz. This is the frequency range that covers most of the frequencies of speech. In **packet switching**, voice or data is converted into a stream of bytes that is divided into packets of a fixed size. These packets are stored in the RAM of each network device along the path from sender to receiver, and are passed to the next device along the path when that path is available. Such packets are sent using one of the following methods:

- Virtual circuit. Before any packets are sent, a virtual circuit is established. This method is somewhat similar to circuit switching, except that the circuit is not dedicated to one sender/receiver pair. The circuit is shared by other sender/receiver pairs. The circuit is called **virtual** because it appears to any sender/receiver pair that they are the only pair using the physical circuit. This method is used by the Transmission Control Protocol (TCP) of the Transport layer of the TCP/IP protocol stack.

- Datagram. A virtual circuit is not established. Packets are sent when ready and may take any available physical circuit between the sender and receiver. Throughput is increased because a router, for example, can choose to use an output circuit that has a shorter queue of packets, or one that uses a less congested physical circuit. Disadvantages of the datagram method are that packets may arrive out of order and have to be reassembled, and that packets may get lost. This method is used by the User Datagram Protocol (UDP) of the Transport layer of the TCP/IP protocol stack.

Today, the use of packet switching and TCP/IP dominates communication on the Internet.

This chapter explains the TCP/IP protocols. These protocols will be used with Windows NT 4.0 to provide network communication. Prior to looking at the details of the TCP/IP protocols, we will examine the client/server model in the next section. This is the conceptual model of communications on the Internet and on most intranets.

CLIENT/SERVER MODEL

First, client/server model concepts are examined. Then, the methods that the model uses are considered.

CLIENT/SERVER MODEL CONCEPTS

The client/server *architecture*, which was introduced in Chapter 1, "Communications Architectures," was defined to be one in which central storage and resources are controlled by a server computer and are accessed by a client computer. In contrast, the client/server *model* demonstrates how one process obtains service from another process. A process becomes a *client* when it sends a request message to a server process and awaits a reply. The *server* process runs and waits for a request from a client. Any computer can run client or server processes. Windows NT provides two operating systems: Windows NT Server and Windows NT Workstation. The former includes more utilities for providing services than the latter, and thus it is the one typically installed on a computer that will run the client/server model server processes. The demands on the computer running the server processes are much greater, because many clients may have to be serviced "simultaneously."

However, unless the computer running the server processes has more than one processor, real simultaneous processing is not possible. In a single-processor computer, the processor switches rapidly between processes that are providing different services to different clients. This makes the server computer appear to be serving multiple clients simultaneously. Thus the faster the processor, the better server the computer will be. Also, as was mentioned in Chapter 1, a computer that runs server processes will typically have more RAM that can be allocated to buffering request packets from a large number of clients.

CLIENT/SERVER MODEL METHODS

A **system call** is a request for service from the operating system on which an application program is running. The application program makes a system call by executing a line of code that specifies the name of a function and perhaps function arguments, which specialize it for a particular task. This function is part of the Application Program Interface (**API**), shown in Figure 4-1.

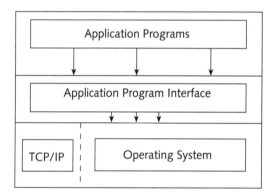

Figure 4-1   Application Program Interface (API)

Typical API functions such as Open, Close, Read, Write, and Seek cause the local operating system to take some action related to a file. However, it is possible to call API functions using different parameters that will access the TCP/IP stack as if it were another file. This was how TCP/IP was accessed when it was originally added to the BSD UNIX operating system. In this case the system call is actually a request for service from a remote operating system.

 IP addresses are discussed in Chapter 5: "IP Addressing."

Instead of depending on system calls designed for service from the local operating system, in order to access a protocol stack, application programs can use new functions that have been added to the API. These functions are specialized to the particular local operating system and the particular protocol stack, as indicated in Figure 4-2.

4

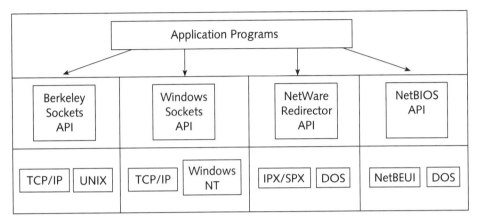

Figure 4-2   APIs for different operating systems and protocol stacks

Three new terms in Figure 4-2 are socket, NetBIOS, and NetBEUI. A **socket** is an address pair. The first address in the pair is the IP address of the computer. The second address of the pair is called a port. The **port** is a number that is assigned to either a client or server process. When a packet is received, the port identifies the process to which the packet should be delivered. **NetBIOS** is an API function that originally provided a monolithic network communications protocol for DOS. **NetBEUI** (NetBIOS Extended User Interface) is an IBM enhancement of NetBIOS. It is the default transport protocol stack for Microsoft Networks. Windows Sockets is based on Berkeley Sockets. Windows Sockets is a standard that defines a networking API that application developers use to create application programs for the entire family of Microsoft Windows operating systems, not just Windows NT. Windows Sockets provides a single-standard programming interface that is supported by all major vendors implementing TCP/IP for Windows systems. Windows Sockets allows application programs written for UNIX to be ported to Windows NT. The NetWare redirector shown in Figure 4-2 is one written for a NetWare client. It captures requests for service from a DOS application program and passes them either to DOS for local service or to the NetWare protocol stack for remote service. This redirector is called NETX in NetWare 3.11 and becomes a set of modules—called Virtual Loadable Modules (**VLMs**)—in version 3.12 and later.

Figure 4-3 indicates how the Windows NT 4.0 environment provides access for application programs to the Windows NT operating system and to multiple transport protocol stacks.

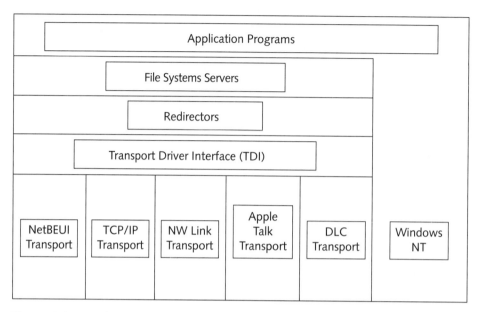

Figure 4-3   Application program access to the Windows NT operating system and to multiple transport protocol stacks

As you saw in Chapter 1, the Transport Driver Interface (TDI) provides a common interface to all transport stacks. The redirectors are functions used by application programs as APIs that provide information to the TDI layer necessary for it to switch the request to the desired transport stack; the file system servers map packets presented in formats used by other file systems into NTFS format, and map the NTFS format into the "foreign" format when that is necessary to provide services to a client.

Now that the communication framework that the TCP/IP protocol suite supports has been discussed, in the next section the details of the TCP/IP protocols and their implementation will be examined.

THE TCP/IP PROTOCOL STACK

The left side of Figure 4-4 shows the DOD TCP/IP protocol stack. The right side of the figure shows specific protocols that are found in the layers of the stack. The layers in a TCP/IP protocol stack are currently referred to by the names Application layer, Transport layer, Internet layer, and Network Interface layer. These terms, instead of the original DOD terms, will be used in this book from this point on.

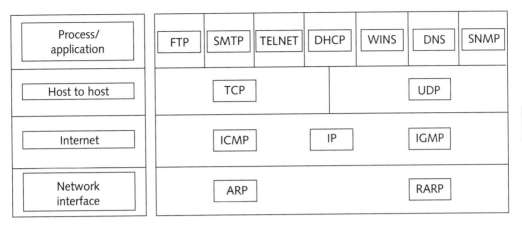

Figure 4-4   Layers of the DOD TCP/IP protocol stack and specific protocols in
the layers

THE APPLICATION LAYER

The Application layer of the TCP/IP protocol stack contains protocols that provide services
often needed by many application programs. This arrangement minimizes the need for each
application program to include all of these services in its code. Among the many TCP/IP
Application layer protocols, those shown in Figure 4-4 are probably the ones used most often.

- File Transfer Protocol (FTP). FTP provides an excellent example of the client/
  server model implementation discussed in the last section. The server FTP process
  requests its local operating system to "open" its well-known port. The operating
  system binds the process to the well-known port ID, on which the server process
  will receive control packets. For FTP, the port ID = 21. A **well-known port ID** is
  the ID of a process that is used so often that it has been assigned a unique ID. An
  application program wanting to use the FTP service will call the specific API function that accesses the TCP/IP protocol stack that starts the client FTP process. A
  port with an arbitrary ID is bound by the client operating system to the FTP client
  process. By means of the TCP and IP protocols, a control packet containing the IP
  address of the computer on which the FTP server process is running, and the
  server process well-known port ID (21), the IP address of the computer on
  which the FTP client process is running and the port ID of the client process
  are sent to the server computer. When the server process receives the request, it
  asks its operating system to open another well-known port with the ID = 20,
  which will be used for further communications between itself and this client.
  This second port is opened so that the server FTP process can receive control
  packets from other clients while sending files to the previous client.
- Simple Mail Transfer Protocol (SMTP). An SMTP client process on one host
  transfers electronic mail to a mailbox managed by a server process on another
  host. The process is initiated when the client sends the HELO command and the
  domain name of its host to the server process at Port 25. The server process sends
  a reply that includes the domain name of its host. The client then sends a series of

frames containing the e-mail addresses of the sender and the recipient(s). The client then sends a frame containing the mail message. The server sends a reply frame with a command, indicating that the message was received without error, or a command that requests a retransmission.

- Telnet. Telnet is a protocol that allows the local computer to logon to a remote computer as if the local computer were a terminal directly attached to the remote computer. A user of an application program invokes the Telnet process by typing the command Telnet at the MS-DOS prompt or by clicking on the command in a Windows based application program, followed by an argument that can either be the domain name of the remote machine or of its IP address. The request will be delivered to the Telnet server process at a well-known port with ID = 23. The Telnet server process creates a port for the client process to use to send commands to a Telnet server process and sends that port ID and a logon prompt to the client process. Commands on the remote computer can now be executed.

- Dynamic Host Configuration Protocol (DHCP). DHCP was devised to automate configuration of TCP/IP protocols for large networks. This automation is especially useful now that there are so many portable computers moving between networks. When a client computer that has the DHCP protocol installed starts up, it broadcasts a request for an IP address. A server that has the DHCP service installed sends a reply message that includes a unique address that can be used. This address is taken from a range of IP addresses assigned to the server. The address is not permanent but leased for a time set by the DHCP service.

- Windows Internet Name Service (WINS). Communication between a WINS sever and a WINS-enabled client creates a dynamic database of mappings of NetBIOS names to IP addresses. When a WINS-enabled client starts, it sends a name registration request message to the WINS server. This message includes the NetBIOS names of the computer and processes running on that computer and the IP address of the computer's interface. The WINS server uses these name registration requests to establish a current database for the local network to which the server is attached. WINS servers on different networks communicate with each other automatically and periodically in order to maintain a consistent intranet-wide database. Applications using the NetBIOS name of a destination computer obtain a mapping to the IP address of that computer by sending a name query request to the local WINS server. DHCP can be used to provide IP addresses to a WINS-enabled client. These IP addresses are then transmitted to the WINS server when the client starts.

The Domain Name System (DNS) and domain names will be discussed in detail in Chapter 9: "Name Services."

4

- Domain Name System (DNS). If the IP address of a computer on which a server process resides is not available to a client process, but the domain name of the computer is known, the following steps are taken:

1. The client process makes a call to another local client process called a name resolver.

2. The name resolver sends the domain name to a computer on the local network that is running a DNS server. A typical **domain name** might be "unity.ncsu.edu," where edu (educational institution) is the top level in the domain label, ncsu (North Carolina State University) is the label of the subdomain, and unity is the name of the computer that is running the DNS server. If this computer does not have the IP address corresponding to the domain name in its database, it will provide the name resolver with the IP address of another DNS server.

3. The result of this iterative process is an IP address that is delivered to the original client process.

4. The original client process can now communicate with the intended server process, using the IP address and the well-known port of the server process.

- Simple Network Management Protocol (SNMP). SNMP is a protocol that is used to obtain statistical information about a network device. Any network device, such as a computer or router or hub, can be loaded with software that can store and access information about the usage of the device. Such software is called an **agent**. It is a server process that provides information requested by a network management application client process. The management client process can also request that the agent process change device configuration parameter values. For example, a management client process can send an SNMP message that disables a device.

Application layer protocols must also perform the functions of protocols included in the Session and Presentation layers of the OSI Reference Model. As you have seen in the discussion of that model in Chapter 1, these functions include translating between different computer representations of data, translating from the ASN.1 syntax used by Application layer protocols to the transfer syntax used by the transport protocols, and encryption and decryption of data.

Table 4-1 provides a brief summary of the functions of the Application layer protocols that have been discussed.

Table 4-1   Summary of Functions Provided by Principal TCP/IP Application Layer Protocols

Protocol	Acronym	Function
File Transfer	FTP	Client and server processes that communicate to transfer files from the FTP server process to the FTP client process
Simple Mail Transfer	SMTP	Client and server processes that communicate to provide reliable transfer of e-mail to a mailbox
Telnet	TELNET	Client and server processes that communicate to establish a remote logon capability for the client computer
Dynamic Host Configuration Protocol	DHCP	Client and server processes that communicate to provide a leased IP address for the client
Domain Name System	DNS	Client and server processes that communicate to map a domain name into an IP address
Simple Network Management	SNMP	Client and server processes that communicate to provide network device statistics
Windows	WINS	Client and server processes that communicate to map a NetBIOS name to an IP address

THE TRANSPORT LAYER

There is good overlap of the functions provided by the TCP/IP Transport layer and the OSI Transport layer that was discussed in Chapter 1. The TCP/IP Transport layer consists of two protocols: the TCP and the UDP. The Application layer protocols FTP, SMTP, Telnet, and DHCP use TCP, while WINS, DNS, and SNMP use UDP. TCP will be discussed first.

Figure 4-5 shows the Ethernet II frame that was first introduced as Figure 1-14 in Chapter 1. Figure 4-5 also shows IP and TCP headers. When UDP is used, its header replaces the TCP header. First, TCP and its header are discussed.

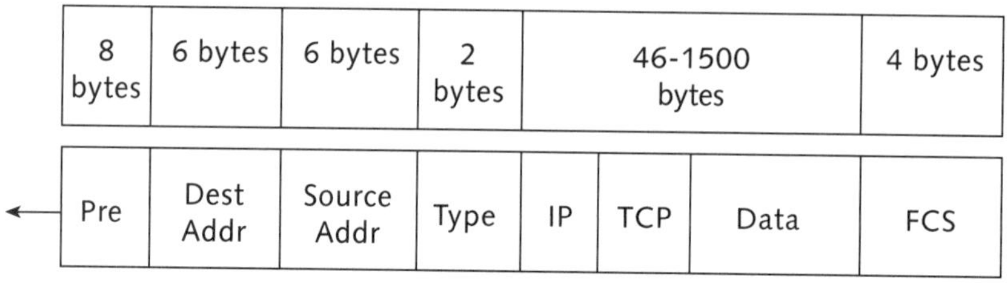

8 bytes	6 bytes	6 bytes	2 bytes	46-1500 bytes	4 bytes
Pre	Dest Addr	Source Addr	Type	IP	TCP	Data	FCS

Figure 4-5   Ethernet II frame

The Transmission Control Protocol (TCP)

The primary function of TCP is to provide reliable communication between the source application program and the destination application program. This reliability is called end-to-end reliability, and it is more encompassing than the point-to-point reliability that is provided by the Data Link layer of the OSI model. Point-to-point reliability ensures error-free communication only between two devices on a network. End-to-end reliability means that a packet sent by the Application layer port in the source computer is exactly the packet received by the Application layer port in the destination computer. To be sure that this is the case, TCP compares the bit pattern in the received packet to the bit pattern in the transmitted packet before passing it to the Application layer port. If an error has occurred in transmission, TCP constructs an error packet and sends it to the source computer, requesting packet retransmission. For the source to be able to send the packet again it must have kept a copy of the frame sent.

Flow control of packets between source and destination is another function provided by TCP. TCP sends control packets between computers to establish communication procedures that are acceptable to both computers. During this "hand-shaking" process, one of the parameters that is negotiated is the "sliding window" size. The details of how the sliding window is used are extensive, but we can describe its essence by referring to Figure 4-6.

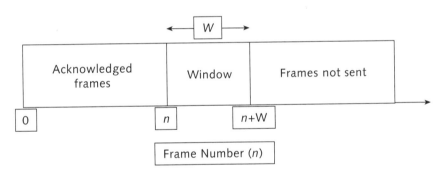

Figure 4-6 Sliding window

Both the sending and receiving computers count the number of frames they send and receive. Both computers send acknowledgment (**ACK**) and negative acknowledgment (**NAK**) frames in response to frames that they receive. In Figure 4-6, one computer has sent n frames and has received n ACKs of those frames. The window size, W, is the number of frames that one machine is allowed to send without receiving an ACK. Typical window sizes are in the range of 7–128 frames. As a computer sends frames, if no ACKs are received, the window gradually closes with each frame sent, until there is no more window. No further frames can be sent until an ACK is received. In this way the computer receiving the frames maintains control over the rate at which it can process received frames.

TCP is implemented by the header of the TCP segment. The fields in the TCP segment and how they are used are described in Table 4-2.

Table 4-2 Fields of the TCP Segment

Section	Field	Bits	Description
Header	Source Port	16	ID of the Application layer process port that is sending a packet
	Destination Port	16	ID of the Application layer process port that is receiving the packet
	Sequence Number	32	Identifies, in units of 32 bits, the location of the data in this segment relative to the start of the user's message
	ACK Number	32	Specifies the sequence number of the next byte that the source expects to receive next from the destination machine. This is how the destination machine knows if any packets get lost during transmission.
	Header Length	4	An integer that specifies the TCP header length in units of 32 bits. From this information, the receiving TCP can determine where the data field starts.
	Reserved	6	Field reserved for future use
	Code Bits	6	Setting of a code bit to 1 specifies: (1) the Urgent Pointer field is valid, (2) the ACK Number field is valid, (3) the segment requests a Push, (4) connection abort, (5) synchronize sequence numbers, and (6) end of byte stream.
	Window	16	Specifies how many bytes the sending machine can accept without loss of packets. The buffer size should be equal to the number of bytes in the initial size of the sliding window.
	Checksum	16	A binary addition by the sender, in 16-bit units, over the TCP segment and a TCP pseudoheader, both padded with zeros to be an integral number of 16-bit units. The pseudo header is not transmitted. The IP layer in the receiver creates this pseudoheader again and passes it to the TCP layer so that it can calculate the checksum and compare it to the received checksum. The pseudoheader contains the IP addresses of the sending and receiving machines. This information assures TCP that the packet is assigned to the right connection.
	Urgent Pointer	16	When the first bit in the Code Bits field is set to 1, the urgent pointer points to the end of urgent data in a TCP segment, measured in bytes from the sequence number. Segments containing urgent data are processed before any other segments.
	Options	variable	This field contains one byte for the option number, the number of bytes in the option, and a number of option bytes. There are only two option numbers: 0 specifies the end of the option list, and 2 specifies that the option gives the maximum segment size that the sending machine can handle.
	Padding	variable	Because the Options field is variable, this field is used to make the TCP segment header an integral number of 32-bit units.
Data	Data	variable	Contains the Application layer header and the application program data

The User Datagram Protocol (UDP)

As you have seen from the discussion of the TCP segment in the previous section and Table 4-2, the control procedures implemented by TCP generate many bytes of communication overhead, the TCP segment header. There are many communications that do not require so much reliability. When this is the case, UDP is used. UDP may not apply any of the control methods just discussed. Different packets may traverse different physical circuits to the destination computer and may arrive out of order. It is then up to the Application layer process to reorder them. Packets may get lost, and packets may not be checked for errors incurred in transmission. However, UDP usually works well because of the low error rates introduced by today's communications hardware. The fields in the UDP segment are shown and described in Table 4-3.

Table 4-3 Fields in the UDP Segment

Section	Field	Bits	Description
Header	Source Port	16	ID of the Application layer process port of the sending computer
	Destination Port	16	ID of the Application layer process port of the receiving computer
	Message Length	16	Total number of bytes in the UDP segment
	Checksum	16	Binary addition of 16-bit units in the UDP segment. This may or may not be used.
Data	Data	variable	Contains the Application layer header and the application program data

Whether it is the TCP or UDP header that is used by the transport segment, the header is included in the data section of the IP segment constructed by the IP protocol.

THE INTERNET LAYER

 The Internet Group Management Protocol (IGMP) will be discussed in Chapter 5: "IP Addressing." Details of IP routing are the subject of Chapter 6: "Bridging and Routing."

The Internet layer contains three protocols: the Internet Protocol (IP), the Internet Control Message Protocol (ICMP), and the Internet Group Management Protocol (IGMP). IP is discussed first.

The Internet Protocol (IP)

IP is a connectionless protocol. A **connectionless** protocol is one that includes no mechanisms for providing reliability. It provides no error checking, requests for retransmission, or flow control. IP is concerned only with routing packets between networks. IP provides the IP addresses of the source and destination networks, and of the source and destination computers attached to those networks. If a packet is to be passed to another network, the router connecting the networks (1) reads the network part of the destination IP address in the IP header, (2) searches its **routing table** for the network that maps to the network part of the destination address, (3) creates a frame with new source and destination hardware addresses, (4) encapsulates the IP segment in the new frame, and then (5) transmits the new frame onto the next network along the path to the destination network.

IP is implemented by the header of the IP segment. As you will see in Table 4-4, the Data section of the IP segment encapsulates all other packet headers as well as the data generated by an application program. Thus an Ethernet II frame consists of a MAC header, the IP segment, and a MAC trailer. Table 4-4 describes the fields in the IP segment.

Table 4-4 Fields of the IP Segment

Section	Field	Bits	Description
Header	Version	4	The version of IP that created the segment header. It is currently version 4, but version 6 will provide more IP addresses. All devices check the version number to be sure the header is processed correctly.
	Header Length	4	The length of the IP header in units of 32 bits
	Service Type	8	This field contains five subfields. They are used to request: (1) precedence (3 bits), (2) delay (1 bit), (3) throughput (1 bit), (4) reliability (1 bit), and (5) unused (2 bits).
	Total Length	16	This is the total length of the IP segment. The length of the Data section of the segment is then obtained by subtracting the header length.
	Identification	16	A number that specifies the IP segment. When segments are fragmented, this number is put into the header of each fragment. **Fragmentation** is the breaking up of segments into smaller packets that can be handled by all devices on the network.
	Flags	3	The high-order bit is set to 1 if the segment may not be fragmented. The two low-order bits control fragmentation, when it is used. The lower-order bit of this pair is set to 1 if more fragments of this segment are to follow.
	Fragment Offset	13	The offset in bytes of the data in this fragment, from the start of the data in the segment, before fragmentation
	Time to Live (TTL)	8	This field is used to keep an IP segment from remaining on the network indefinitely. Each router through which the segment passes reduces TTL by 1. Also, for every second that a segment waits for service in a router, TTL is reduced by 1. The segment is discarded if TTL reaches 0.

Table 4-4   Fields of the IP Segment (continued)

Section	Field	Bits	Description
	Protocol	8	The ID of the protocol that was used to create the Data section of the IP segment. This might be TCP or UDP, for example. The ID is 6 for TCP, and 17 for UDP.
	Header Checksum	16	Produced by binary addition of 16-bit units in the IP header. This calculation is repeated by each router through which the segment passes, and at the destination computer.
	Source IP Address	32	The IP address of the source computer. It is distinct from the hardware address.
	Destination IP Address	32	The IP address of the destination computer
	Options	variable	This field will be described after this table.
	Padding	variable	Bytes of zeros to ensure that the header contains an integral number of 32-bit units
Data	Data	variable	Contains all other headers and application program data

The subfields of the IP header Options field are shown in Figure 4-7 and are described in Table 4-5. Options are included in the IP header primarily for testing and debugging of the network.

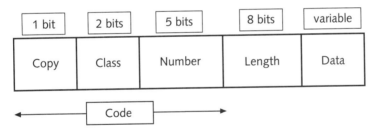

Figure 4-7   IP header options field

Table 4-5   The IP Header Options field

Subfield	Bits	Description
Copy	1	If segment fragmentation is used, this bit is set to 1 if the Options field is to be copied into all fragments. It is set to 0 if the Options field is to be copied only into the first fragment.
Class	2	Only two classes are currently used: 0 and 2. (See text that follows.)
Number	5	This is the number of a specific option in the class.
Length	8	The length in bytes of the Options field
Data	variable	The option's data

The following are three options that are often used in the IP header:

- Record route. This is a Class 0, Number 7 option. In this case the option data is an empty list in which each router on the path to the destination network records its IP address.

- Source Routing. This is a Class 0, Number 9 option. In this case the option data is a list of router IP addresses that the segment must use to reach the destination network.

- Time stamp. This is a Class 2, Number 4 option. In this case the option data is an empty list in which each router through which the segment passes specifies the time at which it handled the segment, expressed in milliseconds past midnight Universal Time.

These options might, for example, be specified by arguments included in a command typed by the user at the MS-DOS command prompt or in the configuration of an application program such as e-mail.

The other Internet layer protocol that will be examined in this chapter is ICMP. This protocol makes it possible for network devices to inform one another of network conditions.

The Internet Control Message Protocol (ICMP)

You made use of ICMP in Chapter 3, "Windows NT 4.0 Utilities," when Network Monitor was used to capture a frame generated by the PING.EXE application. The PING command invokes Echo Request and Echo Reply types of ICMP messages. Its execution causes a set of Echo Request messages to be sent to the IP address used as the argument of the Ping command. The corresponding number of Echo Reply messages from the destination indicate that there is an IP network between source and destination. In this section, you will examine the structure of ICMP. ICMP can generate many types of messages. These messages are primarily used by routers to report to the source computer that an IP segment cannot be delivered to the destination network or computer. There are also message types that request information or request that a source computer decrease the rate at which it is sending frames. ICMP messages are generated by IP in one machine and received by IP in the destination machine.

The Echo Request and Echo Reply ICMP message types will be used as examples of a specific ICMP message format. Table 4-6 describes the fields in the ICMP Echo Request message.

Table 4-6   Fields in the ICMP Echo Request Message

Section	Field	Bits	Description
Header	Type	8	There are eleven message types. The Echo Request Type field has the value 8.
	Code	8	There are thirteen codes that can be used to give meaning to the message type. The Echo Request code has the value 0.
	Checksum	16	The binary addition of 16-bit units in the ICMP message.
	Identifier	16	A number used to identify which Echo Request
	Sequence Number	16	A number that identifies the specific Echo Request when multiple requests are sent in sequence to the same destination IP address.
Data	Optional Data	variable	If sent, the data sent is returned in the Echo Reply message from the destination machine.

If the intended destination receives the Echo Request message, an identical ICMP message is returned as an Echo Reply message, except that the Type field is set to 0. If an Echo Reply is not received within a time set by IP, IP in the computer that sent the Echo Request generates a "destination unreachable" message.

Whenever any IP segment cannot be delivered by a router, the router will send an ICMP message, containing the fields described in Table 4-7, to the source computer.

Table 4-7   Destination Unreachable ICMP Messages

Section	Field	Bits	Value	Description
Header	Type	8	3	Destination unreachable
	Code	8	0	Network unreachable
			1	Host unreachable
			2	Protocol unreachable
			3	Port unreachable
			4	Fragmentation needed but "Don't Fragment" bit set
			5	Source route failed
	Unused	32	0	32 zero bits
Data	Data	variable		The IP header plus the first 64 bits of the IP data segment section

When IP in the source machine receives one of these messages, it uses the Data section to evaluate the problem. In addition to the IP header, the first 64 bits of the IP segment Data section are returned because those bits include the source and destination protocol ports in the TCP header.

The Internet Group Management Protocol (IGMP)

Because this protocol is contained in the Internet layer, it is mentioned in this chapter for the sake of completeness. However, the subject relates to IP addressing and therefore will be discussed in Chapter 5. Briefly, ICMP is a protocol that is used to manage IP multicasting. **Multicasting** is the specification of an IP address that is recognized by a group of machines. Broadcasting is a special case of multicasting, in which all machines process the received message.

In the next section, the Network Interface layer (the last of the TCP/IP protocol stack layers) is examined.

THE NETWORK INTERFACE LAYER

The Network Interface layer is a layer that was designed to isolate the higher layers in the TCP/IP protocol stack from the details of accessing a specific network, such as an Ethernet network. Remember, it was the intention of the TCP/IP designers to build a logical end-to-end connection that was to be independent of physical implementation. This layer provides an interface only between the higher-layer protocols and established media access protocols that are appropriate for the medium to be accessed. The functionality of this layer is therefore much simpler than that of the higher layers in the TCP/IP protocol stack.

The Network Interface layer includes software that provides an interface between multiple protocol stacks and a particular NIC driver. Two standard interfaces are the Network Device Interface Specification (NDIS) Standard and the Open Data-Link Interface (ODI) Standard. Also required by specifications for this layer are mechanisms for providing a database that includes parameter values such as: a number for the NIC, the number of different types of packets received, the IP address, and the hardware address. It is this database that the SNMP agent on the machine accesses on request from a network management application program. The Network Interface layer also includes the protocols ARP and RARP, which are used to map IP and hardware addresses into one another. ARP and RARP will be discussed in Chapter 5.

When a packet is received by the NIC, the NIC informs the CPU by means of a hardware interrupt. The operating system makes a function call to the driver to collect the packet and to deposit it either in a buffer in main memory set aside for that NIC or in RAM on the NIC. Processing by IP then begins. The hardware interface to the physical network depends on the type of network to which the NIC is attached. For example, if the interface is to an Ethernet network, the ISO/IEC 8802-3 standard is followed in constructing the header and trailer of the frame, and the CSMA/CD media access method is used to transmit the frame onto the Ethernet medium. If the IP segment must traverse a router, the router will encapsulate the IP segment into a frame that is appropriate for the next network, and another medium access method will be used. For example, if the next network is a remote link of a WAN, the point-to-point protocol (PPP) might be used to encapsulate the IP segment. By means of encapsulation methods that are appropriate for each network that the IP segment must traverse, the IP segment is delivered to the destination network in the same form in which it was created in the source computer.

CHAPTER SUMMARY

- The history of the development of the TCP/IP suite of protocols and the rationale behind its development by the DOD agency ARPA were reviewed.

- You saw that this development was originally intended to provide a set of protocols that would establish a consistent approach to communication on a network of computers used in academic institutions. However, the wide distribution of this protocol suite led to its adoption by many other organizations, and today the TCP/IP protocol suite dominates communications on the Internet.

- Client/server model concepts and methods were discussed because this model provides the framework for communications on the Internet and because the TCP/IP protocol suite is most often used to implement the methods that support this model.

- You saw that a client is a process that requests service from a server process. The client initiates a request by making a system call. The system call is a call to a function in the Application Program Interface (API). This function results in a service being initiated by the local operating system. This service may be provided by a local process or may entail access to a remote operating system and a remote process.

- An excellent example of the implementation of the client/server model is the chain consisting of an FTP client process, the Windows Socket API, the Windows NT Workstation operating system, the TCP/IP protocol stack, the Windows NT Server operating system, and an FTP server process.

- The protocols associated with the Application, Transport, Internet, and Network Interface layers of the TCP/IP protocol stack were discussed.

- You learned that the implementation of a protocol is accomplished by the field in the header of the protocol segment.

- The fields in the headers of the IP, TCP, UDP, and ICMP segments were examined, and descriptions of the functions that each performs were provided.

REVIEW QUESTIONS

1. What was the original goal of the ARPA-sponsored TCP/IP research?
   a. To add TCP/IP to the UNIX operating system
   b. To establish a standard set of protocols for communications on a network of computers at academic institutions
   c. To build a protocol stack for the Internet

2. Which of the following is true?
   a. Circuit switching bandwidth is reserved.
   b. Packet switching allows network bandwidth to be shared only by datagrams.
   c. Packet switching does not allow virtual circuits.

3. Which of the following is true? Datagram packet switching increases throughput by:
   a. Sharing of links by packets from multiple sources
   b. Using only links that have short queues
   c. Using only links that are constructed of optical fibers

4. Why are TCP/IP protocols considered de facto standards?
   a. They are approved by standards organizations.
   b. They are used for only one purpose.
   c. They have been established by a consensus of users.

5. Which of the following is true?
   a. Client/server architecture assumes an unbalanced distribution of network resources.
   b. The client/server model assumes the existence of the server architecture.
   c. When the client/server model is employed, one computer, the server, must always execute the server processes.

6. An Application Program Interface (API) function is called by an application program to:
   a. Provide access to the services of another process
   b. Control the hard drive on a computer
   c. Access the Windows Sockets program

7. What is a socket?
   a. A hardware address
   b. A specific IP address
   c. An IP address/port address pair

8. A port is:
   a. A number that identifies the address of a program
   b. A connector on an NIC
   c. Another name for a socket

9. The purpose of the Windows Transport Device Interface (TDI) is to:
   a. Provide access to the NIC driver
   b. Provide access for an application program to the TCP/IP protocol stack
   c. Provide a common interface to the transport protocol stacks for the redirector APIs

10. The purpose of specific APIs, such as Windows Sockets, is to:
    a. Eliminate the need for NetBIOS
    b. Allow an application program to "open" a specific network connection as if it were opening a file
    c. Redirect the system call of an application program to the local operating system

11. How many protocol layers are there in the TCP/IP protocol stack?
    a. 7
    b. 4
    c. 6

12. What are the names of the protocols in the Transport layer?

    a. TCP

    b. TCP and UDP

    c. TCP, UDP, and ICMP

13. What are the names of the protocols in the Internet layer?

    a. IP

    b. IP and ICMP

    c. IP, ICMP, and IGMP

14. What are the names of the protocols in the Network Interface layer?

    a. ARP

    b. RARP

    c. ARP and RARP

15. If a computer knows the domain name of another computer with which it wants to communicate using the TCP/IP protocol stack, what information must it *first* obtain in order to communicate?

    a. The hardware address of the remote computer

    b. The IP address of the remote computer

    c. The IP address of the default router

16. If a computer needs the IP address of a remote computer with which it wants to communicate, how does it obtain the IP address if it does not know the hardware address of the remote computer?

    a. It sends the domain name of the remote computer to the default router.

    b. It sends the domain name of the remote computer to the DNS server on the local domain.

    c. It sends the domain name of the remote computer to the DNS server on the network of the remote computer.

17. How does the TCP protocol on the destination computer control the flow of packets from the source computer?

    a. It sends no acknowledgment messages to the source computer.

    b. It discards all received messages when its receive buffer is full.

    c. It limits the number of frames a source can send without receiving an acknowledgment.

18. What is the minimum length of the header of a TCP segment in bytes?

    a. 17

    b. 256

    c. 1500

19. What is the minimum length of the header of a UDP segment in bytes?

    a. 8

    b. 16

    c. 32

20. What is the minimum size of the header of an IP segment in bytes?

   a. 20

   b. 32

   c. variable

CASE PROJECT

The status of the case project after completing Chapter 3, "Windows NT 4.0 Utilities," is shown in Figure 4–8.

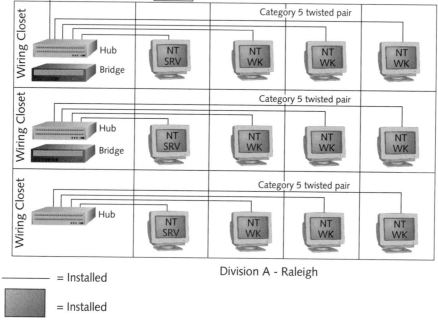

————— = Installed

▨ = Installed

Figure 4-8   Case Project environment prior to Chapter 4

Each department has a network that is physically connected through the hub in that department, and each computer has an operating system installed. No communication is possible because no networking software has been configured to provide the logical connection that was discussed in this chapter. In Exercise 1 that follows, you will install a logical connection to the network for the server. You will then proceed to configure networking software on the other machines in the Raleigh division. Computers on the same floor will then have the hardware and software resources required to communicate. In Exercise 2, you test the connectivity of the network. In Exercises 3, 4, 5, and 6, you analyze an FTP session and the TCP/IP headers.

EXERCISE 1—CONFIGURATION OF THE TCP/IP INTERFACE

In this exercise, you will perform the configuration on another computer that has the Windows NT 4.0 Server operating system installed. If possible, perform a similar installation on your computer. From the Start menu, select **Settings** and then click **Control Panel**. In the Control Panel Window, double-click on the **Network** icon. This produces the Network dialog box, which has five Tabs at the top. Click the **Adapters** tab and then the Properties button to obtain Figure 4-9.

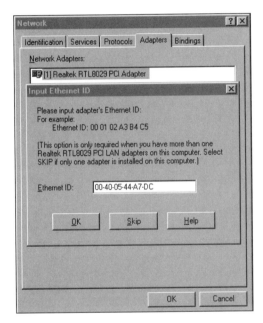

Figure 4-9   Network adapter dialog box

The Adaptor configuration Network Adapters: text box in Figure 4-9 shows that Windows NT detected the *Realtek RTL8029 PCI Adapter* during the installation. This is an NE 2000-compatible Ethernet "plug-and-play" adapter for the PCI bus of this computer. A **plug-and-play adapter** is one that is automatically configured by the operating system. You are asked to specify the Ethernet ID (the hardware address) of the adapter card. Because there is only one Realtek adapter on this server, the driver will not be confused about which adapter to communicate with. However, you should have a record of all hardware addresses of the network you administer, so take the opportunity now to find out what the address is. On computers with either Windows NT 4.0 Workstation or Windows NT 4.0 Server installed, you can find the hardware addresses of the NICs installed, and the services that use them, by doing the following:

1. Click **Windows NT Diagnostics** on the Administrative Tools (common) menu.

2. Click the **Network** tab.

3. Click the **Transports** button to see the hardware addresses and the services they are bound to.

You can also obtain this information by typing the name of the TCP/IP diagnostic tool **ipconfig** with the switch **/all** at the command prompt. The hardware address of this server's network adapter is 00-40-05-44-A7-DC. Hardware addresses are written in the hexadecimal number system using 12 digits. This number is stored in ROM on the adapter, and sometimes it is written on the adapter. Each pair of hexadecimal digits is equivalent to 8 binary digits, or 1 byte. Thus the hardware address has 6 bytes. This is the address that is used in the Source and Destination fields of an Ethernet frame.

Having obtained the harware address of your computer:

1. In the Ethernet ID:, enter the hardware address.

2. Click **OK** to obtain the dialog box shown in Figure 4-10.

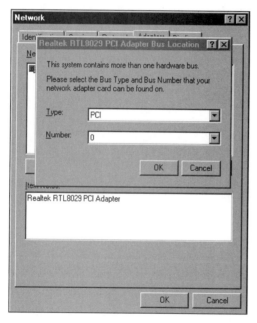

Figure 4-10   Selection of bus for the network adapter

The dialog box in Figure 4-10 for the Realtek adapter says that the installation process detected that there is more than one bus in this server. That is true. There is an **ISA** (Industry Standard Architecture) bus and a **PCI** (Peripheral Component Interface) bus in this server. The text boxes are used to type in the bus type and the bus number. The Realtek adapter is plugged into bus 0 on this server. Thus all communications with it should be placed on bus 0. Click **OK** to have your selections stored. You are returned to the Network dialog box. Click the **Protocols** tab, and you are presented with the window shown in Figure 4-11.

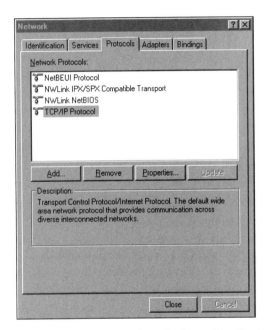

Figure 4-11   Protocol stacks bound to the Windows NT 4.0 operating system

The text box shows that three protocol stacks and NWLink NetBIOS were selected during installation of this server for binding to the Windows NT 4.0 Server operating system. These protocol stacks and NWLink NetBIOS will be loaded when the operating system starts up. However, that action is not enough for them to be usable. Because you are going to use TCP/IP, highlight it and then click the **Properties** button. You are presented with the Microsoft TCP/IP Properties dialog box. This dialog box allows you to determine how you want to configure the interface bound to the TCP/IP stack. Click the **IP Address** tab. The resulting dialog box is shown in Figure 4-12.

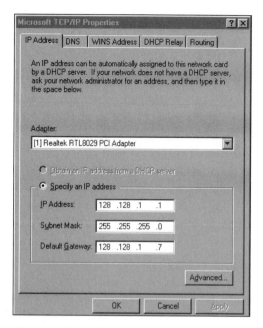

Figure 4-12   Microsoft TCP/IP Properties dialog box

This window serves as an introduction to the next chapter, "IP Addressing." The dialog at the top of the box can be ignored for now. DHCP (Dynamic Host Configuration Protocol) is the subject of Chapter 7. An IP address is typed into the "IP address" text boxes. The IP address for the Realtek RTL8029 Adapter is given the value 128.128.1.1. This is a typical IP address, which consists of four sets of decimal digits separated by dots. Each set can have values from 0 to 255. We will discuss Subnet Mask and Default Gateway in Chapter 5. Every adapter attached to a network that uses the IP protocol must have an IP address. Click **OK** to store this configuration and to bind it to the hardware address of the adapter. You are returned to the Network dialog box. Click the **Bindings** tab, and you see the Window shown in Figure 4-13.

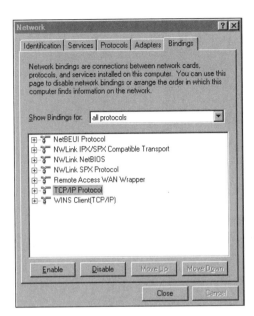

Figure 4-13   Bindings of protocols, services, and NIC

The text at the top of the Bindings tab is instructive. Selecting bindings is what establishes the logical network. Every installation step up to this point has provided the pieces to be bound. There are two types of bindings going on here. One is a binding between protocol stacks and the driver of the network adapter. The other is the binding between application layer processes and the protocol stacks. By means of these bindings, the pieces being bound are provided with locations in memory where they can talk to one another to establish the logical connection. If you click a ⊞ box, you are shown a list of the services to which that particular protocol is bound. If you select "all adapters" in the Show Bindings for textbox, adapters in your computer are listed. You click the ⊞ box next to an adapter to obtain a list of the protocols bound to it.

EXERCISE 2—TESTING THE CONNECTIVITY OF THE IP NETWORK

After the procedures described in Exercise 1 have been implemented on each of the work-stations on the network, all users on the network should be able to communicate. To see if this is really so, execute PING.EXE. To execute PING.EXE and see if there is an Echo Reply packet, click the **Start** button, select **Programs**, and then click **Command Prompt**. At the prompt, type in **ping** followed by a space and the IP address of the destination machine. Example Echo Reply messages from a machine are shown in Figure 4-14.

```
Command Prompt                                                    _ □ ×

C:\>ping 128.128.1.6

Pinging 128.128.1.6 with 32 bytes of data:

Reply from 128.128.1.6: bytes=32 time<10ms TTL=128
Reply from 128.128.1.6: bytes=32 time<10ms TTL=128
Reply from 128.128.1.6: bytes=32 time<10ms TTL=128
Reply from 128.128.1.6: bytes=32 time<10ms TTL=128

C:\>
```

Figure 4-14   ICMP Echo Reply messages

Using Figure 4-14, complete the following table:

Table 4-8   The Ping Exercise

Question	Answer
What machine IP destination address was used in the Ping command?	
How do you know a connection was made?	
How much time did it take for the Request message to reach the destination machine and for the reply to be received?	
What does TTL mean?	
What was the length of the ICMP Data field?	

Figure 4-15 shows the status of your case project environment, now that you have completed Exercises 1 and 2. Only the Raleigh division Engineering Department is shown, but it is assumed that the status of the networks on the other floors is the same.

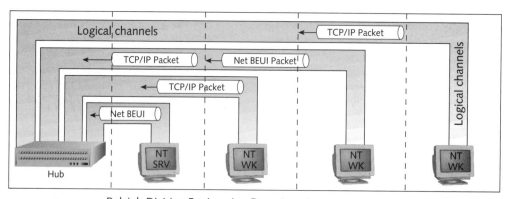

Raleigh Division Engineering Department

⬭ = Installed logical channels

Figure 4-15   Case Project environment after completing Exercises 1 and 2

The diagram says that you have configured two logical channels that can be used to communicate on this network. There is a TCP/IP channel and a NetBEUI channel. Although the arrows all point to the hub, packets with arrows pointing the other way are implied because all machines communicate through the hub.

The communication shown in this diagram assumes that each machine has a unique IP address. In Chapter 5, you will design an IP address map for the machines in the Raleigh division.

4

EXERCISE 3—USING FTP

Using FTP is a good way to exercise the TCP/IP protocol stack that you have studied and installed in this chapter. FTP is the quintessential TCP/IP Application layer protocol because it once accounted for most of the traffic on the Internet. Also, the FTP methodology and its commands and responses have their counterparts in other Application layer protocols. Thus you will get a feel for how these other Application layer protocols work when you use FTP.

Windows NT 4.0 Server includes the Microsoft Internet Information Service (IIS). This service will be discussed in detail in Chapter 10: Networking Services. IIS is used to setup access to files on your server for Internet users. In this exercise, you will make use of the FTP server component of IIS that has been installed on a computer with which you will establish an FTP session. Once IIS is installed, establishing an FTP connection is very simple.

Figure 4-16 shows an FTP session between an FTP client and the IIS FTP server. This session is actually taking place on a LAN but is identical to what would be happening if the client computer were accessing a remote server. The session in Figure 4-16 starts with the command

ftp 192.192.192.244

to make a connection to a computer with the IP address 192.192.192.244, which hosts the FTP server. The numbers at the left of each line are the commands parsed by the client or server. The text serves as a reference for the human user.

1. Access the FTP RFC # 0959 from ds.internic.net. You can accomplish this by completing either Step (a) or Step (b):

   a. Use URL ftp://ds.internic.net on the WWW

   b. Use FTP itself and an application such as Fetch. In the first screen that Fetch shows, you enter:

   - HOST NAME: ds.internic.net

   - USER ID: anonymous

   - PASSWORD: your e-mail address

2. Use the information in RFC # 0959 and Figure 4-16 to complete the following table:

```
FTP                                                              _ | & | ×
Auto        ▼   [ ] 🗎 🖹 🔳 🗎 🗎 A

C:\>ftp 192.192.192.244
Connected to 192.192.192.244.
220 ibmsv Microsoft FTP Service (Version 2.0).
User (192.192.192.244:(none)): anonymous
331 Anonymous access allowed, send identity (e-mail name) as password.
Password:
230 Anonymous user logged in.
ftp> ls
200 PORT command successful.
150 Opening ASCII mode data connection for file list.
ACCOUNT POLICY.rtf
226 Transfer complete.
20 bytes received in 0.00 seconds (20000.00 Kbytes/sec)
ftp> get accoun~1.rtf
200 PORT command successful.
150 Opening ASCII mode data connection for accoun~1.rtf(4416 bytes).
226 Transfer complete.
4416 bytes received in 0.00 seconds (4416000.00 Kbytes/sec)
ftp>
```

Figure 4-16   FTP Session between a Microsoft Internet Information Service (IIS) Server and an FTP client

Table 4-9   FTP Session

Command	Meaning
220	
331	
230	
200	
226	
150	
ls	
get	

EXERCISE 4—FTP SESSION FRAMES

Figures 4-17 through 4-20 show frames captured by Network Monitor during the FTP session shown in Figure 4-16. As you saw in Chapter 3, the top panel in these figures shows some of the frames captured and the middle panel is an analysis of the hexadecimal format of the frame shown in the bottom panel. Taking Figure 4-17 as an example, and referring back to Table 4-2, you see that the lines in Figure 4-17 following (-TCP) are the fields in the TCP header of the captured frame. Using Figure 4-17 and Table 4-2, complete Table 4-10:

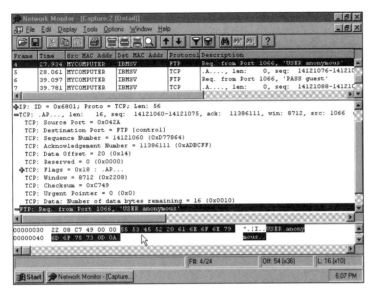

Figure 4-17   Network Monitor Capture Detail of an FTP client "USER anonymous" Request frame

Table 4-10   TCP Header of FTP Session Frame in Figure 4-17

Question	Answer
What is the length of the TCP header in bytes?	
What is the length of the FTP segment in bytes?	
What is the length of the TCP segment?	
What is the length of the IP segment?	
What is the length of the IP header?	
What is the decimal number of the FTP client port?	
What is the length of the FTP server port (see discussion in the text for this answer)?	
What is the number of the well-known FTP server port? (See discussion on page 91 for this answer.)	
What is the ratio of FTP message bytes to the total number of bytes in the frame?	

EXERCISE 5—SESSION MESSAGES

The first line of the FTP section in the middle panel in Figures 4-17 through 4-20 shows the messages sent by the FTP client to the FTP server. In the following table, relate these messages to the server response command numbers shown in Figure 4-16.

Table 4-11   Session Messages

Command	Meaning
331	
230	
200	
226	

EXERCISE 6—HEXADECIMAL CODE TRANSLATION

When you highlight a line in the middle panel of the Capture Detail window, the corresponding hexadecimal code is highlighted in the bottom panel. Convince yourself that the text in the middle panel is an accurate translation of the hexadecimal code by completing the following table:

Table 4-12   Hexadecimal Code to Text Translation

Text	Hexadecimal	Binary
'USER anonymous'		

To complete the table above, find a table that gives the ASCII binary representation of letters. Use it to convert 'USER anonymous' to binary code, translate the binary code to hexadecimal code, and compare to the highlighted hexadecimal code in the bottom panel.

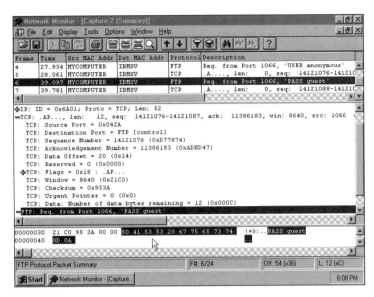

Figure 4-18   Network Monitor Capture Detail of an FTP client "PASSguest"
Request Frame

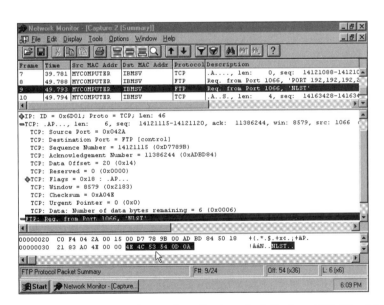

Figure 4-19   Network Monitor Capture Detail of an FTP Client NLIST Request
Frame

Figure 4-20   Network Monitor Capture Detail of an FTP Client RETR accou~1.rtf
Request Frame

Figure 4-21 shows the status of the Case Project at the Division level after this chapter. The
cylinder represents the hard drive. The cylinder platters represent the protocols that have
been installed and configured.

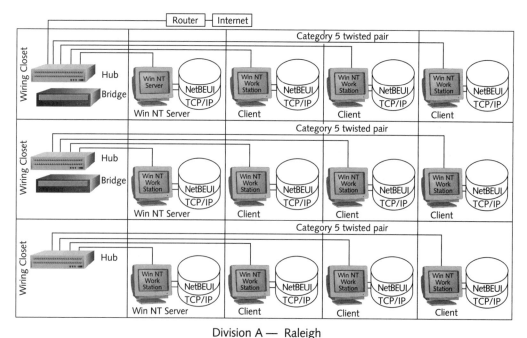

Division A — Raleigh

Figure 4-21   Status of the Case Project after Chapter 4

CHAPTER FIVE

IP ADDRESSING

In this chapter you will learn how IP addresses are obtained and how they are structured. You will learn how to use IP addresses and a subnet mask to divide a network into subnets. You will also see how the ARP and RARP protocols are used to obtain hardware and IP addresses.

IP ADDRESS CLASSES

 Information about InterNIC can be obtained at http://www.internic.net

The hardware address that is entered in the destination field of an Ethernet frame is necessary for the frame to be recognized by the NIC of the destination device. If the NIC does not recognize the hardware address, it discards the frame. The Ethernet hardware address is a 6-byte, 48-bit address. It is typically written in the hexadecimal number system. It is a "flat" address in that it has no structure. Devices that communicate using TCP/IP protocols must have an additional address, the IP address. The IP packet in the Data part of the Ethernet frame will not be processed by the TCP/IP protocols unless the IP address is recognized. The IP address is a 4-byte, 32-bit address. The IP address is a "structured" address that contains both network and device information. Figure 5-1 compares these address formats and gives an example of each type.

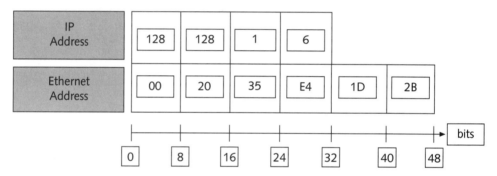

Figure 5-1   Comparison of Ethernet hardware address and IP address formats

The IP address is typically written in the decimal number system, as shown in this figure. The Ethernet address is typically written in the hexadecimal system. Each field in either address can be expressed by eight binary digits. The binary digits are of course the ones that are used by network devices. When you see these addresses written, they look like the following:

128.128.1.6

00-20-35-E4-1D-2B

There is no relationship between these formats. They are distinct ways of representing the address of a network device, but both are necessary to effect communication on a network that uses Ethernet LANs and TCP/IP protocols. Now let's look at the format of IP addresses in more detail.

The format of the IP address was chosen so that it would unambiguously specify both the address of a device and the address of the network to which the device is attached. Thus, an IP address has a network part and a device (host) part. The network part of the address is what a router uses to select the network interface to which a packet should be routed. Five **classes** of IP addresses have been defined by the InterNIC. They are labeled A through E. D and E are special classes that will be described later in this chapter. These are the classes that you will encounter most often. Each class contains a different number of networks and allows a different maximum number of devices on each network. Thus, the InterNIC can assign an organization a network from a class that maps to its needs most efficiently. Figure 5-2 will help you to understand Classes A, B, and C.

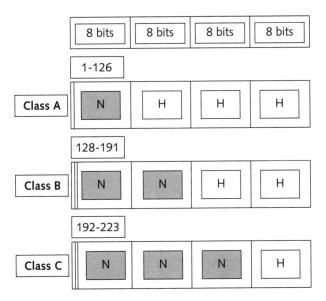

Figure 5-2   IP address classes

As was mentioned previously, an IP address is usually displayed as four fields of decimal numbers. The letters **N**(etwork) and **H**(ost) in the figure distinguish fields that are used to specify a network ID from fields that specify a device ID, respectively. The **vertical lines** in the first field in each class represent the bits that identify the class ID. The first bit in the first field of a Class A address is 0. The decimal number in the first field is determined by this bit and the values of the remaining 7 bits. The decimal number in the first field specifies the network ID. The decimal numbers in the remaining three fields specify the device ID. The first two bits in the first field of a Class B address are 1 and 0. These two bits and the remaining 6 bits determine the decimal number in the first field. The first and second fields specify the network ID of a Class B address. The decimal numbers in the last two fields specify the device ID. The first three bits in the first field of a Class C address are 1, 1, and 0. These three bits and the remaining five bits determine the decimal number in the first field. The first, second, and third fields specify the network ID of a Class C network. The decimal number in the last field specifies the device ID. Table 5-1 provides more specific information about these numbers and the ranges that are available.

Table 5-1   IP Address Classes, Field Values, Numbers of Networks, and Numbers of Hosts (Shaded Fields Specify Network ID)

Class	Class ID Bits	Field 1 Range	Field 2 Range	Field 3 Range	Field 4 Range	Number of Networks	Number of Hosts
A	0	1 – 126	0 – 255	0 – 255	0 – 255	126	16,777,216 – 2
B	10	128 – 191	0 – 255	0 – 255	0 – 255	16,384	65,536 – 2
C	110	192 – 223	0 – 255	0 – 255	0 – 255	2,097,152	256 – 2

An example of a Class B address is:

$$128.128.1.6$$

This notation is referred to as dotted decimal notation because a decimal point separates the four numbers, and because the decimal number system is used to represent the numbers. This is the IP address that you used in the last chapter with the Ping application to check the connectivity of the TCP/IP network. Except for the constraints imposed by the Class ID bits and some other constraints that will be discussed, each number can, in principle, be in the range from 0 to 255 because eight bits are available to represent each number. The bits are of course what a machine on the network reads. The decimal number is just a convenient representation for us human beings.

Let's look at some example binary IP addresses that correspond to the decimal addresses shown in Table 5-1.

Table 5-2   Binary IP Addresses Corresponding to the Decimal IP Addresses Shown in Table 5-1

Class	Class ID Bits	Field 1 Range	Field 2 Range	Field 3 Range	Field 4 Range	Number of Networks	Number of Hosts
A	0	00000001 to 01111110	00000000 to 11111111	00000000 to 11111111	00000000 to 11111111	126	16,777,216 – 2
B	10	10000000 to 10111111	00000000 to 11111111	00000000 to 11111111	00000000 to 11111111	16,384	65,536 – 2
C	110	11000000 to 11011111	00000000 to 11111111	00000000 to 11111111	00000000 to 11111111	2,097,152	256 – 2

The binary digits in bold identify the class. You will notice in Tables 5-1 and 5-2 that not all possible numbers in the network and host ranges are included. The missing numbers comprise the "special IP addresses" that will be discussed shortly. The special addresses and the Class ID bits limit the range of possible values for specifying IP addresses. Class A, Field 1 is limited to the decimal numbers between 1 and 126 (the binary numbers between 00000001 and 01111110). As you will see, this limitation is due to the special addresses 0 and 127 in the first field. Therefore, the number of Class A networks that it is possible for the InterNIC to distribute is 126.

In principle, the number of possible hosts on a Class A network is:

$$256 \times 256 \times 256 = 16,777,216$$

However, no host is allowed to have an ID of all zeros or all ones, because those IDs are part of special addresses. So the number of hosts on a Class A network is $16,777,216 - 2$ as shown in Table 5-2. A host ID of all zeros indicates that the IP address is a network address. A host ID of all ones indicates that the message is being broadcast to all hosts. Following the same reasoning, there are two fewer host connections on Class B and Class C networks than the product of the field ranges would suggest.

You will not often be concerned about special addresses, but you do need to recognize them, and not use one unintentionally. Table 5-3 describes these special addresses in general, and Table 5-4 provides binary examples.

Table 5-3   Special IP Addresses

Network Fields	Host Fields	Description
network IP address	all ones	A broadcast to all devices on "Network IP Address"
all ones	all ones	A broadcast to all devices on "this" network, where "this" means the network to which the source is attached. Cannot be a source address.
all zeros	host IP address	A source address used when the source does not yet know its network IP address. Cannot be a destination address.
all zeros	all zeros	The address of "this" host on "this" network, that is, the host is referring to itself on its network.
network IP address	all zeros	The IP address of a network
127	anything	This is called the loopback address. It is used for communication between processes on the same computer. A packet with this destination IP address does not leave the source computer. This address is used for testing internal connectivity.

Table 5-4 shows five Class B examples and one Class A example of the special addresses in Table 5-3.

Table 5-4   Binary Examples of the Special Addresses Listed in Table 5-3 (Xs in the Table Can Have Either Binary Value)

Class	Field 1	Field 2	Field 3	Field 4	Description
B	10XXXXXX	XXXXXXXX	11111111	11111111	A broadcast to all devices on the network specified
B	11111111	11111111	11111111	11111111	A broadcast to all devices on the network to which the source is attached
B	00000000	00000000	XXXXXXXX	XXXXXXXX	Used as a source address when the source does not yet know its network address
B	00000000	00000000	00000000	00000000	Indicates the host is referring to itself on its network
B	10XXXXXX	XXXXXXXX	00000000	00000000	The address of the network
A	01111111	XXXXXXXX	XXXXXXXX	XXXXXXXX	The loopback address

There are two other IP address classes defined: Class D and Class E. Class E was reserved for future use and has not as yet been used. Class D is assigned to multicast addresses. Multicast addresses are used and are coming into greater use because of distributed systems and emphasis on distance education. Table 5-5 shows the format and range of Class D IP addresses.

Table 5-5   Class D Multicast IP Addresses

Class D ID Bits (4 bits)	Class D IP Address Range (28 bits)
1110	224.0.0.0 through 239.255.255.255

This IP address range is not divided into network addresses and host addresses, as is done in Classes A, B, and C. An address in the Class D IP address range identifies a group of computers or processes that has joined the group specified by the address. In addition to processing packets addressed to itself and the broadcast packet, an interface that has joined the group specified by the address will process a packet if it has been configured to recognize the group address. There are two special addresses: 224.0.0.0 and 224.0.0.1. The first is reserved.

The second is assigned to the "all hosts group." The all hosts group address can be used to reach all hosts on the network local to the source that are participating in any multicast group. There is no "all hosts group" address that refers to all hosts on the Internet. Host interfaces and gateways have to be configured to recognize multicast addresses. Multicast hosts and gateways use the Internet Group Management Protocol (IGMP), referred to in Chapter 4, "The TCP/IP Protocol Suite," to communicate group membership information. **IGMP** is a TCP/IP Internet layer protocol. Hosts send IGMP messages to their local multicast gateway when they join a group. Local multicast gateways poll multicast hosts periodically to see if there are still multicast hosts in that group on the local network. When the multicast gateway finds that there are no multicast hosts in a given group on the local network, it no longer distributes information about that group to other multicast gateways.

5

IP ADDRESS FORMAT

In the previous section, you saw that Class A, B, and C IP addresses consist of two parts—a network part and a host part. The InterNIC assigns the ID of the network part to an organization wishing to connect its network to the Internet. The network administrator of the organization decides how to assign the host IDs. The network administrator has further flexibility. He or she may want to divide the organization's network into subnets. One reason for doing so, which was discussed in Chapter 1, "Communication Architectures," is to provide each department in the organization with its own subnetwork to which local traffic is confined. People in the Marketing Department, for example, do not need to communicate with people in the Engineering Department on a daily basis. Therefore, why should packets that are only of interest to people in the Marketing Department be seen by people in the Engineering Department? (This type of control can also be accomplished by bridges, as you will see in the next chapter.) There is also the question of security. Some departments may work on files that are company proprietary or require need-to-know access. Traffic of this type should be contained within the subnet, and access from other subnets should be controlled. The creation of subnetworks is one way of accomplishing these goals.

Let's consider the IP address:

128.128.8.6

This is a **Class B** address for which the network ID is **128.128** and the host ID is **8.6**. Let's say that the network administrator for the company has been assigned the Internet address 128.128.0.0 by the InterNIC. This address has a host "space" of 65,534 hosts, as shown in Table 5-1. The network administrator wants to create subnets and distribute some of this host "space" to subnets. The situation that exists is described in Figure 5-3.

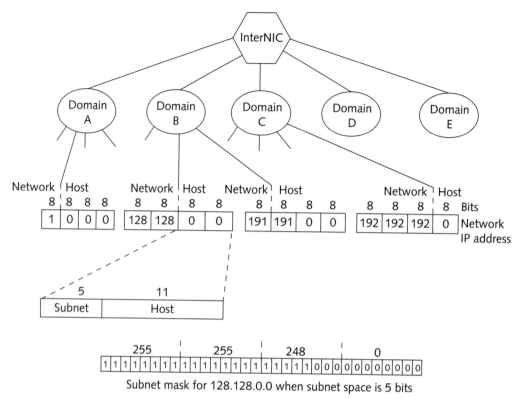

Figure 5-3   Creating subnets for the IP network 128.128.0.0

The host space of network 128.128.0.0 is 16 bits. Let's say the network administrator decides that, at some time in the future, as many as 28 subnets may be needed by the organization. Thus a subnet space of at least five bits is necessary to plan for this future contingency. The administrator therefore divides the host space into a subnet subspace of five bits and a host subspace of 11 bits, as shown in Figure 5-3. The subnet mask for this new configuration is shown at the bottom of Figure 5-3. The **subnet mask**, which will be described further in the next section, uses 2 one bit to specify which bits in the IP address correspond to the network and subnet address spaces. The decimal value of 248 for the third field of the subnet mask requires some explanation.

In the binary number system, the third field is:

$$2^7 \ \ 2^6 \ \ 2^5 \ \ 2^4 \ \ 2^3 \ \ 2^2 \ \ 2^1 \ \ 2^0$$
$$1 \ \ \ 1 \ \ \ 1 \ \ \ 1 \ \ \ 1 \ \ \ 0 \ \ \ 0 \ \ \ 0$$

The decimal value of the field is therefore $128 + 64 + 32 + 16 + 8 = 248$. The possible binary values for network 128.128.0.0 subnets when the high-order five bits of the host space are given over to subnet space and the corresponding decimal value of the third field of the subnet mask are given in Table 5-6.

Table 5-6   Possible Subnet IDs for the Network 128.128.0.0 with a Subnet Space Consisting of the High-Order Five Bits of the Host Space

Number of Subnets	2^7	2^6	2^5	2^4	2^3	2^2	2^1	2^0	Decimal Value of Third Field of Subnet Mask
1	0	0	0	0	1	0	0	0	8
2	0	0	0	1	0	0	0	0	16
3	0	0	0	1	1	0	0	0	24
4	0	0	1	0	0	0	0	0	32
5	0	0	1	0	1	0	0	0	40
6	0	0	1	1	0	0	0	0	48
7	0	0	1	1	1	0	0	0	56
8	0	1	0	0	0	0	0	0	64
9	0	1	0	0	1	0	0	0	72
10	0	1	0	1	0	0	0	0	80
11	0	1	0	1	1	0	0	0	88
12	0	1	1	0	0	0	0	0	96
13	0	1	1	0	1	0	0	0	104
14	0	1	1	1	0	0	0	0	112
15	0	1	1	1	1	0	0	0	120
16	1	0	0	0	0	0	0	0	128
17	1	0	0	0	1	0	0	0	136
18	1	0	0	1	0	0	0	0	144
19	1	0	0	1	1	0	0	0	152
20	1	0	1	0	0	0	0	0	160
21	1	0	1	0	1	0	0	0	168
22	1	0	1	1	0	0	0	0	176
23	1	0	1	1	1	0	0	0	184
24	1	1	0	0	0	0	0	0	192
25	1	1	0	0	1	0	0	0	200
26	1	1	0	1	0	0	0	0	208
27	1	1	0	1	1	0	0	0	216
28	1	1	1	0	0	0	0	0	224
29	1	1	1	0	1	0	0	0	232
30	1	1	1	1	0	0	0	0	240

5

SUBNETS AND ROUTING

Figure 5-4 shows the network 128.128.0.0 divided into two subnetworks.

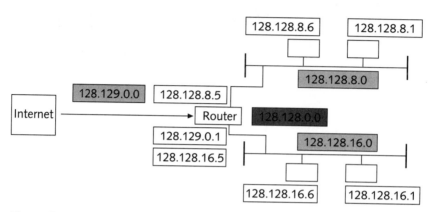

Figure 5-4   Two subnets of the network 128.128.0.0

The first two subnet IDs from Table 5-6 have been used for these two subnets. The only information in Figure 5-4 known to the Internet is that it should use network 128.129.0.0 to reach network 128.128.0.0. The organization has one Class B network, and its IP address is **128.128.0.0**. It is up to the router to know which subnet should receive a packet that arrives from the Internet. Routers maintain a routing table. (See Table 5-8.) Routing will be discussed in detail in Chapter 6, "Bridging and Routing," but a routing table is simply a table in which the router looks up the interface to use in forwarding the packet to the next network. This router is connected to two subnets. The routing table contains the subnet mask, which is **255.255.248.0**. Figure 5-4 shows that the network administrator has assigned the addresses **128.128.8.0** and **128.128.16.0** to these subnets. On subnet 128.128.8.0 there are two hosts with addresses **128.128.8.1** and **128.128.8.6**. On subnetwork 128.128.16.0 there are two hosts with addresses **128.128.16.1** and **128.128.16.6**. Table 5-7 summarizes information for the node with the address 128.128.8.6.

Table 5-7   IP Addresses and Subnet Mask for the Node 128.128.8.6 on the Network Shown in Figure 5-4

	Field 1	Field 2	Field 3	Field 4
Node Address (decimal)	128	128	8	6
Node Address (binary)	10000000	10000000	00001000	00000110
Subnet Mask (decimal)	255	255	248	0
Subnet Mask (binary)	11111111	11111111	11111000	0
Network Address (decimal)	128	128	0	0

5

The first and second fields of the subnet mask are all ones in binary notation. According to IP subnet mask rules, any bit in the subnet mask that is set to one means that the corresponding bit in the IP address belongs to either the network part or subnet part of the IP address. The first two fields of the subnet mask are all ones because the network is a Class B network. The ones in the third field of the subnet mask tells the router (1) that there are subnets, and (2) which bits in the IP address represent the subnet address.

Table 5-8 shows the information in the routing table of the router in Figure 5-4. If the destination IP address of a packet received by the router from a network interface does not have the same network address as the network from which it was received, the router uses its routing table to route the packet to another network interface. (The column labeled Distance will be explained in Chapter 6, "Bridging and Routing.")

Table 5-8   Routing Table for the Default Router in Figure 5-4

Node Address	Subnet Mask	Interface	Subnet Address	Distance
128.128.8.1	255.255.248.0	128.128.8.5	128.128.8.0	0
128.128.8.6				
128.128.16.1	255.255.248.0	128.128.16.5	128.128.16.0	0
128.128.16.6				
	255.255.0.0	128.129.0.1	128.129.0.0	0

 A logical AND is a binary addition in which the result is 1 if both the binary digits being added are 1. The result is 0 otherwise.

For example, when the default router receives a packet from the Internet in which the first two fields have the decimal values 128, it knows that the packet is for this network. It then must decide which subnetwork should receive the packet. To make this decision it looks in its routing table (Table 5-8) to get the subnet mask value. It then does a bit-by-bit logical **AND** of the IP destination address in the received packet and the subnet mask. It compares the result to the subnet addresses in the routing table (Table 5-8) and then routes the packet to the interface that maps to that subnet address. Let's look at Figure 5-5 to see how this works.

IP Address	128.128.8.6	10000000	10000000	00001000	00000110
Subnet Mask	255.255.248.0	11111111	11111111	11111000	00000000
	Binary AND	10000000	10000000	00001000	00000000
	Decimal AND	128	128	8	0

Figure 5-5   Logical AND of the subnet mask and the IP address 128.128.8.6

The first row contains the 32-bit binary representation of the IP address 128.128.8.6. The second row contains the binary representation of the subnet mask 255.255.248.0. The third row contains the binary AND of the first two rows. The fourth row is the translation of the binary AND to decimal format. The correct result is achieved, and the packet will be routed to interface 128.128.8.5.

THE ADDRESS RESOLUTION PROTOCOL (ARP)

ARP is used to obtain the hardware address of another computer on the same network. For example, when the router that connects the subnets in Figure 5-4 has decided to which subnet should receive the packet, it is necessary for the router to create a frame containing the destination hardware address of the particular host on the subnet for which the packet is destined. If the router does not know that hardware address, it uses ARP to obtain it.

As you saw in Figure 4-4 of Chapter 4, ARP is a TCP/IP Network Interface Layer protocol. When a process on one computer wants to send a packet to a process on another computer, the hardware address of the remote computer must be placed in the destination address field of the frame that is being sent. When that hardware address is not known, the packet is stored and the process makes a call to ARP. ARP places the IP address of the destination computer in the ARP message, and the frame is broadcast on the network. On Ethernet, the frame that is sent would look like that shown in Figure 5-6.

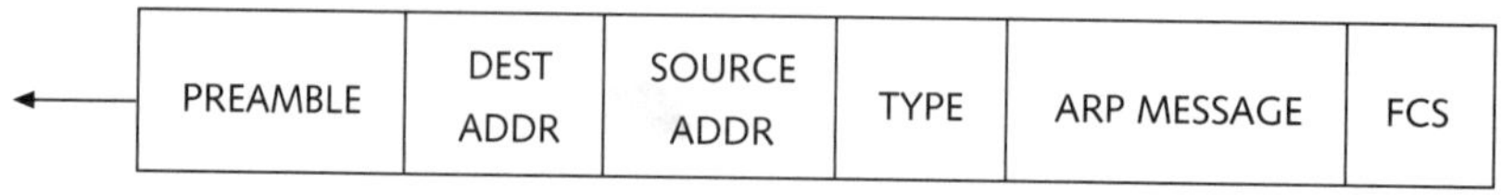

PREAMBLE	DEST ADDR	SOURCE ADDR	TYPE	ARP MESSAGE	FCS

Figure 5-6   ARP message in an Ethernet frame

The Destination Address field contains the hardware broadcast address consisting of 48 1 bits. The Source Address is the hardware address of the sending machine. The Type field contains the hexadecimal value of 0806hex, the ID of ARP. FCS is the frame check sequence. Table 5-9 explains the fields in the ARP message.

Table 5-9   Fields in the ARP Message

Field	Number of Bits	Description
Hardware Type	16	Hardware interface type for which the sender seeks a hardware address. For the Ethernet hardware interface, the value = 1.
Protocol Type	16	Specifies the type of high-level address that the sender is supplying. For IP, the ID is hexadecimal 0800.
HLEN	8	Specifies the length of hardware address in bytes. For Ethernet, the length would be 6.
PLEN	8	Specifies the length of the high-level protocol address in bytes. For IP, the length would be 4.
Operation	16	Specifies an ARP request or ARP response value. ARP request value = 1. ARP reply value = 2.
Sender HA	variable	The sender's hardware address
Sender network protocol address	variable	The address used by the sender's network layer protocol
Target HA	variable	(To be determined)
Target network protocol address	variable	The address used by the target's network layer protocol

When the message is read by the target machine, it fills in the missing hardware address (Target HA), swaps the target and sender hardware address pairs, changes the operation to a reply, and returns an **ARP Reply** message. The ARP reply provides the destination hardware address so that the source can send the packet that has been stored awaiting the destination hardware address. In addition to sending the packet, the source stores the target IP address/hardware address pair in a database called the ARP table. The next time this source wants to communicate with the same target, it can look up the hardware address in this table. Similarly, the target stores the source IP address/hardware address pair in its ARP table.

The ARP table is dynamic. If an IP address/hardware address pair is not updated within a time determined by a timer, the pair is deleted from the table. This is done in case machines go down or move to another IP address. Figure 5-7 shows the MSDOS command prompt window and an ARP table.

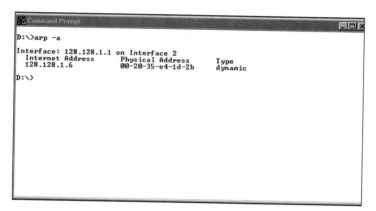

Figure 5-7   An example of an ARP table

This information was obtained by typing **arp -a** at the command prompt. Interface: 128.128.1.1 is the IP address of the computer on which the arp -a command was executed. Interface 2 indicates that this is only one of the interfaces on this computer. The Internet Address 128.128.1.6 and the Physical (hardware) Address 00-20-35-e4-1d-2b belong to another computer on subnet 1. ARP was used to obtain the hardware address, and the IP address/hardware address pair was then stored in the ARP table shown in Figure 5-7. You also see that the Type of the entry in the ARP table is dynamic, which means that this entry will only be retained in the table for a time that has been configured in ARP.

When you executed the Ping command in an exercise in Chapter 4 to test the connectivity of the network, that application first made a system call to ARP to obtain the hardware address of the target of the Ping. If you had looked at the ARP table of the machine that executed the Ping application, you would have seen that it contained the hardware address of the target, which had to be obtained prior to sending the Ping message.

THE REVERSE ADDRESS RESOLUTION PROTOCOL (RARP)

RARP does the opposite of ARP. The RARP client knows the target's hardware address and requests the IP address from a RARP server. RARP was designed to provide a mechanism for a diskless machine to obtain its IP address from another machine on its network, and then access an image of an operating system remotely. A process on a computer that provides mappings of hardware addresses to IP addresses is called a **RARP server**. The RARP request is broadcast on the local network. The RARP message contains the hardware address of the source and a field in which an IP address should be entered by the RARP server. The format of the RARP message is similar to that of the ARP message. In the RARP format, however, both the source and target hardware addresses are that of the source. The RARP reply contains the IP address of the source.

CHAPTER SUMMARY

In this chapter you learned that:

- The Internet Protocol (IP) standard defines five IP address classes labeled A through E. These classes provide different numbers of networks and hosts on each network.

- IP addresses are written in what is called dotted decimal notation, in which there are four fields, each containing a decimal number, separated by dots. Each field has values in the range 0 to 255.

- High-order bits in the first field of an IP address are used to designate the class of the address. Routers read these bits to get information about which fields in the address specify the network address.

- Some IP addresses are used for special purposes and are not to be included in the general pool of IP addresses that can be assigned. These addresses were listed and described.

- Class D IP addresses are multicast addresses. Hosts use these addresses to send messages to multicast groups. Group members are processes that reside on computers that have been configured to recognize a multicast address.

- The Internet Group Management Protocol (IGMP) is used by multicast hosts and gateways to communicate group membership information.

- A network can be divided into subnets. To do this, the network administrator uses some of the network host "space" to create a number of subnets. Subnets are connected by a router. Each subnet has an IP address.

- Routers connecting subnets use a subnet mask, the IP address of a packet, and the routing table to determine which subnet should receive the packet received by the router.

- The Address Resolution Protocol (ARP) is used by a computer to obtain the hardware address of another computer on the same network, when the IP address of that computer is known.

- The Reverse Address Resolution Protocol (RARP) is used by a computer that knows its hardware address to obtain its IP address from a RARP server on the network to which the computer is attached.

REVIEW QUESTIONS

1. Why does the IP address of a machine change when you move it to another subnet?
   a. Because the hardware address changes
   b. Because the subnet address changes
   c. Because the network address changes

2. When does a network have to get its network address from the InterNIC?
   a. When the network is to have subnets
   b. When the network is a Class A network
   c. When the network will be part of the Internet

3. How many classes of IP addresses have been defined?
   a. 5
   b. 3
   c. 4

4. When a computer uses the third byte of its IP address for subnets, how many subnets can be assigned to a Class B network?
   a. 255
   b. 256
   c. 254

5. Why could the InterNIC not assign more than 126 Class A networks?
   a. Because the Class A ID is zero
   b. Because of the number of bits in Field 1
   c. Because of the location of the Class A ID bit in Field 1 of the address

6. Why is a host ID of all ones not allowed?
   a. Because all ones is a broadcast address
   b. Because it is the address of RARP servers only
   c. Because all ones is the loopback address

7. Why is a subnet mask necessary when the network is divided into subnets?
   a. To select addresses for the subnets
   b. To determine which machines are on which subnet
   c. To provide an automatic mechanism for selecting the correct subnet for packet delivery

8. When an ARP request message is transmitted from a source that is attached to an Ethernet, what is the address that is placed in the destination field of the Ethernet frame?

   a. The hardware address of the destination machine

   b. FFFFFFFFFFFF

   c. The hardware address of the default router

9. What is the information that is being requested in an ARP message?

   a. The IP address of the destination machine

   b. The hardware address corresponding to the target's IP address.

   c. The IP address of the source machine

10. What is the ID of ARP?

    a. 0800hex

    b. 0806hex

    c. 0812hex

11. What is the information that is being requested in a RARP request message?

    a. The IP address of the source machine

    b. The IP address of the RARP server

    c. The hardware address of the RARP server

12. What is the decimal value of the first field of the loopback address?

    a. 128

    b. 127

    c. 255

13. What is the binary value of the first field of the loopback address?

    a. 00000001

    b. 01111110

    c. 10000000 ?

For questions 14, 15, and 16, assume that you are a network administrator who has decided to use part of the host space of your InterNIC-assigned Class B network address to create subnets for the divisions in your organization.

14. You want to be able to create eight or fewer subnets. What should be the binary value of the subnet mask?

    a. 11111111 11111111 11110000 00000000

    b. 11111111 11111111 11100000 00000000

    c. 11111111 11111111 11111000 00000000

15. What will be the decimal value of the subnet mask corresponding to the binary value you selected in question 14?

   a. 255.255.248.0

   b. 255.255.240.0

   c. 255.255.224.0

16. How many hosts can be accommodated by each subnet?

   a. 4096

   b. 4094

   c. 8190

17. When the host fields of an IP address are zero, what does the address refer to?

   a. A subnet address

   b. A network address

   c. The address of a special host on the network

18. What does it mean when the network fields of an IP address have the value zero?

   a. The source is sending a packet to all networks

   b. The source has just started up and does not know its IP network address

   c. The source is sending a packet that should only be received by devices on its local network

19. What is multicasting?

   a. Sending a packet to a specified set of subnets

   b. Sending a packet to all hosts on the local subnet that are members of a multicast group

   c. Sending a packet to all hosts on the Internet that are members of a multicast group

20. How many subnets can a Class D IP address have?

   a. 255

   b. Network addresses are not defined

   c. 4096

CASE PROJECT

In Chapter 4, you installed TCP/IP and then established the logical connectivity of the network in each department of each division of the company and tested the connectivity of each department's network. Figure 5-8 shows the current status of the Case Project environment.

As you have seen in this chapter, testing of connectivity actually requires the use of ARP and IP addresses, which were not discussed in detail in Chapter 4. In the exercises that follow, you will design the IP address hierarchy for the Raleigh division of your company, configure IP addresses and subnet masks, create an ARP table, and use the Windows NT 4.0 Network Monitor to analyze ARP frames.

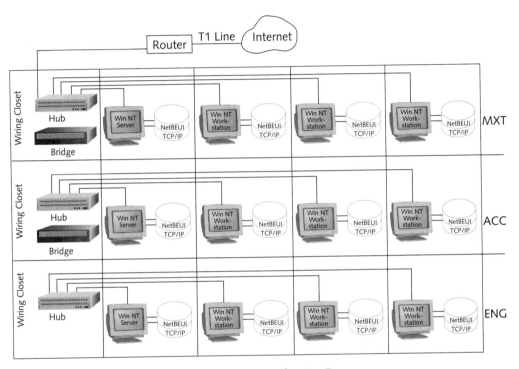

Figure 5-8   Case Project environment prior to Chapter 5

EXERCISE 1—DESIGN THE IP ADDRESS HIERARCHY OF THE RALEIGH DIVISION

Using Figure 5-8 as a guide, lay out the IP and hardware address hierarchy of the Raleigh division by completing the following table. Assume that the InterNIC has assigned you a Class C network ID of 192.192.192.0. If you have an actual network for which you can build a table like this, include the hardware addresses of the devices on that network, and enter vender identification information in the Description column. There are no subnets used in this example.

Table 5-10   Addresses of Devices on the Raleigh Division Network

Device	IP Address	Hardware Address	Description
PDC			
BDC 1			
BDC 2			
Hub 1			
Hub 2			
Hub 3			
Bridge 1			
Bridge 2			
Wk 1			
Wk 2			
Wk 3			
Wk 4			
Wk 5			
Wk 6			
Wk 7			
Wk 8			
Wk 9			
Router			

As has been done in Table 5-10, it is a good idea to list all devices on a network even if those devices do not require you to configure IP addresses. This is the case for hubs and bridges, for example. You can use the table to make comments about such machines for future reference. Each computer must have a distinct name that will be used to identify it to a domain name server (DNS), Windows Internet Name Server (WINS), and the server for which it will be the actual address on a Microsoft Network. These concepts will be discussed in Chapter 9, "Windows NT Domain Concepts."

EXERCISE 2—CONFIGURE IP ADDRESSES FOR A SERVER

1. Select **Settings** from the START Menu of a Windows NT 4.0 workstation.
2. Click **Control Panel**.
3. Double-click the **Network** icon.
4. In the Network Dialog box, click the **Adapters tab**.
5. In the text box of the Dialog box for the Adapter tab, type in the hardware address of the workstation. Click the **OK** button.
6. In the Dialog box that results, enter the type of bus on which your network adapter is installed.
7. Click on the **OK** button.
8. In the Network window, click the **Protocols tab**.
9. Highlight the TCP/IP protocol and click the **Properties** button.
10. In the resulting IP Address tab window, complete the "Specify an IP address" text boxes by entering the IP addresses of the server, the default gateway, and the subnet mask. (A **default gateway** is a router that forwards packets to another network.)

EXERCISE 3—CREATE AN ARP TABLE FOR A WORKSTATION

1. Select **Programs** from the START menu.
2. Click **MSDOS Command Prompt**.
3. Type **arp** to get the list of arp commands.
4. Type **arp -a** to get a view of the arp cache for the workstation. What is the response?
5. Type **arp** again to get a list of arp commands.
6. Using the format provided by the list of arp commands, type the command that will bind the hardware address of the workstation with its IP address.
7. Type the command **arp -a** to get an arp table listing. In this table you should see the Ethernet address/IP address pair you created. What is the listing?
8. The listing gives an interface IP address. This is the IP address of which computer?
9. What does the listing mean by specifying that the entry is of Type static?

EXERCISE 4—VIEW AND ANALYZE ARP PACKETS USING THE WINDOWS NT 4.0 SERVER NETWORK MONITOR

1. On a computer on which Windows NT 4.0 Server has been installed, select **Programs** from the Start menu.

2. Select **Administration Tools (common)** on the Programs menu.

3. Select **Network Monitor** on the Administration Tools (common) menu.

The window that appears suggests that the Network Monitor provides a lot of information about traffic on your network. It is an invaluable tool for seeing what is actually inside frames you send and receive. The Windows NT 4.0 Network Monitor is an example of the types of network monitors that are on the market today. Perhaps the most well known of these is the Network General Sniffer. The Sniffer is a separate device that is attached to the network to monitor traffic. The Windows NT 4.0 Network Monitor is more specifically an example of a monitor that is implemented only in software. Some monitors operate in *promiscuous* mode. That is they capture and read *all* frames that are on the network. In contrast, the Windows NT 4.0 Network Monitor runs only on the server and captures and displays only frames for which it is the destination or the source.

4. From the Capture menu of Network Monitor, click **Start**. This will initiate the capture of frames by Network Monitor.

5. Leave the Network Monitor window on the screen and return to the Windows NT Server Start menu.

6. From the Start menu, select **Programs**.

7. Click the **MSDOS Command Prompt**.

8. Type **PING <IP Address>**, where IP address should be the address of another computer on the network. Then press **Enter**.

9. Close the MSDOS Command Prompt window to return to the Network Monitor.

10. On the Capture menu, click **Stop and View**.

11. You are presented with a list of frames captured. Search down the list for a frame that has ARP in the Protocol column and highlight that line.

12. Notice that immediately after the ARP Request and ARP Reply frames in the list, there are a number of Echo Request and Echo Reply frames. Explain why the PING command that you gave produced the ARP and Echo frames.

13. What is the MAC address of the source of the ARP Request?

14. What is the MAC address of the destination of the ARP Request?

15. Double-click the highlighted **ARP Request frame** to obtain Detail of the fields in the frame.

16. Why does the target of the ARP Request have the same IP address as the target of your PING command?

17. Expand the ARP Request Detail by clicking the **(+)** next to it.

18. Explain each of the fields in the ARP Request packet. (Refer back to Table 5-9.)

19. In the upper panel of the Detail window, double-click the **ARP Reply line** to get the ARP Reply Detail.

20. Expand the ARP Reply Detail by clicking the **(+)** next to it.

21. Explain each of the fields in the ARP Reply packet. (Refer back to Table 5-9.)

Figure 5-9 shows the status of the Case Project environment after completing this chapter. The completed exercises resulted in the selection of static IP addresses for the PDC and the BDCs on a Class C network. In completing Exercise 1, you may have given static IP addresses to the workstations as well. Another option, which will be discussed in detail in Chapter 7, "The Dynamic Host Configuration Protocol (DHCP)," is to allow workstations to be assigned dynamic IP addresses by a DHCP server. You have documented the hardware addresses of each of the computers on your network, and you have created a subnet mask for the servers. In the next chapter, you will examine in detail how to add and use bridges to control interdepartment traffic and a router to connect to your company intranet.

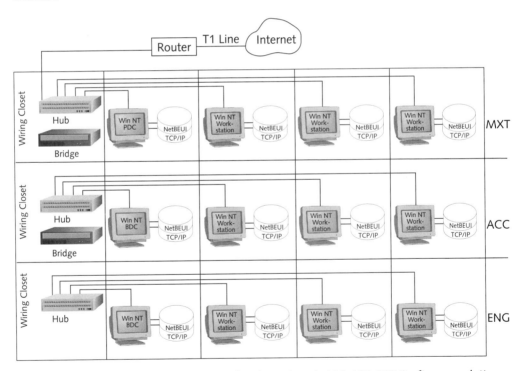

Figure 5-9   Case Project environment for the network 192.192.192.0 after completing Chapter 5

BRIDGING AND ROUTING

A network can be defined as a connected set of two or more nodes. Such nodes may be hosts, bridges, routers, repeaters, hubs and switches, for example. Bridges, routers and switches connect networks. The Internet is a set of networks connected by such devices. Although bridges, routers and switches perform related functions, they use different hardware, protocols and software to perform those functions. The device chosen depends on the requirements of the connection being implemented.

This chapter covers bridging and routing concepts, configuration and implementation. A serial link between a serial port on a computer and the console port on a Cisco combination bridge/router and Windows NT Hyperterminal is used to configure the network interfaces of the bridge/router. The bridge/router is first configured to operate as a bridge using a spanning tree protocol. The bridge/router is then configured to operate as a router that uses RIP and OSPF routing protocols.

IN THIS CHAPTER YOU WILL:

LEARN ABOUT BRIDGES

LEARN ABOUT ROUTERS

LEARN ABOUT THE RIP ROUTING PROTOCOL

LEARN ABOUT THE OSPF ROUTING PROTOCOL

LEARN ABOUT CONFIGURING RIP

LEARN ABOUT CONFIGURING OSPF

BRIDGES

In the first part of this section, bridge concepts and functions will be explained. In the second part, a bridge will be configured and used to connect two segments of a network.

BRIDGE CONCEPTS AND FUNCTIONS

Bridges are used to link two segments of a network, two networks of the same media type, or two networks of different media types. The typical bridge has two ports. It differs from a repeater in that the bridge makes a decision about what to do with a frame that it receives, whereas the repeater always retransmits the exact frame that it receives. Bridges are further classified as local and remote bridges. A **local bridge** makes a direct connection between two LANs. **Remote bridges** connect two LANs by means of a WAN. Multiport bridges also exist. They are known as **switches**. Multiport bridges can operate on more than one packet at the same time. Multiport bridges will not be discussed in this book.

The purpose of a bridge is to isolate two network segments or networks. Types of networks that can be connected by bridges include Ethernet, Token Ring, and FDDI. Figure 6-1 shows two examples of how bridges are used.

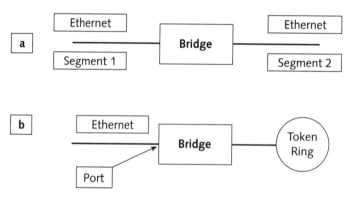

Figure 6-1   Using a bridge to connect two Ethernet segments (a) and an Ethernet and a Token Ring network (b)

The isolation function of a bridge keeps some traffic on one network from reaching the other network to which it is connected; that is, the traffic is filtered. Likewise, errors and collisions that occur on one segment or network are not seen by the other segment or network.

When a bridge is powered on, it has no knowledge of the devices on the networks attached to it. Any frame that it receives is retransmitted out of both ports. However, the bridge uses the source hardware addresses in these frames to build a bridge table. The **bridge table** consists of entries that include the source address of the frame received and the port through which it was received. The bridge table is then used to determine the segment or network from which the frame arrived. If the destination address of the frame is the same as an address on that segment from which the frame arrived, the bridge discards the frame. Otherwise, the frame is forwarded to the next segment or network.

Now let's take a somewhat closer look at how a bridge operates. Figure 6-2 shows the protocol stacks of a bridge and of two computers on connected segments.

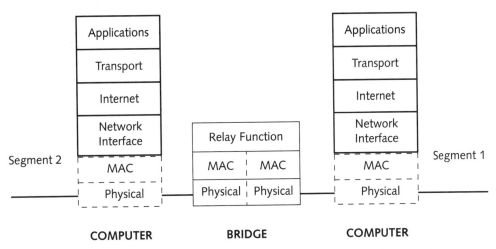

Figure 6-2   Protocol stacks of a bridge and computers on connected segments

The figure shows that the operation of the bridge depends on the Data Link layer MAC protocol and the Physical layer protocol for communication with the network. The bridge is often called a "layer 2" device because its action is determined only by the MAC part of the OSI protocol stack. When the bridge receives a frame, it reads the source address in the MAC header and makes an entry in the bridge table consisting of the source address and MAC address of the port at which the frame was received. Subsequently, if the bridge receives frames with that address as a destination address, it discards the frame. Otherwise, the bridge forwards the frame to its other port. These actions are the **filtering** and **forwarding** (relay) actions of a bridge, respectively. If the bridge is connected to two networks of the same type, the frame is forwarded "as is." This is called **transparent bridging**. If the bridge connects dissimilar networks, such as Ethernet and Token Ring networks, frame translation is required. The bridge then maps the information in the MAC header of the Ethernet frame into the MAC format of the Token Ring header. The source and destination addresses are unchanged. This mapping, which is performed by the bridge **Relay process**, is known as **translational bridging**. When a bridge connecting two segments of a network receives a frame in which the destination address is the broadcast address (FFFFFFFFFFFFh), it always forwards the frame so that the frame will be received by all devices on the attached segments or networks.

BRIDGE CONFIGURATION

The network shown in Figure 6-3 will be used to examine the functions performed by bridges and routers.

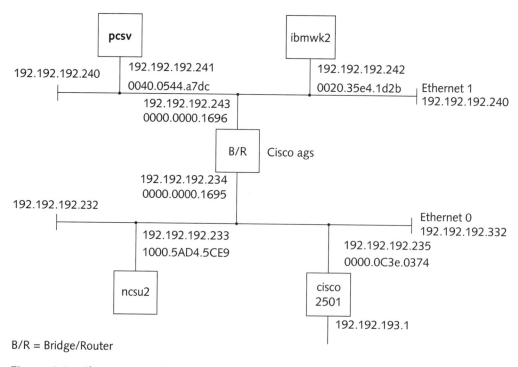

B/R = Bridge/Router

Figure 6-3   Class C network 192.192.192.0 with subnet mask 255.255.25.24 used to examine bridge and router functions

The network in Figure 6-3 contains the primary domain controller **pcsv**, two workstations **ibmwk2** and **ncsu2**, and two Cisco bridge/routers **ags** and **2501**. Ags and 2501 can be configured as either bridges or routers. The ags connects subnet 192.192.192.240 (Ethernet 1) to subnet 192.192.192.232 (Ethernet 0). The 2501 is attached only to the subnet 192.192.192.232 (Ethernet 0). Table 6-1 lists these devices and their associated parameters.

Table 6-1   Summary of Parameters of Devices Shown in Figure 6-3

Devices	Hardware Address	IP Address	Subnet	Interface	Bridge Group	Bridge Area
pcsv	0040.0544.a7d7	192.192.192.241	192.192.192.240	Ethernet 1	1	2
ibmwk2	0020.35e4.1d2b	192.192.192.242	192.192.192.240	Ethernet 1	1	2
ncsu2	1000.5ad4.5ce9	192.192.192.233	192.192.192.232	Ethernet 0	1	1
ags	0000.0c00.1696	192.192.192.243	192.192.192.240	Ethernet 1	1	2
ags	0000.0c00.1695	192.192.192.234	192.192.192.232	Ethernet 0	1	1
2501	0000.0c3e.0374	192.192.192.235	192.192.192.232	Ethernet 0	1	1

(The terms Bridge Group and Bridge Area are discussed below). Figure 6-4 shows an actual bridge table for ags when it was operating as a bridge. A bridge table is displayed by entering the command **show bridge** at the Executive-level ags-small # prompt shown in the figure (ags-small is the name that was given to the ags router when it was configured). The format of bridge commands will be discussed subsequently.

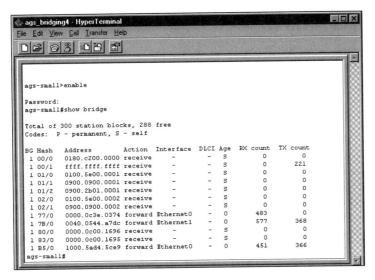

```
ags_bridging4 - HyperTerminal
File  Edit  View  Call  Transfer  Help

ags-small>enable

Password:
ags-small#show bridge

Total of 300 station blocks, 288 free
Codes:  P - permanent, S - self

BG Hash    Address        Action   Interface  DLCI Age  RX count  TX count
 1 00/0    0180.c200.0000 receive     -         -   S       0        0
 1 00/1    ffff.ffff.ffff receive     -         -   S       0       221
 1 01/0    0100.5e00.0001 receive     -         -   S       0        0
 1 01/1    0900.0900.0001 receive     -         -   S       0        0
 1 01/2    0900.2b01.0001 receive     -         -   S       0        0
 1 02/0    0100.5e00.0002 receive     -         -   S       0        0
 1 02/1    0900.0900.0002 receive     -         -   S       0        0
 1 77/0    0000.0c3e.0374 forward Ethernet0     -   0     483        0
 1 7B/0    0040.0544.a7dc forward Ethernet1     -   0     577       368
 1 80/0    0000.0c00.1696 receive     -         -   S       0        0
 1 83/0    0000.0c00.1695 receive     -         -   S       0        0
 1 B5/0    1000.5ad4.5ce9 forward Ethernet0     -   0     451       366
ags-small#
```

Figure 6-4   A bridge table for bridge AGS

The first column in the bridge table shown in Figure 6-4 is the list of **bridge groups (BG)**. Bridge network interfaces are members of bridge groups (bridge groups are discussed later in this section). The second column provides the location of the interface entry in the hash table. Records stored in a **hash table** are indexed according to an algorithm that speeds the search for the record. The **Address** column contains the hardware addresses that the bridge knows either because these hardware addresses are those of ags interfaces or because ags has learned these addresses from the frames it has read. **Action** means the action to be taken when a frame with the associated hardware address arrives at the bridge. The default action is to **forward** the frame if the destination hardware address is not the address of one of the interfaces on the network from which the frame arrived at the bridge. As you will see, there is a command to discard a frame with a particular hardware address. If this command has been used, the word **discard** will appear in the Action column next to that address. The **Interface** column contains the label of the network (subnet) to which the device is attached. **DLCI** is a term that is relevant when the bridge is connected to a frame relay network. **Age** is the number of minutes since a frame was sent to or received from the address in the Address column. The letter **S** indicates that the age, when shown, has been determined and recorded by the router from frames it has read. Bridges can be configured to drop addresses from the table if the address has not been active for a configured period of time. This procedure is used to avoid having frames forwarded to bridges that are no longer in use. The two columns **RX count** and **TX count** are the number of bytes that have been received or transmitted respectively by devices with addresses in the Address column. The five hardware addresses at the bottom of the table are the addresses of devices shown in Figure 6-3. The ibmwk2 address is not shown because this device was not active at the time at which this bridge table was current.

We will now examine the steps necessary to configure a bridge. The Cisco AGS bridge referred to previously will be used as an example. First, it is necessary to establish a serial connection between the console port on the bridge/router and a serial port on a computer. In this example, **Windows NT HyperTerminal** will be used to establish the virtual terminal connection with the AGS console port. HyperTerminal provides dialog boxes in which you configure the serial communication mode (modem or COM port), connection speed, stop bits, parity, and flow control of the serial link. Having completed the configuration, you turn on the bridge/router and are automatically presented with an introductory screen and a prompt. Figure 6-5 shows what this screen will look like after the introductory material is scrolled off the screen.

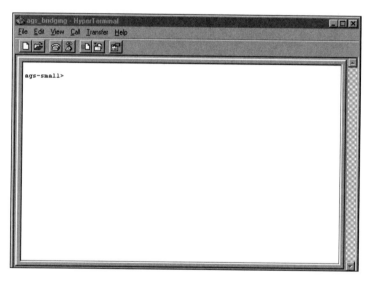

Figure 6-5   User-level prompt of the AGS bridge/router

In this case the AGS Bridge/Router has been configured to have the name ags-small. The prompt **ags-small>** is called the user-level prompt. The bridge/router cannot be configured at this access level. As shown in Figure 6-6, typing **enable** at the user-level prompt brings up a request for a password.

If the correct password is entered, the executive-level prompt **ags-small #** appears. All commands for configuring the system are now available. To begin configuring, the **configure** command is entered. The system then displays the message "Configuring from terminal, memory or network [terminal]?" Terminal is the default that is selected by pressing Enter. The system then displays the next two lines, and actual configuration begins. There are many bridge/router configuration commands and subcommands. Although only a few of the basic commands and subcommands can be discussed here, these will be sufficient for you to understand bridge/router configuration principles. When you configure a bridge or router for use in a production network, you will need to carefully review the product manuals for details about exactly how to use the many other configuration commands available to you.

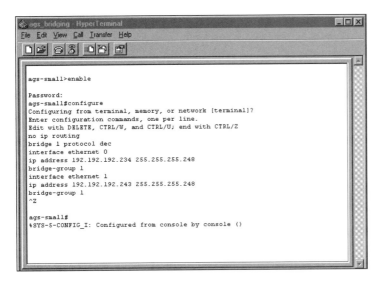

Figure 6-6 Executive-level prompt of the AGS bridge/router

Following is a list that describes commands or subcommands entered in Figure 6-6.

1. **no ip routing** A global command that turns off all ip routing protocols. The bridge/router then functions as a bridge.

2. **bridge 1 protocol dec** A global command that is described as follows:
   - **Protocol dec** The spanning-tree algorithm, designed by Digital Equipment Corporation (DEC), will be used to control the connectivity of bridges on the network. The **spanning-tree** algorithm is so named because it ensures that there are no loops in the network created by the bridges. Such loops can cause unending traffic. This algorithm will disable bridge ports if necessary to achieve the spanning-tree configuration in which the number of links necessary to provide complete connectivity is minimized.
   - **Bridge 1** 1 is the bridge group number assigned to the group of bridge interfaces that will be bridged by the DEC spanning-tree algorithm. Assigning bridge interfaces to groups also makes it possible to execute global commands that apply to all interfaces in the group.

3. **interface ethernet 0** A subcommand that specifies that all commands that follow apply to the interface with the label ethernet 0.
   - **ip address 192.192.192.234 255.255.255.248** A subcommand that specifies the ip address of the bridge interface ethernet 0 on subnet 192.192.192.232 and the subnet mask 255.255.255.248.
   - **bridge-group 1** Assigns this interface to bridge group 1.

4. **interface ethernet 1**   A subcommand that specifies that the commands that follow apply to the interface with the label ethernet 1.

   ■ **ip address 192.192.192.243   255.255.255.248**   A subcommand that specifies the ip address of the bridge interface ethernet 1 on subnet 192.192.192.240 and the subnet mask 255.255.255.248.

   ■ **bridge-group 1**   Assigns this interface to bridge group 1.

5. **<control> Z**   Signals completion of the configuration and the binding of values to configuration variables.

6. **write memory**   Although not shown in Figure 6-6, this command should be used to copy the configuration file into nonvolatile memory. If this command is not executed, the configuration information is lost when the bridge/router is powered off.

Commands 1 to 5 are sufficient to convert the bridge/router into a transparent bridge that forwards frames between interfaces in group 1. Bridges that are members of one group will not forward frames to bridges that are not members of that group.

Another important global command is **show interfaces**. When this command is made specific to an interface, for example by typing **show interface ethernet 0** at the Executive-level command prompt, it produces a screen of the type shown in Figure 6-7.

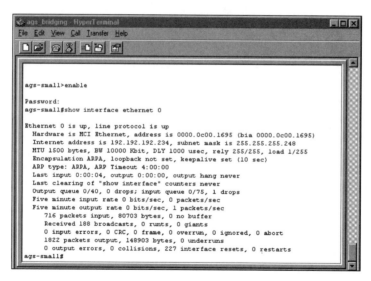

Figure 6-7   "Show interface ethernet 0" command

The result is a complete description of the configuration parameters of the interface and some interface statistics. The meaning of some of this information is as follows. The statement **Ethernet 0 is up** means that the adapter is functioning correctly. **Line Protocol is up** means that communication is taking place between this interface and the one to which it is connected. Both of these conditions are necessary. **Encapsulation ARPA** indicates that this interface will encapsulate packets in the Ethernet II frame. **ARP type: ARPA** indicates that the default IP ARP is being used.

There are many other commands that can be used to configure the filtering action of a bridge. The bridge can filter on hardware addresses, IP addresses, frame types, and protocols, for example. A specific example of a command that is used to filter on a hardware address is the command:

```
bridge <group>    address <MAC address>    [forward | discard]
```

where:

- **<group>** is the group of which the interface is a member.

- **<MAC address>** is the hardware address of the interface.

- Including the parameter **forward** ensures that frames to or from <MAC address> will be forwarded.

- Including the parameter **discard** causes frames to or from <MAC address> to be discarded by the bridge.

The proper configuration and implementation of network connectivity with bridges is a complex subject that has only been touched on here. Much of the network functionality provided by routers can be provided by bridges. In some ways, networking with bridges is a more complicated subject than is networking with routers. Because this book is focused on TCP/IP, let's now move to the subject of routing.

ROUTERS

The default configuration of the bridge/routers is router with IP routing enabled; this is the configuration assumed for this chapter.

Like bridges, routers isolate network segments into collision domains. In addition, routers isolate networks and subnets by using TCP/IP Internet layer software to determine the destination network or subnet address to which the packet should be delivered. The **routing table** provides a mapping of destination network IP addresses to the IP address of the router interface that should be used to forward the IP packet.

Figure 6-8 is a simple representation of the diagram in Figure 6-3 where R1 is the Cisco ags router and R2 is the Cisco 2501 router.

Figure 6-8   Network connectivity provided by routers

More generally however, Figure 6-8 represents the concept of the Internet or of an intranet, that is, a set of networks connected by routers. As was discussed in Chapter 5, "IP Addressing", each router maintains a routing table with entries that map an IP destination network address in the received packet to the IP address of the router interface that is used to forward the packet. Although Figure 6-8 shows routers with only two interfaces, in general a router will have a number of interfaces that may provide connections to Ethernet, Token Ring, FDDI, X.25, Frame Relay, ISDN, ATM or serial networks.

Figure 6-9 shows the protocols that are used by a router to connect two Ethernet networks.

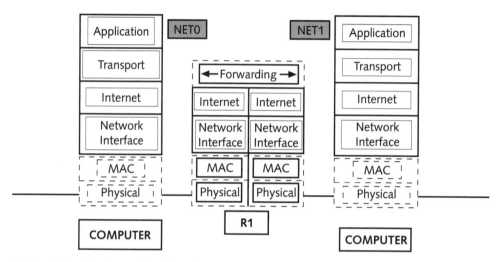

Figure 6-9   Router protocol stock

In addition to the protocols used by a bridge, the router also uses a network layer protocol. When TCP/IP is the protocol stack in use, the Internet layer becomes the network layer. If the frame received by the router contains its MAC address, the IP packet is passed to the Internet layer for processing. The routing table is examined to find a mapping of the packet IP destination network address to the IP address of a router interface. The packet is forwarded to the Network Interface layer protocol for that interface. After processing, the packet is passed to the MAC layer. In the MAC layer the packet is encapsulated in an Ethernet frame in which the source address is that of R1. The destination address depends on whether or not the packet IP destination network address is that of a network directly attached to R1. If the destination network is directly attached, the MAC destination address will be that of the destination host computer. If not, the MAC destination address will be that of the router on the directly attached network, R2 for example, that has used a routing protocol to inform R1 that it can reach the destination network.

Let's continue our examination of routing concepts by reviewing the IP subcommands that can be executed by the router. Figure 6-10 shows a listing of the subcommands that you can see by entering **show ip ?** at the Executive-level prompt. We will examine a number of these subcommands.

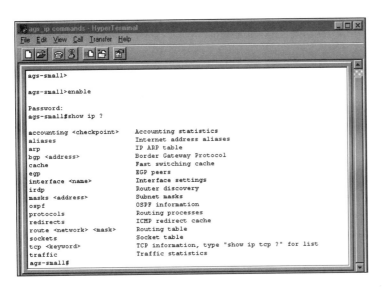

Figure 6-10   Available IP subcommands

Figure 6-11 shows the display provided when we execute the **show arp** subcommand in the list.

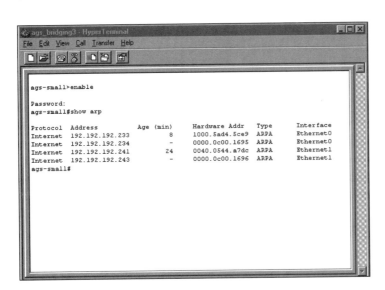

Figure 6-11   The ARP cache

The Protocol column lists the protocols that are using the address format structure shown in the Address column. (ARP is not limited to the IP Internet layer protocol.) In this case these addresses are IP addresses. The Hardware Addr column lists the hardware addresses corresponding to the IP addresses. You can evaluate the correctness of this mapping by looking at Figure 6-3. **Type** is the packet encapsulation format, which is ARPA (Ethernet II). **Interface** is the label for network (or subnet) connection for the corresponding device. **Age** is the time that the particular entry has been in the router's ARP cache. If you look back at

Figure 6-7, you will see a line labeled ARP type. This line shows that "ARP time out" has been set at 4:00:00, or 4 hours, 0 minutes, 0 seconds. This is the default time-out of an ARP cache entry. When the age of an entry reaches this value, the router drops it from the ARP cache. If you enter "show arp" a number of times in succession, you will see that the value of "age" for an entry increases. A dash (-) next to an entry refers to a router interface that does not age.

Another useful IP subcommand from the list in Figure 6-10 is **show protocols**. Entering this command at the Executive-level prompt produces a screen like that shown in Figure 6-12.

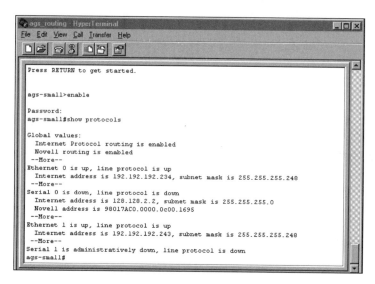

Figure 6-12   Show Protocols command

Under Global values, you see that Internet Protocol and Novel1 routing are enabled. In this list, you also see that the router Ethernet interfaces 0 and 1 are both "up" and that two serial interfaces are not in use.

A related subcommand is **show ip protocols**, which only provides information about IP protocols and is more detailed. Entering this subcommand at the Executive-level prompt produces, in the case of our experimental network 192.192.192.0, the screen shown in Figure 6-13 for the Routing Information Protocol (RIP).

```
Routing Protocol is "rip"
  Sending updates every 30 seconds, next due in 29 seconds
  Invalid after 180 seconds, hold down 180, flushed after 240
  Outgoing update filter list for all interfaces is not set
  Incoming update filter list for all interfaces is not set
  Redistributing: rip
  Routing for Networks:
    192.192.192.0
  Routing Information Sources:
  Distance: (default is 120)

  --More--
```

Figure 6-13   Show IP Protocols command

ROUTING PROTOCOLS

 For more information about Exterior Gateway Protocols (EGP), start with RFC 904.

Before we begin to look into the details of specific routing protocols such as RIP, some discussion of routing protocols in general is needed. For a small network that is generally static, static routing tables for the routers on the network can be configured manually. On networks that are dynamic and large this is not possible because too many changes in network topology occur too rapidly. Thus a mechanism for providing updates to routing tables is needed and is the reason routing protocols exist. A simple routing table contains the information shown in Table 6-2.

Table 6-2   Contents of a Routing Table

Destination (IP Network address)	Mask for	Route (IP Interface address)	Distance (hops)
Network 1	Network 1	A	0
Network 2	Network 2	B	0
Network 3	Network 3	C	1
Network 4	Network 4	D	1
Network 5	Network 5	E	2
Network 6	Network 6	F	3
Network 4	Network 4	G	2

The **Destination** column contains destination networks that the router knows about. The router will use a mask to determine a destination network IP address. The **Distance** column contains the number of hops to that destination network. The **Route** column contains the IP address of the router interface that should be used to forward the packet so as to reach the destination network in the number of hops shown in the Distance column. The number 0 in the Distance column for Network 1 and Network 2 means that the router is directly connected to Network 1 through Route A and Network 2 through Route B. The number 1 in the Distance column for Networks 3 and 4 means that Network 3 and Network 4 can be reached by traversing one router using Routes B and C, respectively. Notice that the table indicates that Network 4 can be reached via two routes, Route D and Route G. This is a redundancy that occurs in some routing tables, depending on the routing protocol that is used. Route G would only be selected by the routing algorithm if Route D were down.

Because of changes in network topology and because devices are not always active, the contents of all three columns in Table 6-2 are subject to change. Routing protocols are used to share router table information between routers in order to keep the information in routing tables as current as possible. When a router receives an update of routing information known by another router, the router that receives this information updates its routing table if the information that is provided results in routes that are "shorter." The meaning of "shorter" depends on the routing protocol that is used. In Table 6-2 "shorter" means fewer hops are required to reach the destination network.

Routing protocols are divided into Interior Gateway Protocols (IGP) and Exterior Gateway Protocols (EGP). These names are relative to what are called autonomous systems (AS). An **autonomous system** is an administrative entity that manages the communication between networks in that system. Autonomous systems use **IGPs** to do that management. The Internet is made up of many autonomous systems. **EGPs** are used to manage communication between autonomous systems. **Boundary** routers are routers that communicate reachability information about networks in one autonomous system to another autonomous system.

In the following sections, two IGPs and their configuration and implementation are described: RIP and OSPF. RIP is the routing protocol that dominates the transfer of routing information on the Internet. RIP uses a vector-based algorithm in which the minimum number of hops to a network determines what information is kept in a routing table and which route is chosen by the RIP algorithm. The Open Shortest Path First (OSPF) protocol has many advantages over RIP. It has been in existence for some time, and efforts to implement it are now more widely in progress.

ROUTING INFORMATION PROTOCOL (RIP)

 For more information about RIP, see RFC 1058.

You see in Figure 6-13 that RIP sends "updates every 30 seconds." In actuality, RIP sends the complete routing table every 30 seconds whether or not there have been any changes to it. The next line says "Invalid after 180 seconds." This statement specifies that any route becomes invalid if an advertisement for it has not been received from another router within this time period. On the same line, "flushed after 240 seconds" means that the invalid route will be dropped from the routing table 240 seconds after it has been declared invalid. "Hold down" refers to the time that a route must be kept in the routing table after it has been declared unreachable. This procedure minimizes the chances for instability when route change information propagates slowly throughout a large network. After the line "Routing for Networks," the IP numbers of networks that are using RIP are shown. In our case there is only one network, 192.192.192.0. The next line refers to "Routing Information Sources." There may be more than one routing information protocol being employed by the network. The reliability of routing information sources is given a rating between 0 and 255. This is called the **administrative distance**. The higher the number, the lower the reliability. RIP has a rating of 120 on this scale.

To see the contents of a routing table, you would enter the subcommand **show ip route** at the Executive-level prompt. Figure 6-14 shows the screen that results for our case when this subcommand is entered on Cisco router 2501, for which the Executive-level prompt is **test#**.

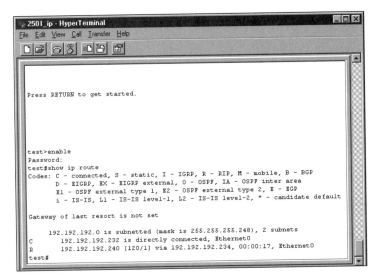

```
Press RETURN to get started.




test>enable
Password:
test#show ip route
Codes: C - connected, S - static, I - IGRP, R - RIP, M - mobile, B - BGP
       D - EIGRP, EX - EIGRP external, O - OSPF, IA - OSPF inter area
       E1 - OSPF external type 1, E2 - OSPF external type 2, E - EGP
       i - IS-IS, L1 - IS-IS level-1, L2 - IS-IS level-2, * - candidate default

Gateway of last resort is not set

     192.192.192.0 is subnetted (mask is 255.255.255.248), 2 subnets
C       192.192.192.232 is directly connected, Ethernet0
R       192.192.192.240 [120/1] via 192.192.192.234, 00:00:17, Ethernet0
test#
```

Figure 6-14   Routing table of the Cisco 2501 router

The first four lines next to "Codes:" are definitions of the letters that appear in the next four lines of the routing table. The table tells us that the network 192.192.192.0 has been subnetted, that the subnet mask is 255.255.255.248, and that there are two subnets. The code **C** on the next line says that the subnet 192.192.192.232 is directly connected to the router and that the connection label is ethernet 0. The next line is more interesting. The code **R** tells us that router Cisco 2501 learned about the subnet 192.192.192.240 via a RIP broadcast that it received from its connection to the router interface 192.192.192.234 to ethernet 0. **[120/1]** in the last line tells us that the administrative distance is 120 and that the hop metric is one. A **hop metric** of one means that one router must be traversed in order to reach subnet 192.192.192.240 from subnet 192.192.192.234.

Figure 6-15 shows the routing table for the Cisco router ags.

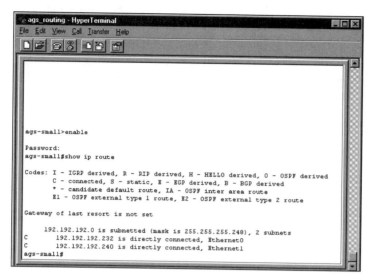

Figure 6-15 Routing table of the Cisco AGS router

The two lines above the Executive-level prompt ags-small # at the bottom of the figure show two routing table entries. Both entries are known because the router is directly connected (indicated by code **C**) to those subnets. There is no entry advertised by Cisco router 2501 because this router is not connected to a remote network. Configuration of RIP to obtain information of the type shown in Figures 6-14 and 6-15 is simple. For the Cisco AGS router the commands are:

```
ags-small> configure

router rip

network 192.192.192.0
```

Now let's look at the format of the RIP frame that is used to communicate between routers. Figure 6-16 shows this format.

PREAMBLE	DESTINATION ADDRESS	SOURCE ADDRESS	TYPE	IP	UDP	RIP MESSAGE	FCS

Figure 6-16 RIP Ethernet II frame

The router broadcasts this frame to directly connected networks (subnets) every 30 seconds. The RIP message contains the routing table of the router that is the source of the message. Routers update their routing tables on the basis of the information in the RIP message. These routers in turn send updates to routers on networks to which they are directly connected. The result is that routing updates are propagated throughout the network. The destination address in a RIP frame is the broadcast address FFFFFFFFFFFFh. Thus it will be processed by any attached router. The format of the RIP message is shown in Table 6-3.

Table 6-3   RIP Message Format

Section	Field	Bits	Description
Header	Command	8	1 = Request for partial or full routing information 2 = Response containing network/distance pairs
	Version	8	Currently version 1
		16	All bits are zero.
Data	ID of Network Family 1	16	The ID of the Network-layer protocol being used. IP has the value 2.
	Network Address of Net 1	16	
	Network Address of Net 1	32	Only these 32 bits of the available 112 (16 + 32 + 32 + 32) bits are used if the network protocol is IP. The other Network Address bits will be set to 0.
	Network Address of Net 1	32	
	Network Address of Net 1	32	
	Distance to Network Address	32	An integer that specifies the number of hops to Network Address. Maximum is 16 for IP. The number of **hops** is the number of routers that must be traversed in order to reach Network Address.
	Network Address of Net N	16	
	⋮		
	Network Address of Net N	32	
	Distance to Network Address	32	
	ID of Network Family 2	16	
	Network Address of Net 1	16	
	⋮		
	Network Address of Net 1	32	
	Distance to Network Address	32	

As the table indicates, more than one network protocol family, not just IP, may be active. Under each family ID, there are **network address/distance to network address** pairs. These pairs have been learned from RIP messages received from other routers connected to the same network. These routers have, in turn, received their information from other routers.

Although RIP is a very popular and useful protocol, it has three major drawbacks: (1) messages are sent every 30 seconds whether or not the routing table has been updated, (2) the whole routing table is sent, and (3) the only "cost" metric used is distance (hops). The development of the OSPF Protocol was initiated to address these and other deficiencies of RIP. The next section examines OSPF.

OPEN SHORTEST PATH FIRST (OSPF) PROTOCOL

OSPF is a comprehensive protocol. It takes a considerable amount of time to gain an appreciation for its many aspects.

Configuration of the OSPF protocol.   This section begins with a basic configuration of the protocol on the routers shown in Figure 6-3. Understanding this configuration will provide you with a better appreciation for the OSPF message format that is presented later.

Table 6-4 lists features that are part of OSPF and not available in RIP.

Table 6-4   Distinguishing OSPF features

OSPF Features
Includes Type of Service (TOS) routing. The router uses both the destination address and the TOS fields in the IP header to choose a route.
If multiple routes to a destination that have the same cost are configured, the traffic is distributed equally over these routes.
A site is allowed to partition its networks and routers into **areas**. The topology in one area can be configured independently of those in other areas.
Routers may be authenticated. Only trusted routers may propagate routing information.
Routing tables are not broadcast. Instead, routers that use OSPF send **link state messages** about the links to which they are directly attached. Routers use these messages to independently create their routing table, which consists of a tree of routes to all destination networks.
On multiaccess networks, OSPF assigns designated routers. These **designated routers** send link status messages for all routers on that network.
OSPF allows routers internal to the autonomous system (AS boundary routers) to distribute information obtained from routers external to the autonomous system. Message format distinguishes between information obtained from routers internal and external to the AS.

Figure 6-17 shows the commands used to configure the AGS router for OSPF routing.

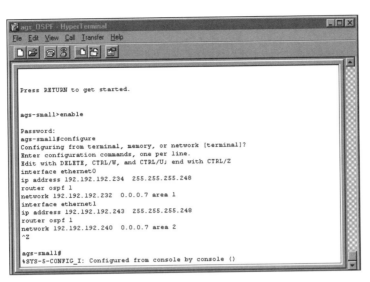

```
ags_OSPF - HyperTerminal
File  Edit  View  Call  Transfer  Help


Press RETURN to get started.


ags-small>enable

Password:
ags-small#configure
Configuring from terminal, memory, or network [terminal]?
Enter configuration commands, one per line.
Edit with DELETE, CTRL/W, and CTRL/U; end with CTRL/Z
interface ethernet0
ip address 192.192.192.234  255.255.255.248
router ospf 1
network 192.192.192.232  0.0.0.7 area 1
interface ethernet1
ip address 192.192.192.243  255.255.255.248
router ospf 1
network 192.192.192.240  0.0.0.7 area 2
^Z

ags-small#
%SYS-5-CONFIG_I: Configured from console by console ()
```

Figure 6-17   Configuring OSPF routing on the Cisco AGS router

Table 6-5 lists these commands and what they do.

Table 6-5   Commands to Configure OSPF Routing on the Cisco AGS Router

Line	Command	Description
1	interface ethernet0	The interface subcommand that specifies the interface (ethernet0) to which the following commands apply
2	ip address 192.192.192.234	The IP address of the router interface to ethernet0
3	255.255.255.248	The subnet mask for network 192.192.192.0
4	router ospf 1	The command that is required to initiate OSPF configuration on this router interface. 1 is the ID of the routing process.
5	network 192.192.192.232	The first argument of the router ospf 1 network subcommand It is the subnet address to which IP addresses will be compared.
6	0.0.0.7	The wildcard mask for network 192.192.192.232. It determines which interfaces are in the area that is defined by the command on line 7.
7	area 1	An interface is said to be in area 1 if its IP address satisfies the area 1 criteria defined by lines 5 and 6. These criteria will be explained in the text that follows this table.
8	interface ethernet1	The interface subcommand that specifies the interface (ethernet1) to which the following commands apply
9	ip address 192.192.192.243	The IP address of the router interface to ethernet1

Table 6-5   Commands to Configure OSPF Routing on the Cisco AGS Router (continued)

Line	Command	Description
10	255.255.255.248	The subnet mask for network 192.192.192.0
11	router ospf 1	The command that is required to initiate OSPF configuration on this router
12	network 192.192.192.240	The first argument of the router ospf 1 network subcommand. It is the subnet address to which IP addresses will be compared.
13	0.0.0.7	The wildcard mask for network 192.192.192.243
14	area 2	An interface is said to be in area 2 if its IP address satisfies the area 2 criteria defined by the previous lines 12 and 13.

As implied by lines 5, 6, and 7 in the table, the interfaces that are in OSPF area 1 are determined by the subcommand:

network 192.192.192.232   0.0.0.7   area 1.

Let's examine the three steps that the algorithm uses to determine membership in area 1.

1. The router computes the logical OR of 192.192.192.232 with 0.0.0.7.

2. The router computes the logical OR of the <IP Address> with 0.0.0.7.

3. The router compares the results of each logical OR. If the results are the same, the IP address is in area 1.

Let's look at Step 1. The logical OR of the first three fields returns 192.192.192. The logical OR of 232 with 7 in binary looks like:

11101111 (232)

00000111 (7)

11101111 (232)

The result of Step 1 is therefore 192.192.292.232. The logical OR of an IP address with 0.0.0.7 will always match the result of **Step 1** as long as the IP address does not differ from 192.192.192.232 except in the last three bits. Thus any IP address in the range 192.192.192.232 to 192.192.192.239 is defined to be in area 1. Therefore, the interfaces 192.192.192.233, 192.192.192.234, and 192.192.192.235 in Figure 6-2 are in area 1. A similar analysis shows that the interfaces 192.192.192.241, 192.192.192.243, and 192.192.192.242 are in area 2. Figure 6-18 shows the resulting OSPF routing environment for the network shown in Figure 6-3.

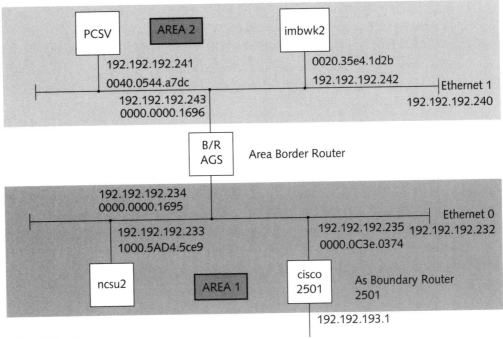

Figure 6-18 OSPF routing environment configured for the network shown in Figure 6-3

In the language of OSPF, the following routing topology has been generated:

- Area 1. Includes one interface of the border router Cisco AGS the workstation ncsu2 interface, and one interface of the boundary router Cisco 2501. A **border router** is one that has interfaces in more than one area. A boundary router is one that connects autonomous systems.

- Area 2. Includes one interface of the border router Cisco AGS, the server pcsv interface, the workstation ncsu2 interface, and the workstation ibmwk2 interface.

An **autonomous system** is one in which the topology is transparent to all other autonomous systems.

A useful command for viewing the result of configuring an OSPF router interface is, for example, for the ethernet0 interface of the router Cisco 2501:

```
show ip ospf interface ethernet0
```

which produces the information shown after the command in the lower half of the screen displayed in Figure 6-19.

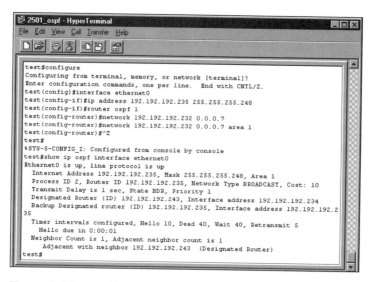

Figure 6-19   Configuring OSPF on Cisco 2501 router and results of executing the command "show ip ospf interface ethernet0"

Table 6-6 describes the information displayed in Figure 6-19.

Table 6-6   OSPF Configuration Status of the Cisco 2501 Router Interface Ethernet0

Parameter	Description
Ethernet0 status	Status is up. Interface is functioning correctly.
Line protocol	Status is up. The link is active.
Internet Address	192.192.192.235 is the address of the ethernet0 interface of the router.
Mask	255.255.255.248 is the IP subnet mask.
Area	Area 1 is the area to which interface ethernet0 has been assigned.
Process ID	The ID assigned to the OSPF routing process.
Router ID	192.192.192.235 is the ID of the router that originates the OSPF routing protocol packet. It uniquely identifies the router in the autonomous system. An **autonomous system** is a group of routers exchanging information using a common routing protocol.
Network Type	Ethernet is a BROADCAST-type network.
Cost	An integer, greater than 0, that gives the relative cost of the link. **Cost** is a measure of the type of service (TOS) that can be provided by the link. A Cost = 10 is the default for TOS 0.
Transmit Delay	The time allowed for a link state advertisement to be effective.
State	The State of this router is backup designated router (BDR). This router becomes the designated router (DR) if the DR fails.
Interface address	The IP address of the designated router on the network to which it is attached. You will see this address in the **link state advertisement** format shown in the next section.

Table 6-6   OSPF Configuration Status of the Cisco 2501 Router Interface Ethernet0
(continued)

Parameter	Description
Hello timer interval	"Hello10" means that Hello messages are sent to maintain communication between neighboring routers every 10 seconds.
Dead timer interval	"Dead 40" is the time interval in seconds that a neighbor router will wait to hear a Hello message from another router before declaring it dead.
Wait timer interval	"Wait 40" is the time interval in seconds that is waited before a new designated router is elected if the current designated router fails.
Retransmit timer interval	"Retransmit 5" is the time in seconds between link state advertisement retransmissions if a link state acknowledgment is not received.
Hello due	Router expects another hello message in 1 second.
Neighbor Count	The number of routers that are neighbors of this router. In this case only one router, Cisco AGS, is a neighbor. A **neighbor** is a router directly connected to the same network.
Adjacent neighbor count	The number of routers with which this router has established adjacencies. In this case, only one adjacency exists, with the Cisco AGS router. An **adjacency** between routers means that routers have agreed to let one of the group, the **designated router**, advertise the link status of each of them.
Adjacent with	The IDs of routers with which this router is adjacent. In this case it is the designated router with ID 192.192.192.243.

Figure 6-20 shows the results of the commands `show ip ospf interface ethernet0` and `show ip ospf interface ethernet1` on the CISCO AGS router.

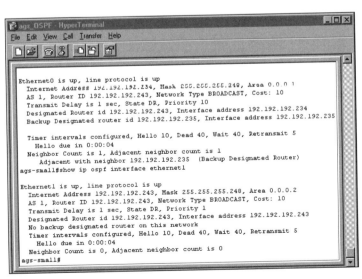

Figure 6-20   Results of executing the commands "show ip ospf interface ethernet0" and "show ip ospf interface ethernet1" on the Cisco AGS router

The format of the information is the same as that displayed in Figure 6-19. The items of interest in this figure are the following:

- Internet address 192.192.192.234 of the AGS router is in area 1.

- Internet address 192.192.192.243 of the AGS router is in area 2.

- The AGS router has one neighbor and one adjacent neighbor. Both are the 2501 router with ID 192.192.192.235.

A border router in Figure 6-18 may be part of a backbone area. A **backbone area** contains connected routers that connect other areas, such as AREA1 and AREA2. The backbone area has area number 0. Router 2501 is an AS boundary router. A router that has interfaces in only one area is called an **internal router**.

Now that you have seen how OSPF is configured and how it can be used, let's look at the format of OSPF messages.

OSPF Message Format

 The comprehensive nature of the OSPF message makes it necessary to use a number of tables to describe it. See RFC 2179 for more details about OSPF.

Figure 6-21 shows the Ethernet II frame that is used to transport the OSPF message on a multiaccess network.

PREAMBLE	DESTINATION ADDRESS	SOURCE ADDRESS	TYPE	IP	OSPF PACKET	FCS

Figure 6-21   OSPF Ethernet II frame

The OSPF packet is encapsulated in the IP segment of the Ethernet II frame. Neither the TCP nor UDP protocol is used. OSPF is IP protocol number 89. There are five distinct OSPF packet types. These are listed in Table 6-7.

Table 6-7   OSPF Packet Types

Type	Packet	Description
1	Hello	Sent by routers to find neighboring routers on the network
2	Database Description	Sent by routers to communicate their database topology to all other routers
3	Link State Request	Sent by a router to request an update on specific links
4	Link State Update	Sent by a router to provide an update on links in its routing table
5	Link State Acknowledgment	Sent by a router to acknowledge receipt of Link State Request and Link State Update packets

Every OSPF packet type starts with a common 24-byte OSPF header. This header is described in Table 6-8.

Table 6-8   Common Header of an OSPF Packet

Section	Field	Bits	Description
Header	Version	8	Version of the protocol. The current version is 2.
	Type	8	One of the types listed in Table 6-7
	Packet Length	16	The number of bytes in the OSPF packet, including the header
	Router ID	32	The ID for the packet source. This ID depends on the type of packet being sent.
	Area ID	32	The ID of the area that this router belongs to
	Checksum	16	16-bit ones complement of the ones complement sum of all 16-bit words in the packet, including the header but excluding the 64-bit Authentication field
	Authentication Type	16	Described in Table 6-9, which follows
	Authentication	64	See Table 6-9, which follows

6

Table 6-9   OSPF Authentication Types

Type	Authentication	Description
0	Null authentication	No password is used, and the Authentication field is ignored by the router that receives the packet.
1	Simple password	The authentication is used to enter a password up to 64 bits in length. This password is network-specific. It is a password in the clear, which is vulnerable. It is intended to keep routers from joining the network without being configured to join the OSPF communication.
2	Cryptographic authentication	Each router on the network has a shared secret key. This key and the message generate a message digest, which is attached to the end of the packet. The Authentication field is used to specify key ID information.

The packet of Type 1 in Table 6-7 is the Hello packet. Table 6-10 describes the fields that are added to the OSPF common header to form the Hello packet. Hello packets are multicast to the AllSPFRouters address, which is 224.0.0.5. **SPF** stands for shortest path first, the precursor of the OSPF algorithm.

Table 6-10   Description of the Fields in the Hello Packet

Section	Field	Bits	Description
Common		192	OSPF Common header in Table 6-8
Hello	Network Mask	32	The network mask associated with this interface
	Hello Interval	8	The interval in seconds between sending Hello messages
	Options	8	Used to advertise optional capabilities. Can be used to route packets around reduced functionality routers. Currently, only the third (E-bit) and fourth (T-bit) bits are used. If T = 0, the router is only capable of TOS = 0. When E = 0, the router does not send or receive AS external link advertisements.
	Rtr Pri	8	This router's priority. Used in the determination of the designated router.
	RouterDeadInterval	32	The number of seconds before this router will declare a router dead when it does not get a Hello packet from the router in the Hello interval
	Designated Router	32	The IP address of the designated router on this network. The **designated router** advertises the routing tables of other routers on this network.

Table 6-10   Description of the Fields in the Hello Packet (continued)

Section	Field	Bits	Description
	Backup Designated Router	32	The IP address of the backup designated router on this network. The **backup designated router** becomes the designated router if the designated router fails.
	Neighbor1 IP Address	32	The IP address of a neighbor router from which a Hello message has been received in the last RouterDeadInterval seconds
	Neighbor2 IP Address	32	The IP address of another neighbor router
	⋮	⋮	⋮
	NeighborN IP Address	32	The IP address of the Nth neighbor

Let's now consider OSPF packet Type 4, The **Link State Update packet**. Its description will provide insight into most of the OSPF packets, aside from that generated by the Hello packets. Link State Update packets are multicast on networks that support multicast or broadcast. For reliability, these packets are acknowledged by **Link State Acknowledgment packets**. If retransmission of a Link State Update packet is necessary, a unicast Link State Update packet is sent. Five types of link state advertisements can appear in a Link State Update packet. These are listed in Table 6-11.

Table 6-11   Types of Link State Advertisements

LS Type	Advertisement	Description
1	Router Links	Data depends on what the router is connected to. For example, if connected to a network, the data contains the IP address of the interface.
2	Network Links	The designated router advertises its ID and the IDs of all adjacent routers on the network.
3	Summary Link	Originated by area border routers. The Type 3 advertisement is sent to a network in another area.
4	Summary Link	Originated by area border routers. The Type 4 advertisement is sent to an autonomous system (AS) boundary router.
5	AS External Link	Originated by AS boundary routers. The announcement is sent all AS boundary routers external to this AS that are known to the router.

Table 6-12 describes the fields in the Link State Update packet.

Table 6-12   Description of the Fields in the Link State Update Packet

Section	Field	Bits	Description
OSPF Common Header		192	OSPF Common header in Table 6-8
	Number of Advertisements	32	The number of link state advertisements included in this update packet
Link State Advertisement Header		160	See Table 6-13, which follows this table. This header is included with every type of link state advertisement.
Link State Advertisement		variable	One of the link state advertisements listed in Table 6-11. See Table 6-13.

The Link State Advertisement header, referenced in Table 6-12 above is described in Table 6-13. This header precedes every link state advertisement.

Table 6-13   Link State Advertisement Header

Section	Field	Bits	Description
	LS Age	16	The time in seconds since the link advertisement was sent
	Options	8	The options supported by the routers in the domain of addresses being advertised
	LS Type	8	The five types are described in Table 6-11.
	LS ID	32	Depends on the LS Type. For example, if the advertisement is Type 2, Network Links, the LS ID is the IP address of the designated router.
	Advertising Router	32	The ID of the advertising router
	LS Sequence Number	32	Successive instances of a link state advertisement are given incremental sequence numbers to identify the most recent update.
	LS Checksum	16	Includes the entire link state advertisement except the Link Age field. This header is included.
	Length	16	Length in bytes of the link state advertisement, including this header

Table 6-14   Link State Advertisement Router Links LS Type (LS Type 1 in Table 6-11)

Section	Field	Bits	Description
Router Links		8	Contain two 0 bits and bits V, B, and E. *Bit V* is set to 1 if the router is an endpoint of an active virtual link. A **virtual link** is one that is not part of the backbone area but provides a link between areas. *Bit E* is set to 1 if the router is an AS boundary router. *Bit B* is set to 1 if the router is an area border router.
	Number of Links	24	The number of router links being advertised
Link 1	Link ID	32	The ID of the object that the router links to, e.g. another router or a network. Depends on the Type field listed below. For example if Type = 2, connection to a transit network, the ID is that of the designated router on that network.
	Link Data	32	Data here depends on the Type field listed below. For Type = 2, it is the router's IP address on the network.
	Type	8	Type 1 = point-to-point connection to another router. Type 2 = connection to a transit network. Type 3 = connection to a stub network. A **stub** network is not a transit network, i.e. it is a dead end. Type 4 = Virtual link
	Number of Types of Service (TOS)	8	The number of TOS metrics that are available on this link in addition to TOS 0
TOS Metrics for Link 1	TOS 0 Metric	16	The cost of using TOS 0 on this link. The default is 10.
	TOS 1	8	An IP Header TOS option number
	0	8	8 zero bits
	TOS 1 Metric	16	The cost of using TOS 1 on Link 1
	TOS N	8	An IP Header TOS option number
	0	8	8 zero bits
	TOS N Metric	16	The cost of using TOS N on Link 1
Link 2	Link ID		The ID of the object that the router links to
Link 2	Link Data		Data here depends on the Type field
⋮	⋮	⋮	⋮
⋮	⋮	⋮	⋮
Link N	Link ID		The ID of the object that the router links to

6

Similar tables can be developed for the four other types of link advertisements listed in Table 6-11, but most of the concepts and fields have been covered by the previous discussion about Link State Update packets for router advertisements.

The discussion of the OSPF configurations that were examined prior to this section exposed you to the basics of configuring an OSPF router. There are of course many other OSPF configuration commands that were not discussed, but which provide tools for implementing more comprehensive features of OSPF routing that have been described in this section. Implementation of OSPF routing in a production environment requires a careful study of the details of RFC 2178.

CHAPTER SUMMARY

In this chapter you learned several important concepts about bridging and routing:

- Bridges use source and destination hardware addresses to control the flow of traffic across their interfaces.

- Bridges isolate segments and networks into collision domains, so that only that segment of the network on which the collision takes place must manage the recovery from the collision.

- Bridges use the OSI Physical and Data Link layer protocols and a Relay process to perform their function.

- A transparent bridge is one that filters and forwards frames between segments and networks that are using the same media access control protocol.

- A translational bridge is one that connects dissimilar networks and translates the MAC header used on one network into the MAC header used on the other network.

- A spanning-tree algorithm is used to manage connectivity of networks connected by bridges. This algorithm ensures that there are no loops created by this connectivity. Bridge interfaces are configured to be members of a group that is managed by the spanning-tree algorithm.

- Bridges can be configured to discard frames sent from or to certain hardware addresses.

- Routers are multiport devices that isolate networks and subnets by using the Internet layer of a protocol stack.

- Routers using the TCP/IP protocol stack map destination network IP addresses to the IP address of the router interface that should be used to forward the packet.

- The routing table of a router can be configured and updated statically or dynamically. In large networks, dynamic configuration is necessary.

- Several protocols may be used to automate the process of providing all routers in a large network with current routing table information.

- Routing protocols are divided into two categories—Interior Gateway Protocols (IGP) and Exterior Gateway Protocols (EGP).

- IGPs are used for communication *in* autonomous systems; EGPs are used for communication *between* autonomous systems.

- An **autonomous system** is an administrative unit consisting of an independent set of networks and routers in a topology that is not visible to other autonomous systems.

- Autonomous systems can be divided into OSPF areas. Area topologies are independent, and communications can be contained within an area.

- OSPF uses area border routers to summarize area information and communicate it to other area boundary routers.

- OSPF uses autonomous system boundary routers to summarize autonomous system information and communicate it to other autonomous systems.

- Routers implementing RIP broadcast messages every 30 seconds to directly connected networks. These messages contain the entire routing table of the source router. Routers use this information to update routes in their routing tables.

- RIP uses only the number of hops to a destination network to determine the best route to take.

- OSPF designated routers multicast link state updates to routers on directly connected networks. These updates contain only new information about the "cost" of reaching a destination network by using the link that is being updated.

- Each OSPF router builds a tree, rooted at itself, that consists of routes to all destination networks.

- OSPF makes use of the types of service (TOS) provided in the IP header to build multiple routes with different TOS to destination networks.

- OSPF will distribute traffic equally over routes that have the same configured TOS.

- OSPF uses five packet types: Hello, Database Description, Link State Request, Link State Update, and Link State Acknowledgment.

REVIEW QUESTIONS

1. What is the main function of a bridge?

    a. To amplify and retransmit the received signal

    b. To detect frames in which the hardware destination address is a broadcast address

    c. To filter traffic destined to a device on the source network

2. How many layers of the TCP/IP protocol suite are required for operating a bridge?

   a. 4

   b. 2

   c. 0

3. Which fields in the Ethernet II frame does a bridge use to filter frames?

   a. Source hardware address

   b. Destination hardware address

   c. Both source and destination hardware addresses

4. How does a bridge know whether or not to relay a frame it receives at a port?

   a. It reads the Type field of the frame.

   b. It reads the hardware destination address.

   c. It compares the hardware destination address to the source addresses that have previously been received by this port.

5. What is one function of a transparent bridge?

   a. To forward frames with IP destination addresses that are not on the network from which the frame was received

   b. To forward frames with hardware source addresses on the network from which the frame was received

   c. To discard frames if the hardware destination address is that of a device on the network from which the frame was received

6. What does a bridge do if it receives a frame in which the hardware destination address is all one bits?

   a. Discards the frame

   b. Sends it to the default router on the source network

   c. Forwards the frame

7. How many ports can a router have?

   a. 2

   b. 3

   c. Any number

8. How many protocols of the TCP/IP suite does a router implement?

   a. 2

   b. 3

   c. 4

9. What address must the router determine in order to forward a packet?

   a. The hardware address of the destination device

   b. The IP address of the destination device

   c. The IP address of the destination network

10. When the router uses static routing, which of the following is true?

   a. The static routing table is constructed automatically by the router.

   b. The static routing table contains the IP addresses of all routers on the route to the destination computer.

   c. The static routing table contains pairs of IP addresses; one is the destination IP address, and the other is the IP address of the interface that should be used to forward the packet.

11. When a router receives a frame, it reads

   a. The IP destination address

   b. The IP source address

   c. The network part of the IP address

12. How is a subnet mask used?

   a. To determine whether or not a destination address is correct

   b. To determine the class of the destination IP address

   c. To determine the network part of an IP address

13. What is a default gateway address?

   a. A multicast address for all routers on the network

   b. The hardware address of the default gateway

   c. The address of a router to which frames are sent when the destination IP network address does not match that of any devices on the local network

14. How does RIP create a dynamic routing table for a router?

   a. Routers broadcast messages specifying the IP addresses of their interfaces.

   b. Routers broadcast messages specifying the IP addresses of all networks on the Internet.

   c. Routers broadcast their routing tables to directly connected networks.

15. What information is kept in both static and dynamic routing tables?

   a. IP addresses of router interfaces

   b. IP addresses of all known IP networks on the Internet

   c. Destination network/interface IP address pairs

16. What is the minimum number of entries required in a routing table?

   a. The number of active router interfaces

   b. One—the IP address of the default router

   c. The number of networks in the router's domain

6

17. Which of the following is true?

    a. A router that uses RIP obtains routing table updates only when it requests them.

    b. RIP selects the router interface that will be used to forward a packet based on the length of the queue for that interface.

    c. RIP provides the routing table with an entry that includes the address of the interface that will result in the shortest distance to the destination network.

18. Which of the following is true about the OSPF routing protocol?

    a. It always provides the routing table with the IP address of the interface that gives the shortest path to the destination network.

    b. It always provides the routing table with the IP address of the interface that gives the highest throughput to the destination network.

    c. It may provide a set of interface IP addresses that map to the type of service (TOS) being requested.

19. Name the five types of OSFP packets.

20. What information is provided by Link State Update packets?

    a. The routing table of the source of the packet

    b. The "cost" to reach a destination network for each interface

    c. The number of neighbor routers that can be reached directly for each interface

CASE PROJECT

The current status of the Case Project environment is shown in Figure 6-22. In this chapter, you have learned how to use bridges to filter traffic on the network segment in each department, and to use a router to subnet and/or connect to the other company divisions. You have also learned to configure a bridge and a router with RIP and OSPF routing protocols. The exercises that follow will provide some practice of the concepts you have learned.

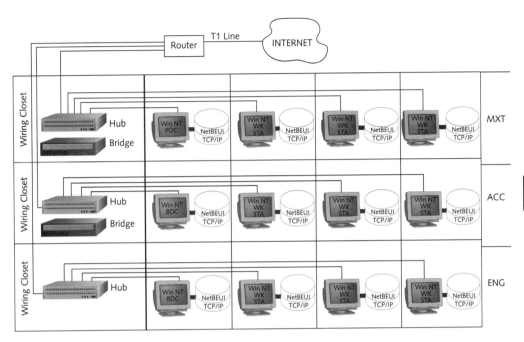

Figure 6-22   Case Project environment prior to Chapter 6

EXERCISE 1—USING THE PING.EXE TCP/IP APPLICATION PROGRAM TO TEST PROPER FUNCTIONING OF THE BRIDGES BETWEEN DEPARTMENTS

This exercise will require one bridge and two protocol analyzers that can operate in promiscuous mode. One analyzer should be installed on each of two network segments.

> The Windows NT 4.0 Network Monitor does not operate in promiscuous mode. Windows System Management Server (SMS), which comes with Windows Back Office, contains an analyzer that does operate in promiscuous mode. Promiscuous mode means that the analyzer will capture all packets regardless of source and destination addresses.

1. Connect a bridge to the hub on its floor and to the hub on the floor below.
2. To test the bridge, install analyzer software, such as that in SMS, NetManage's LANwatch, or Novell's LANalyzer, on a computer on the network segment on the floor that contains the bridge and on a computer on the network segment on the floor below.
3. Start the CAPTURE program on the network analyzer on both computers.
4. From a computer on one segment, PING the IP address of a computer on the other segment.
5. Stop the CAPTURE program on each computer.

6. DISPLAY the captured frames on both analyzers.

7. Find a frame on each analyzer that contains an ICMP request. (PING typically causes four ICMP request messages to be sent, so you should see that many and an equal number of ICMP replies.) You should be able to find an ICMP request frame on both analyzers because you have PINGed the IP address of a computer on the other segment.

8. If you see ICMP frames on both analyzers, you know that the bridge is forwarding frames that it should forward, namely those with hardware destination addresses that are not on the network from which the ICMP frame was received.

9. To see if the bridge is also filtering properly, start the CAPTURE programs on the two analyzers again, and PING the IP address of a computer on the same segment.

10. Stop the CAPTURE programs and DISPLAY the frames captured by both analyzers.

11. You should be able to find ICMP request frames on the analyzer on the network segment from which the PING was initiated.

12. See if you can find the ICMP request frames on the analyzer on the other segment. There should be none, because the bridge should not have passed a frame that had a hardware destination address on the network from which the frame was received.

EXERCISE 2—CREATING SUBNETS

In this exercise, we will assume that instead of having a network consisting of bridged segments, you will make the network on each floor a subnet of the network in the Raleigh building.

1. Use RJ-45 cables to connect each of the three hubs to an Ethernet port on the router. To do this, you may need transceivers that couple the RJ-45 cable to an AUI interface on the router.

2. Make assumptions A, B, and C that follow.

   a. The InterNIC has granted your company three Class C IP networks, one for each division. The Raleigh site network address is 192.192.192.0.

   b. In order to create three subnets at the Raleigh site, you will have to decide how to use some of your Class C host space for subnets.

   c. The router will use a static routing table (constructed in Exercise 3) to route messages from the Internet to the appropriate subnet at the Raleigh site.

3. Create a subnet mask for the IP addresses on your network.

4. Complete Table 6-15.

Table 6-15   IP Address Map for the Raleigh Site

Dept.	Router	Subnet Mask	Server	Wkst. 1	Wkst. 2	Wkst. 3
Marketing						
Accounting						
Engineering						

EXERCISE 3—CONSTRUCTING A STATIC ROUTING TABLE FOR THE ROUTER

Using the IP addresses from Exercise 2, use Table 6-16 to construct a static routing table for the Raleigh site router.

Table 6-16   Static routing table for the Raleigh Site router

Destination Subnet	Subnet Mask	Route	Hops

EXERCISE 4—OSPF CONFIGURATION

Complete Table 6-17 to get some practice in thinking about how to use the OSPF routing protocol for communicating routing information between subnets and company networks. Assume that each Class C site network is in a different OSPF area, and that the company networks comprise an Autonomous System (AS).

Table 6-17   Table for Planning OSPF Routing Between Site Subnets and Between Company Sites

Site (City)	Area	Subnet (IP Address)	Wildcard Mask	Subnet Mask	Border Router (IP Address)	TOS (T1 line)

Figure 6-23 shows the status of the Case Project environment after the completion of this chapter.

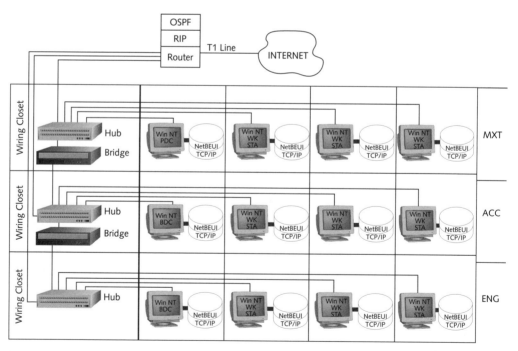

Figure 6-23   Case Project environment after completing Chapter 6

THE DYNAMIC HOST CONFIGURATION PROTOCOL (DHCP)

You have learned that network communication using TCP/IP requires that each device on the network have a unique IP address. If the network is to be attached to the Internet, it is necessary for the network administrator to contact the Internet Network Information Center (**InterNIC**) to obtain an official network ID that is unique. (You can learn more about InterNIC on the Internet at http://www.internic.net/.) It is then the network administrator's responsibility to ensure that IP addresses on the assigned network are unique. This is a difficult problem on a large network. DHCP provides the solution to the problem by having a DHCP server assign an IP address to a DHCP client when the client computer initializes.

IN THIS CHAPTER YOU WILL:

EXAMINE THE FUNCTIONS OF DHCP

INSTALL AND CONFIGURE A DHCP CLIENT AND SERVER

CONFIGURE DHCP SCOPE AND OPTIONS FOR A SUBNET

LEARN ABOUT THE FUNCTION OF THE DHCP RELAY AGENT

ANALYZE DHCP CLIENT/SERVER COMMUNICATION FRAMES

REVIEW OF IP ADDRESSING

Specifications for IP version 6 are described in RFC 1883 and RFC 1884. DHCP is specified by the Internet Engineering Task Force (**IETF**) Requests for Comments (RFCs) 1533, 1534, 1541, and 1542. The IETF is part of the Internet Activities Board (**IAB**), which coordinates the RFC process and sets Internet standards.

You saw in Chapter 5, "IP Addressing," that IP addresses are divided into classes. The number of subnets and hosts that can be attached to a network depends on the class of the IP network address that is assigned to your network administrator by the InterNIC. In IP version 4, the current IP version, all of the Class A addresses and most, if not all, of the Class B addresses have been assigned. Class C addresses allow a very limited number of subnets and hosts. With the rapid expansion of the number of users on the Internet, the availability of unique addresses has become a concern. That is why development of IP version 6 was initiated. The primary new features of version 6 are: (1) IP address size is 128 bits instead of 32 bits, (2) a Priority field has been added, (3) the 16-bit Length field does not include the header, and (4) Header fields that provide for six extension headers have been added.

There is another problem, however. As networks have become much larger and the mobility of computers has increased, it has become too difficult for the network administrator to configure all the devices and maintain an accurate record of IP addresses. DHCP was developed to reduce this complexity.

FUNCTIONS OF DHCP

The purpose of DHCP is twofold: to automate IP configuration and to make more efficient use of available IP addresses. Automation is accomplished by a client DHCP process and a server DHCP process. When the client computer that is DHCP-enabled boots, it broadcasts a message requesting information with which to configure its network interface so that the TCP/IP protocol stack can be used for communication. DHCP servers that receive the message from the client construct and send replies that contain the requested configuration information. The information from the first DHCP server to reply is used by the DHCP client to configure its TCP/IP network interface. The essential pieces of information that must be supplied by the DHCP server are an IP address and a subnet mask. As you will see, other important information can be provided by configuring DHCP server options.

Use of the DHCP protocol not only simplifies and improves the accuracy of TCP/IP configuration but also significantly increases the efficiency of the use of IP addresses. Because most computers on a network need their IP addresses for relatively short periods of time, there really is no need to have these addresses statically bound to those computers. DHCP can be considered a protocol that implements time-sharing of network resources, like the time-sharing of condos. Use of DHCP makes it possible for the pool of IP addresses assigned to a network to be smaller than the number of computers on the network.

DHCP CLIENT INSTALLATION AND CONFIGURATION

Figure 7-1 is an example of the status of a TCP/IP network interface configuration that can be obtained from the TCP/IP utility ipconfig.

```
Command Prompt

Windows NT IP Configuration

        Host Name . . . . . . . . . : ibmwk.raleigh
        DNS Servers . . . . . . . . : 192.192.192.241
        Node Type . . . . . . . . . : Hybrid
        NetBIOS Scope ID. . . . . . :
        IP Routing Enabled. . . . . : Yes
        WINS Proxy Enabled. . . . . : No
        NetBIOS Resolution Uses DNS : No

Ethernet adapter IBMEIWNT1:

        Description . . . . . . . . : IBM EtherJet ISA Adapter
        Physical Address. . . . . . : 00-20-35-E4-1D-2B
        DHCP Enabled. . . . . . . . : Yes
        IP Address. . . . . . . . . : 0.0.0.0
        Subnet Mask . . . . . . . . : 0.0.0.0
        Default Gateway . . . . . . :
        DHCP Server . . . . . . . . : 255.255.255.255
        Primary WINS Server . . . . : 192.192.192.241

Ethernet adapter NdisWan5:

-- More --
```

Figure 7-1   IPCONFIG.EXE display of ibmwk host and interface configuration before DHCP configuration

To obtain a display like this, you would type **ipconfig /all** at the Command Prompt. Figure 7-1 shows the IP configuration of the workstation "ibmwk" and its Ethernet adapter "IBMEIWNT1." The command switch /all causes host information in addition to Ethernet adapter information to be displayed. The state of the information in Figure 7-1 was determined when ibmwk was configured during installation of the Windows NT Workstation operating system. We will review how to set up or change that configuration in a moment. The following is a description of the data in Figure 7-1.

WINDOWS NT IP CONFIGURATION

- The host name is ibmwk, and it is part of the Windows NT domain raleigh.

- The host of the DNS server has the static IP address 192.192.192.241.

Node Type, NetBIOS Scope ID, and NetBIOS Resolution Uses DNS and WINS Proxy will be discussed in Chapter 9, "Name Services."

- IP Routing is enabled on the workstation so that the workstation can forward IP packets.

ETHERNET ADAPTER IBMEIWNT1

- The Ethernet adapter is IBM Etherjet ISA.

- The adapter physical (hardware) address is 00-20-35-E4 1D-2B.

- "DHCP is enabled" means that the workstation will broadcast a request for an IP address to a DHCP server when it initializes.

- IP Address, Subnet Mask, Default Gateway, and DHCP Server address can be assigned by the DHCP server. The DHCP server address shown is the default address used when one has not been specified.

- The Primary WINS Server has the static IP address 192.192.192.241.

The following screens show the steps that are used to configure a computer to have the parameters described in the above list and to obtain the other parameters from the DHCP server.

1. Click **Control Panel** on Settings on the Start menu.

2. Double-click the **Network** icon on Control Panel to display the Network screen. For this workstation, the screen you see is shown in Figure 7-2.

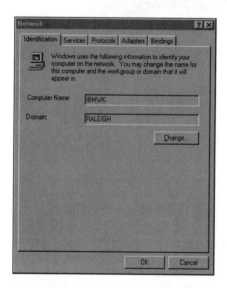

Figure 7-2   Control Panel Network dialog box for IBMWK

The Computer Name is IBMWK, and the Domain is RALEIGH.

3. Click the **Protocols** tab to obtain the list of installed protocols. For this workstation, the screen that opens is shown in Figure 7-3.

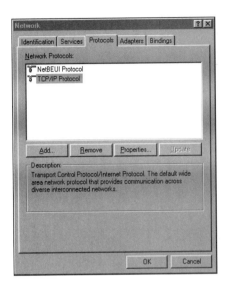

Figure 7-3   Network Protocols dialog box

4. Highlight **TCP/IP Protocol** and click **Properties** to obtain a Microsoft TCP/IP Properties screen. For this workstation, the dialog box that opens is shown in Figure 7-4.

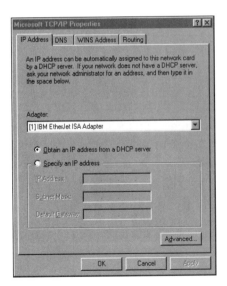

Figure 7-4   Microsoft TCP/IP Properties dialog box

Because we want the rest of the IP configuration of the workstation to be done by the DHCP server, the button **Obtain an IP address from a DHCP server** is clicked. This will cause the workstation to broadcast a DHCP request message on the local subnet when the workstation starts. The DHCP server will then complete the IP configuration of the ibmwk interface. If you did not configure the static information shown in Figure 7-1 during Windows NT installation, you can do so by taking the following steps.

5. Click **Advanced** to obtain the Advanced IP Addressing screen. The screen for this workstation is shown in Figure 7-5.

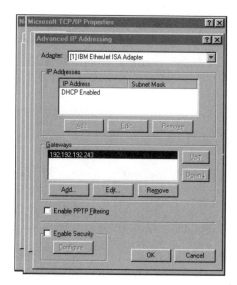

Figure 7-5   Advanced IP Addressing

You see that DHCP is enabled and that a Gateway address of 192.192.192.243 has been added. This is the IP address of the router on the subnet to which this workstation is attached.

6. Click **OK** to return to the Microsoft TCP/IP Properties screen, and then click the **DNS** tab to obtain the screen shown in Figure 7-6, where the address of the host of the DNS server can be entered.

The specified address of the DNS server host is 192.192.192.241, which is the same as the address of the host of the DHCP server. The Host Name is ibmwk. This name refers to the workstation IBMWK that you are configuring. The domain is raleigh, as you have seen. Click **Apply** to confirm the DNS configuration.

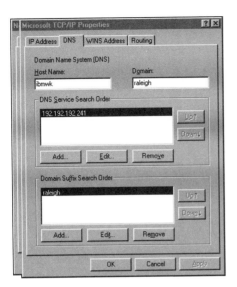

Figure 7-6   DNS dialog box

7. Click the **WINS Address** tab to obtain the screen where WINS can be configured. For this workstation, the screen that opens is shown in Figure 7-7.

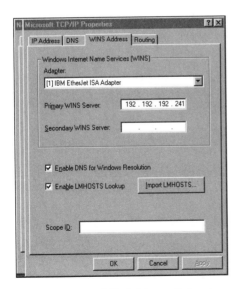

Figure 7-7   WINS Address dialog box

The address of the host of the Primary WINS Server is 192.192.192.241, the same as that of the host of the DHCP and DNS servers. The other items on the screen will be examined Chapter 9.

8. Click the **Routing** tab to obtain the screen shown in Figure 7-8.

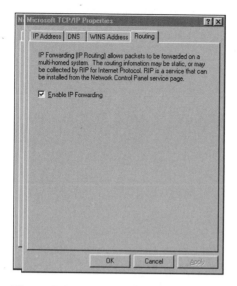

Figure 7-8   Routing dialog box

When you check **Enable IP Forwarding**, if the workstation is multihomed, it will forward packets destined for other subnets or networks, and its routing table will be built by RIP for Internet Protocol messages. A **multihomed** system is one that is connected to more than one network interface.

9. Click **OK**, and you are returned to the screen in Figure 7-2.

10. Click **OK** on this screen, and you will see a message that says that you must restart your workstation in order for your configuration to be saved on the hard drive.

11. Restart the workstation.

Now that the DHCP client workstation is configured, we leave the workstation to configure the DHCP server. After configuring the DHCP server, we will restart the workstation and see if it is properly configured by the DHCP server.

DHCP SERVER INSTALLATION AND CONFIGURATION

Microsoft defines its DHCP server as a process that runs on Windows NT Server and uses the Windows NT TCP/IP protocol stack to communicate with the client DHCP process. DHCP server was installed during the installation of Windows NT Server in Chapter 2, "Windows NT 4.0 Installation." If you did not install it then, you take the following steps:

1. Click **Network** on Control Panel.

2. Click the **Services** tab on the Network screen.

3. If DHCP Server does not appear on the Network Services list, click **Add** to obtain the complete list of services.

4. Highlight **DHCP Server** in this list, then click **OK** to add DHCP Server to the list of services that will be loaded and started when you start the server.

5. Click **Services** on Control Panel, and then check the Service list to see that DHCP Server has started. It should have started automatically.

6. If its Status does not show Started, click **Startup** and set the Startup Type to Automatic, click **OK**, and then click **Start** on the Services screen.

7. Click **Close** to return to Control Panel.

To begin configuration of DHCP Server:

1. Click **Start** on the Taskbar.

2. Select **Programs** on the Start menu.

3. Select **Administrative Tools (Common)** on the Programs menu.

4. Click **DHCP Manager** on the Administrative Tools (Common) menu to obtain the DHCP Manager screen shown in Figure 7-9.

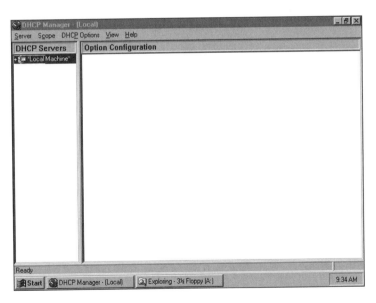

Figure 7-9   DHCP Manager

From this screen you have access to the dialog boxes that allow you to determine what information you want the DHCP server to send to the DHCP client when the client initializes. The next few sections will describe the different components of DHCP Manager and how to use them.

DHCP SERVERS

The DHCP Servers panel on the left of DHCP Manager lists the DHCP servers on your network. In this example (Figure 7-9), you see only the name "Local Machine," which is the computer running the Windows NT 4.0 Server DHCP server process. You can add other DHCP servers to the DHCP Servers list in order to distribute the servicing load or to have back-up DHCP servers. You do this by clicking the **Server** menu and selecting **Add**. You are provided with a dialog box in which you type the IP address of the new DHCP server. When you click **OK** in this box, the IP address of the added server appears in the DHCP Servers list. The added DHCP server can be on another subnet or even on another network if the routers that connect the networks are configured to relay DHCP messages. DHCP Relay Agent will be discussed later in this chapter.

Scope

Scope refers to the range (or pool) of client IP addresses on a subnet that will be managed by a DHCP server. A DHCP server can manage clients on more than one subnet, but a scope is limited to one subnet. To create a scope for the local subnet, you click **Scope** on the menu bar and then click **Create** on the Scope menu. The Create Scope dialog box, shown in Figure 7-10, opens.

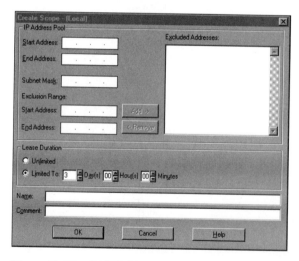

Figure 7-10 DHCP Manager Create Scope dialog box

First consider the IP Address Pool panel of this dialog box. The first two boxes are used to type in the Start and End IP addresses of the scope pool. For example, let's say that you have 10 client computers on the subnet to which this scope applies, and that they are Class C addresses. Then a Start Address could be 192.192.192.1, and an End Address could be 192.192.192.10. When a client on this subnet (configured to use DHCP addressing) initializes, any address in this range can be assigned to the client computer by the DHCP server.

The next box to be completed is Subnet Mask. You may want the DHCP server to service clients on more than one subnet. For each such subnet there would be a different scope, and the subnet mask would have to be configured to accommodate more than one subnet. When the DHCP server replies to a DHCP client request, one of the configuration parameters it sends is the subnet mask.

The next two text boxes are used to type in the Start Address and End Address of the Exclusion Range. The **Exclusion Range** is a range of IP addresses in the IP Address Pool that are configured statically. For example, an Exclusion Range with a Start Address of 192.192.192.2 and an End Address of 192.192.192.4 will exclude machines with the addresses 192.192.192.2, 192.192.192.3, and 192.192.192.4. Examples of addresses you would want to exclude because they are configured statically are those of a router or another server. After you have entered IP addresses into the Exclusion Range text boxes, you click **Add** to tag the exclusions in the DHCP database.

The second panel in the Create Scope dialog box is **Lease Duration**. Here you specify how long the dynamically configured clients are allowed to keep an IP address that has been leased to them by the DHCP server. When the Lease **time to live (TTL)** is half expired, the client will begin a lease renewal process. You can make the lease of unlimited duration or specify the TTL by setting it in the **Limited to** text boxes.

The third panel in the Create Scope dialog box has **Name** and **Comment** text boxes. The Name box must be completed with a string that identifies the scope to the DHCP server and the DHCP clients. Completion of the comment box is not required. Next, you click **OK** to store the scope configuration in the DHCP database and return to the DHCP Manager window. Figure 7-11 shows a completed scope that will be used by the DHCP server on pcsv.

The host pcsv IP address 192.192.192.241 and the address of the router on this subnet, 192.192.192.243, have been excluded because they are statically assigned. The lease duration of the IP addresses in the range 192.192.192.241 to 192.192.192.246 has been set to 10 minutes. The scope has been given the name raleigh1.

7

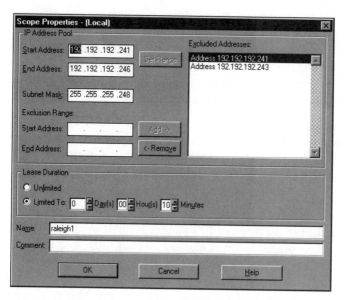

Figure 7-11   Scope for subnet 192.192.192.240

If you double-click **Local Machine** on the DHCP Manager screen, you will see the IP address, 192.192.192.240, of the subnet for which the scope was configured. This is shown in Figure 7-12.

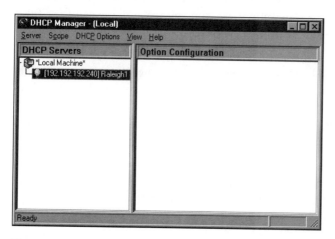

Figure 7-12   Scope Raleigh1 for subnet 192.192.192.240

In addition to the scope properties defined in Figure 7-11, there are DHCP Options that can be added to customize the scope configuration. These options provide further information to a client included in the scope when the DHCP server replies to the request for IP configuration from the DHCP client. These options can be configured to provide the information that was configured statically in Figure 7-1, thus eliminating the need to any static configuration for the DHCP client.

DHCP Options

WINS, DNS, their configuration, and the advantages of their integration will be discussed in Chapter 9, "Name Services."

RFC 1541 defines many DHCP options, 68 of which are supported by Microsoft DHCP Server. However, Windows 95–based, Windows 3.x–based, and Windows NT–based DHCP clients support only some of these options. Third-party DHCP clients may supply others. There are four methods that can be used to set DHCP options. Three of these are accessed from the DHCP Options menu on the DHCP Manager menu bar. These three, Scope, Global, and Defaults, are shown in Figure 7-13. The fourth method configures options for individual clients.

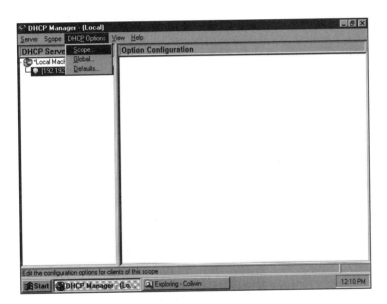

Figure 7-13   DHCP Options

If Scope is selected, the options you set will apply only to the scope that is highlighted in the DHCP Servers list. If Global is selected, the options will apply to all scopes serviced by the selected DHCP server. If Default is selected, you can add options and change the default values of scope or global options. In this chapter, only the Scope method will be used. Clicking **Scope** on the DHCP Options menu produces the dialog box shown in Figure 7-14.

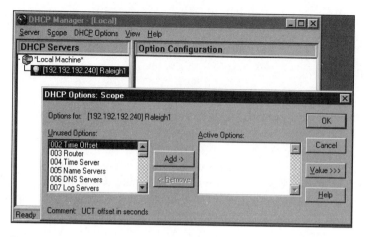

Figure 7-14   DHCP Options: Scope

The dialog box on the left of the DHCP Options: Scope dialog box shows Unused Options from which you can select, and the dialog box on the right shows options that have been made active by clicking **Add**. The ID (e.g., 003 of the Router option) and its value will be included in the Options field of the DHCP packet that is sent to the DHCP client.

Figure 7-15 shows the dialog box that opens when you highlight the 006 DNS Servers Unused Option, click **Value >>>**, and then click **Edit array**.

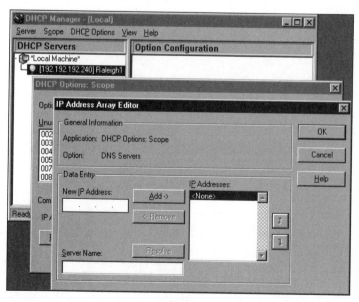

Figure 7-15   IP Address Array Editor for DNS servers

The New IP Address text box is used to enter an IP address for a DNS server on your network. You enter the name of the DNS host, e.g. **pcsv**, in the Server Name box. You could also enter the Server Name and click **Resolve** to let the DHCP server host fill in the IP address for you. Figure 7-16 shows a completed DNS Servers IP Address Array Editor screen for pcsv.

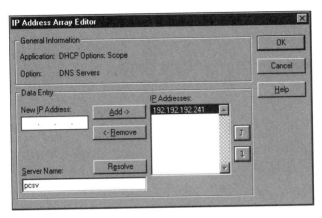

Figure 7-16   DNS Servers IP Address Array Editor dialog box for pcsv

You then click **OK** to return to the DHCP Options: Scope screen where you can select more options.

After selecting and providing values for all desired options, you click **OK** or the DHCP Options: Scope screen to return to DHCP Manager. There, you click the scope in the DHCP Servers list to get a list of the options that have been configured for the DHCP server on host pcsv. These options are listed in the Option Configuration panel. An example list is shown in Figure 7-17.

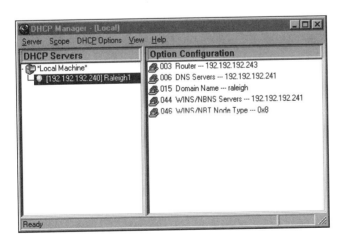

Figure 7-17   Option configuration summary

Router specifies the IP address, 192.192.192.243, of the default router (gateway) for the subnet. **DNS Servers** shows DNS server IP addresses. In this case there is only one, with the address 192.192.192.241. Domain Name System (**DNS**) provides translation between Internet domain names and IP addresses. **Domain Name** is the Windows NT domain name, which is raleigh in this example. **WINS/NBNS Servers** are the IP addresses of computers that are running the WINS/NBNS service. WINS is Windows Internet Name Service, and **NBNS** is NetBIOS Name Service, the precursor to WINS. **WINS** is the service that translates NetBIOS names into IP addresses. **WINS/NBT Node Type** specifies the mode that will be used by clients on the Microsoft Network to propose and establish NetBIOS names. NBT stands for NetBIOS over TCP/IP. These names are mapped to IP addresses in the WINS database. The final step in the configuration of the DHCP server is to activate the scope. On the Scope menu click **Activate**.

The next section describes the function of the DHCP Relay Agent that will be configured on the pcsv server.

DHCP RELAY AGENT

In this chapter, DHCP has been discussed in the context of one subnet, but bear in mind that in general an enterprise intranet will consist of a number of subnets and perhaps more than one network. As was mentioned earlier in this chapter, because of DHCP Relay, it is not necessary to have DHCP servers on every subnet or even on every network. DHCP Relay provides the mechanism for relaying requests for DHCP service between subnets or between networks. Computers running Windows NT Server can provide the DHCP Relay service. The relay service works as follows.

The DHCP client broadcasts a request for IP configuration for the interface on the subnet to which it is attached. If there is no computer running the DHCP server service on that subnet but there is a computer running Windows NT Server and DHCP Relay, that computer will relay the client broadcast to other subnets and networks connected to routers on the subnet. DHCP servers that receive the request will send configuration information to the computer running DHCP Relay, which in turn will forward it to the client that made the request. It is also necessary that the routers support DHCP Relay. The DHCP Relay service is configured from the dialog box shown in Figure 7-18. To open this dialog box:

1. Double-clicking the **Network** icon in Control Panel.
2. Clicking the **Protocols** tab on the Network screen.
3. Highlighting **TCP/IP Protocol**.
4. Clicking **Properties**.
5. Clicking the **DHCP Relay** tab on the Microsoft TCP/IP Properties screen.

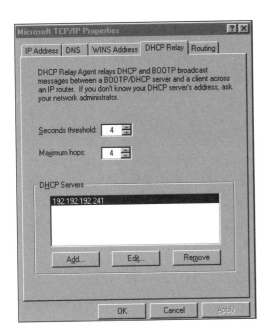

Figure 7-18   DHCP Relay dialog box

In the text at the top of the dialog box, BOOTP is mentioned. **BOOTP** is the boot proto-col that allows a diskless workstation to boot from a remote computer by sending a message to a server that has the desired operating system installed. An image of the operating system is sent to the BOOTP client. DHCP is an extension of BOOTP.

There are three boxes in the DHCP Relay dialog box that require completion. The default and recommended settings for "Seconds threshold" and "Maximum hops" are both 4. **Seconds threshold** is the time at which the DHCP Relay will time out and send a message to the client advising that no DHCP server has replied. **Maximum hops** is the number of hops that a message from the DHCP Relay Agent may take in attempting to find a DHCP server before the message is discarded. The default values should probably be accepted because you do not want the DHCP Relay message "surfing" the network too long or too far, generating excess traffic and processing time. The DHCP Servers list shows the IP addresses of servers that are known. Click **OK** to store the configuration information.

We are now ready for the test of the DHCP client/server system that has been configured. We will restart the DHCP client workstation, type **ipconfig /all** at the workstation Command Prompt, and then compare the dialog box shown in Figure 7-19 with that in Figure 7-1.

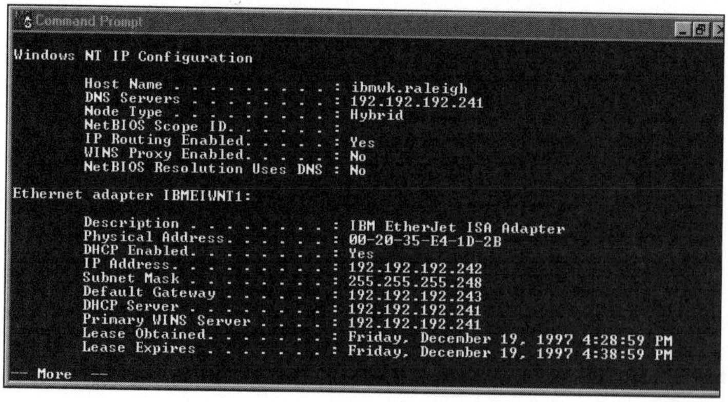

Figure 7-19 IPCONFIG.EXE display of ibmwk host and interface configuration after DHCP configuration

The new information in Figure 7-19, compared to Figure 7-1, tells you that DHCP client/server communication is working correctly. The DHCP Server Scope and Option configurations were sent to the DHCP client. The new information is:

- The IP address of the DHCP client
- The Subnet Mask
- The Default Gateway address
- The DHCP Server address
- The Lease Obtained date and time
- The Lease Expires date and time

DNS server and WINS server addresses, the domain name Raleigh, and the WINS node type were also sent to the DHCP client. However, that information had been statically configured when the DHCP client was configured.

CHAPTER SUMMARY

- Versions 4 and 6 of IP were compared.
- The advantages of using DHCP in today's networking environment were described. These advantages are to automate IP configuration and to make more efficient use of available IP address space.
- The TCP/IP ipconfig utility was used to display the configuration of the interface of a computer running Windows NT Workstation.
- A step-by-step configuration of a DHCP client process on a workstation was described.
- The DHCP server process was configured on a computer running Windows NT Server.

- The workstation was restarted to allow its interface to be configured from the server.
- The IPCONFIG utility was used again to display the workstation interface configuration. It was seen that values provided in the configuration of the DHCP server were sent in DHCP messages to the DHCP client workstation.
- A step-by-step installation of the DHCP server was described.
- DHCP Manager was then used to configure the scope that would be managed by the DHCP server and the options that would be sent to the DHCP client on initialization.
- The DHCP Relay Agent was described. This agent is provided by Windows NT Server. If a DHCP server is not available on a subnet or network, the Agent will relay a request for IP configuration from a DHCP client to a DHCP server on another subnet or network. Routers that the relay message must traverse must be configured to process DHCP Relay Agent messages.

7

REVIEW QUESTIONS

1. What is the current version of IP?

    a. 6

    b. 4

    c. 2

2. What is the address space size in the current version of IP?

    a. 32 bits

    b. 64 bits

    c. 128 bits

3. What will be the address space size in the new version of IP?

    a. 32 bits

    b. 128 bits

    c. 256 bits

4. What organization provides official IP addresses for use on the Internet?

    a. IAB

    b. IETF

    c. InterNIC

5. DHCP improves the *efficiency* of IP address use by doing which of the following?

    a. Leasing IP addresses for a specified time period rather than assigning them to devices permanently

    b. Limiting the number of requests for leases of IP addresses that can be made in a specified time period

    c. Limiting the number of IP addresses that can be distributed

6. Can the number of IP addresses in the address pool for a subnet be smaller than the number of devices on the subnet and still allow all devices access to the Internet?

   a. Yes

   b. No

   c. Yes, if no static addresses are assigned to devices

7. What is the name of the TCP/IP utility that is used to examine the configuration of interfaces in a computer running Windows NT?

   a. WINIPCFG

   b. IPCONFIG

   c. NBSTAT

8. Which of the following sets of steps do you take to reach a screen where you can configure an interface to obtain a DHCP-generated IP address?

   a. Open **Control Panel**; select **Network**; select **TCP/IP Protocol**; and then click **Properties**.

   b. Open **Control Panel**; select **Network**; select **TCP/IP Protocol**; click the **Services** tab; click **Add**; select **Simple TCP/IP Services**; and then click **OK**.

   c. Click **Start** on the Taskbar; select **Programs**; select **Administrative Tools (Common)**; and then click **DHCP Manager**.

9. How many subnets can be included in a DHCP scope?

   a. The number of subnets in the network to which the DHCP server host is connected

   b. The number of subnets indicated by the subnet mask

   c. One

10. How many scopes can be supported by one DHCP server?

    a. One

    b. The number of subnets on the network

    c. Any number

11. What is a "multihomed" computer?

    a. A computer whose network interface has more than one IP address

    b. A computer that has more than one network interface

    c. A computer that has more than one computer name

12. How do you configure another DHCP server on your network?

    a. Add its IP address to the DHCP Manager Servers List

    b. Add its IP address to the DHCP Manager Servers List and configure Scopes for each subnet that this server will service.

    c. Add its IP address to the DHCP Manager Servers List and configure Scopes for the devices on the subnet to which the server is attached.

13. On a subnet with the subnet address 192.192.192.232 and a subnet mask of 255.255.255.248, what is the range of IP addresses that can be assigned to the DHCP scope for that subnet?

    a. 192.192.192.232 to 192.192.192.239

    b. 192.192.192.232 to 192.192.192.238

    c. 192.192.192.233 to 192.192.192.238

14. What do you do about devices whose addresses lie in the range of the address pool assigned to the DHCP server that you do not want the DHCP server to assign?

    a. The assigned pool range cannot include such addresses.

    b. You configure an excluded range of pool addresses that should not be used by DHCP.

    c. You enter each address that you want to have in the pool.

15. Who has the privilege of setting Lease Duration for a scope?

    a. A user in the Administrative Group

    b. Everyone

    c. The administrator

16. What is a disadvantage of setting short lease times?

    a. Too much network traffic is required to renew leases.

    b. Your connection shuts down if the lease expires while you are using the Internet.

    c. You may not get another connection when you need it.

17. How many subnet masks can be assigned to a scope?

    a. The number of subnets on the network

    b. Any number

    c. One

18. Which of the following is an example of a network device that should not have its IP address assigned dynamically?

    a. A router

    b. A client running Windows 3.1

    c. A client running UNIX

19. Which of the following is true about a DHCP Global option?

    a. A Global option will apply to all subnets on one network.

    b. A Global option will apply to all scopes defined for the server.

    c. A Global option will apply to all DHCP servers in the Server List.

20. What is the need for DHCP Relay Agent?

    a. To provide access to a DHCP server on another subnet or network

    b. To be the back-up DHCP server on the subnet

    c. To relay a client's request for DHCP service to a DHCP server on another subnet or network

CASE PROJECT

Figure 7-20 shows the status of the Case Project environment prior to Chapter 7.

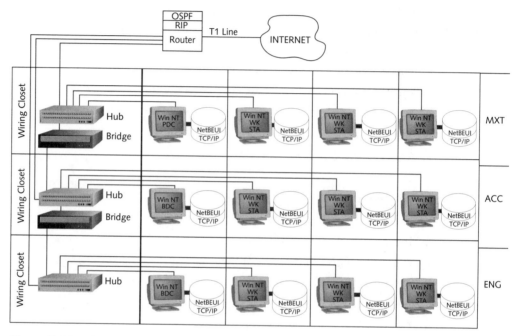

Figure 7-20   Case Project environment prior to Chapter 7

In the exercises at the end of Chapter 6, "Bridging and Routing," you finished connecting all the devices on the network at the Raleigh division site and configured RIP and OSPF routing protocols on the router. Thus, after Chapter 6, the network at the Raleigh site was fully connected both physically and logically. The assumption was also made that the status of the other divisions of the company in Boston and Chicago was the same.

In this chapter, you have learned about the IP configuration convenience offered by the DHCP protocol. The assumption will be made that you want to keep static IP addresses assigned to servers and the router and that you will use DHCP to provide IP configuration for the workstations. In the exercises that follow it is assumed that you have installed DHCP according to the procedures that were covered in this chapter.

For the exercises that follow, there is a computer with the name "pcsv" running Windows NT 4.0 Server and DHCP Server, and a computer named "ibmwk" running Windows NT Workstation, configured as a DHCP client, on the same subnet. Ibmwk has been restarted and initialized. Figure 7-21 shows the statistics of the frames detected by the Network Monitor utility.

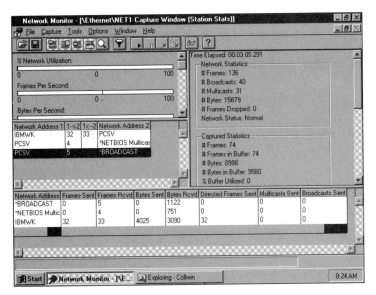

Figure 7-21   Statistics of frames captured by Network Monitor when ibmwk
restarts and reinitializes

There were 74 frames captured between the time that ibmwk was restarted and the time
that an administrator completed logging on to the Raleigh domain. Only a few of these
frames will be examined in the exercises.

EXERCISE 1—USING NETWORK MONITOR TO ANALYZE A DHCP CLIENT DOMAIN REGISTRATION

Although Windows NT Domains and Name Services will not be studied until Chapters 8
and 9, respectively, it is useful to look at two frames sent between ibmwk and pcsv that relate
to ibmwk trying to register its computer name with the server pcsv and the server's response.
Figure 7-22 shows a partial list of captured frames during one such registration.

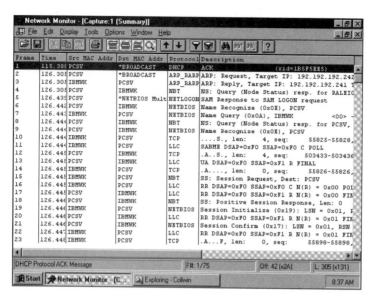

Figure 7-22   Partial list of frames captured by Network Monitor

You double-click a frame on a Capture (Summary) screen like that shown in Figure 7-22 to see its decode. The decode of a frame captured during one registration dialog between pcsv and ibmwk is shown in the middle panel of the screen displayed in Figure 7-23.

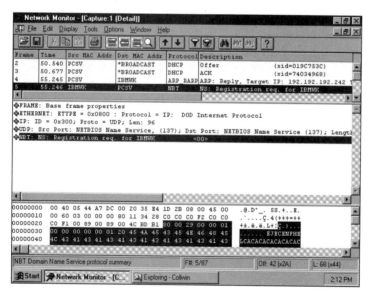

Figure 7-23   IBMWK registration request frame decode

The top panel in Figure 7-23 lists frames 1 through 5, and the bottom panel is the hexa-decimal code of frame #5, which has been translated in the middle panel. When you high-light a line in the middle panel, the corresponding hexadecimal code is highlighted. Using the information in Figure 7-23, try to answer the questions in Table 7-1.

Table 7-1   Questions about the Information in Figure 7-23

Question	Answer
What is the name of the computer that sent the frame?	
What is the name of the destination computer?	
What is the purpose of the frame?	
What Internet layer protocol is being used?	
What Transport layer protocol is being used?	
What is the port number of the NetBIOS name service?	

Clicking the (+) next to NBT (NetBIOS over TCP/IP) in Figure 7-23 opens the screen shown in Figure 7-24.

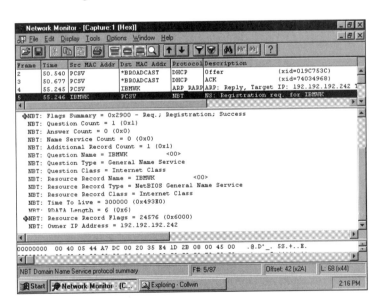

Figure 7-24   NBT fields in frame #5

NBT is what Windows NT uses to transport NetBIOS name information over an IP network. Using the information in Figure 7-24, answer the questions in Table 7-2.

Table 7-2 Questions about the Information in Figure 7-24

Question	Answer
What is the purpose of the line "Question Name = IBMWK"?	
The last line says that the "Owner IP Address = 192.192.192.242." Who is the owner?	

The next two screens, shown in Figures 7-25 and 7-26, contain the contents of the response frame that pcsv sent back to ibmwk. Using the information in Figure 7-26, answer the questions in Table 7-3.

Table 7-3 Questions about the Information in Figure 7-26

Question	Answer
What is the meaning of "Resp.; Registration; Success" in line 4?	
How does this statement relate to the statement in the last line?	

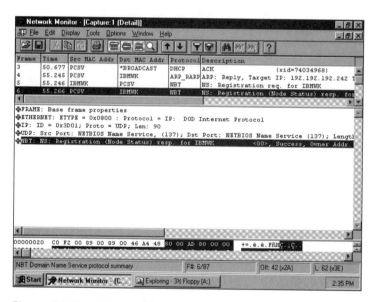

Figure 7-25 PCSV registration response frame decode

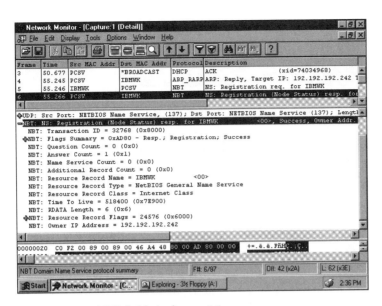

Figure 7-26   NBT fields in frame #6

There is much more to the registration and authentication of computers and their users, as you will see in Chapter 8, "Windows NT Domains."

EXERCISE 2—THE DHCP RESPONSE TO THE DHCP CLIENT

Let's look now to a DHCP reply frame sent by pcsv to ibmwk in response to an ibmwk DHCP client request for IP configuration. The decode of the reply frame is shown in the middle panel of Figure 7-27.

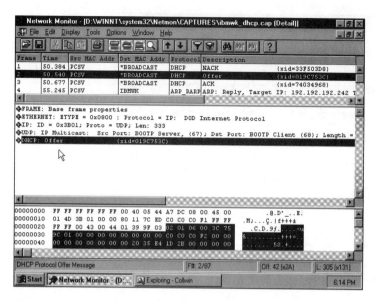

Figure 7-27   DHCP server Offer configuration frame

Notice, in the top panel, that this is frame #2 in the sequence of frames that we've just discussed, and thus was transmitted earlier.

Using the information shown in Figure 7-27, answer the questions in Table 7-4.

Table 7-4   Questions about the Information in Figure 7-27

Questions	Answers
Why does the DHCP client request frame have to precede client registration?	
Why is the frame sent by pcsv a broadcast?	
The description of the frame is "Offer." What does Offer mean?	
What is the destination port value?	
What is the source port value?	
What Transport layer protocol was used in the frame?	

Clicking the (+) next to DHCP opens the screen shown in Figure 7-28.

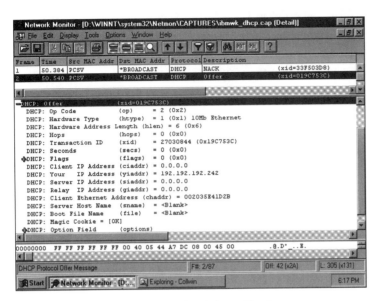

Figure 7-28   DHCP offer fields of the Offer frame

Use Table 7-5 to answer questions about Figure 7-28.

Table 7-5   Questions about the Information in Figure 7-28

Questions	Answers
What is the data rate of the Ethernet medium?	
What IP address was assigned to ibmwk?	
How does the DHCP server know the Client (hardware) Ethernet Address?	
How many hops is the DHCP server from the DHCP client?	

Clicking the (+) next to DHCP: Option Field opens the screen shown in Figure 7-29.

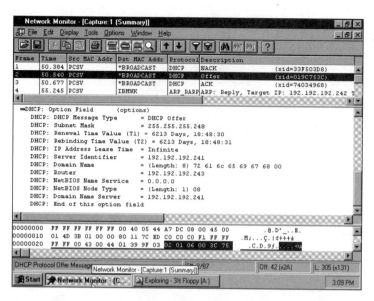

Figure 7-29   DHCP option field of the Offer frame

Answer the questions in Table 7-6 about the information provided in the Option Field of Figure 7-29.

Table 7-6   Questions about the Information in Figure 7-29

Questions	Answers
Is the subnet mask that was assigned by the DHCP server the same as was configured in DHCP Manager?	
What is the IP address of pcsv?	
What is the IP address of the default gateway?	
What is the translation of the Domain Name from hex to English?	
What is the NetBIOS Node Type in hexadecimal notation?	
When does the ibmwk IP address lease expire?	

Use Table 7-7 to make a "before and after" comparison of the data in Figures 7-1 and Figures 7-28 and 7-29. Fill in the **After** column in the table.

Table 7-7   Comparison of the Configuration of the ibmwk DHCP Client Interface Before (Figure 7-1) and After (Figures 7-28 and 7-29) the DHCP Server Reply to the DHCP Client Request

Configuration	Before	After
Physical Address	00-20-35-E4-1D-2B	
DHCP Enabled	Yes	
IP Address	0.0.0.0	
Subnet Mask	0.0.0.0	
DHCP Server	:	
Domain Name Server	192.192.192.241	
Primary WINS Server	192.192.192.241	
Default Gateway	:	
Domain Name	raleigh	
Host Name	ibmwk	
Node Type	Hybrid	
IP Address Lease Time	_____	
Renewal Time Value	_____	

IP configuration for all the workstations in the Raleigh division is now complete.

The current Case Project environment is shown in Figure 7-30.

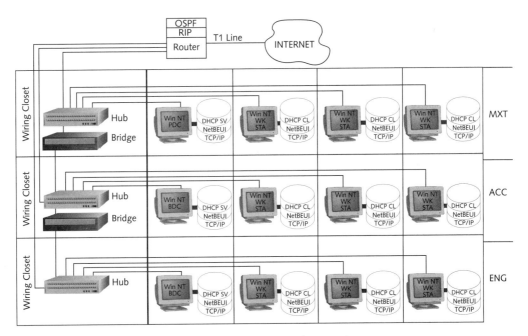

Figure 7-30   Case Project environment after completing Chapter 7

WINDOWS NT DOMAINS

In this chapter you will look at how the networking tools that you have examined so far can be used to construct and use Windows NT domains. You will learn what is meant by a Windows NT domain, why it is a useful concept, and how to implement a domain. Microsoft defines a **Windows NT domain** to be "a logical grouping of network servers and other computers that share common security and user account information to control access to domain resources."

A domain can be of any physical size. Computers in the domain can be connected by LANs, WANs, and/or the Internet. Authenticated users can log on to the domain and thereby access all domain resources. The domain can be monitored and managed from any domain computer.

IN THIS CHAPTER YOU WILL:

EXAMINE DOMAIN SECURITY POLICIES

EXAMINE DOMAIN TRUST RELATIONSHIPS

REVIEW HOW A DOMAIN IS MANAGED

CREATE DOMAIN COMPUTER ACCOUNTS

REVIEW HOW A COMPUTER JOINS A DOMAIN

CREATE DOMAIN USER ACCOUNTS

USE SERVER MANAGER TO MANAGE A DOMAIN FROM A DOMAIN CONTROLLER

SET UP CLIENT DOMAIN MANAGEMENT

DOMAIN SECURITY POLICIES

Figure 8-1 provides a simple picture of a multidomain corporate network to which you can refer as we discuss domain concepts and implementation.

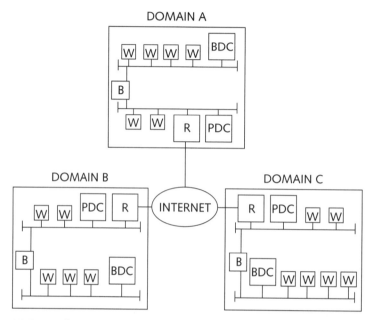

BDC = Backup Domain Controller; PDC = Primary Domain Controller;
R = Router; B = Bridge; W = Workstation

Figure 8-1   Corporate network with three domains

This corporate network has three domains connected by the Internet. Let's start the discussion with the concept of domain security. This is a very important topic because, although domains provide flexibility for users, such flexibility demands robust security practices.

Windows NT security is comprehensive and a subject unto itself. Thus, in this section, we will discuss only the components of security that are necessary for you to appreciate in order to use and manage a domain effectively. These security components and their descriptions are presented in Table 8-1.

Table 8-1   Components of Windows NT Security

Windows NT Security Component	Description
CTRL+ALT+DEL	Starts the program that suspends all user mode processes to prevent password stealing
User Name	User ID that is assigned by Administrator
Password	User password assigned by Administrator and which is bound to the ID

Table 8-1   Components of Windows NT Security (continued)

Windows NT Security Component	Description
Local Security Authority (LSA)	Manager of security policy and implementation on the computer used for logon
Security Account Manager (SAM)	Maintains the user and group accounts database
Security Reference Monitor	Checks that a user or a process has the permissions to access and operate on an object
Security ID (SID)	The index to the record of user credentials
Token	Contains the SID, SIDs of groups belonged to, and special rights assigned to the user
Net Logon Service discovery packets	Packets broadcast by a workstation to find a domain controller on the same domain, and by PDCs and BDCs to find domain controllers in trusted domains
Net Logon Service challenge packets	Packets that verify that a workstation and a domain controller have accounts on the same domain and that trusted domain controllers have computer accounts
Secure communications channel	Session between the verified workstation and the domain controller
Net Logon Service on a domain controller	Authenticates users who log on to the domain

The Windows NT security system starts automatically when the computer is powered up. The operating system presents the initial Logon screen, shown in Figure 8-2, which instructs the user to press the CTRL+ALT+ DEL keys simultaneously.

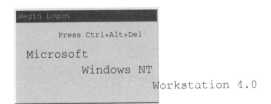

Figure 8-2   Initial Logon screen

This action starts the program Winlogon.exe, which suspends user mode processes which could reveal the user's ID and password in the next step of the logon process. In this next step, the user provides a User name and Password on the screen shown in Figure 8-3.

This action calls the Local Security Authority **(LSA)**, which manages security policy and implementation. The LSA in turn calls an authentication package, which checks the user account to see if the account is local, that is, a user account that was created on the computer used for logon. If the account is not local, the logon request is passed to a domain controller, where another authentication package will authenticate the user. If the user account is validated locally, the Security Account Manager **(SAM)**, which constitutes the directory database of user information on the local computer, returns a user Security ID **(SID)** and SIDs for any groups to which the user belongs, to the authentication package. The authentication package creates a logon session and passes that session and the user's IDs to the LSA. The LSA creates an access **token**, which contains user IDs and user rights. This token is used to validate all future actions taken by the user and becomes the essence of the security process.

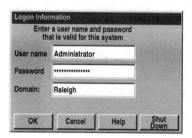

Figure 8-3   User name and Password screen

Up to this point, this description has focused on logging on to the local computer, where validation is confined to processes on one machine. When the user is logging on to a domain at a workstation, the authentication process requires communication between the workstation and a domain controller. When the user logs on, the Net Logon Service on the local computer broadcasts discovery packets in an attempt to find a domain controller on that domain. When a response is received from a domain controller, challenge packets are exchanged. These packets allow each computer to verify that the other computer has a valid account on the domain. Figure 8-4 shows 17 discovery, challenge, and secure session setup packets that were exchanged during a workstation logon and captured by Network Monitor.

Frame	Time	Src MAC Addr	Dst MAC Addr	Protocol	Description
1	4.451	002035E41D2B	PCSV	SMB	C NT create & X, File = \NETLOGON
2	4.454	PCSV	002035E41D2B	SMB	R NT create & X, FID = 0x801
3	4.455	002035E41D2B	PCSV	MSRPC	c/o RPC Bind: UUID 12345678-1234
4	4.456	PCSV	002035E41D2B	MSRPC	c/o RPC Bind Ack: call 0x0 assoc gr
5	4.456	002035E41D2B	PCSV	MSRPC	c/o RPC Request: call 0x1 opnum 0x
6	4.459	PCSV	002035E41D2B	MSRPC	c/o RPC Response: call 0x1 context
7	4.460	002035E41D2B	PCSV	MSRPC	c/o RPC Request: call 0x2 opnum 0x
8	4.464	PCSV	002035E41D2B	MSRPC	c/o RPC Response: call 0x2 context
9	4.466	002035E41D2B	PCSV	MSRPC	c/o RPC Request: call 0x3 opnum 0x
10	4.505	PCSV	002035E41D2B	MSRPC	c/o RPC Response: call 0x3 context
11	4.689	002035E41D2B	PCSV	TCP	.A...., len: 0, seq: 310341-310341
12	9.802	002035E41D2B	PCSV	SMB	C session setup & X, Username = administ
13	9.827	PCSV	002035E41D2B	SMB	R session setup & X, and R tree connect
14	9.828	002035E41D2B	PCSV	SMB	C NT create & X, File = \ntconfig.pol
15	9.831	PCSV	002035E41D2B	SMB	R NT create & X - NT error, System, Errc
16	10.049	002035E41D2B	PCSV	TCP	.A...., len: 0, seq: 310731-31073
17	10.512	PCSV	002035E41D2B	NBT	NS: Registration (Node Status) resp. for
18	0.000	000000000000	000000000000	STATS	Number of Frames Captured = 17

Figure 8-4   Discovery, challenge, and secure session setup packets

As you have seen in previous chapters, Network Monitor can be used to examine the protocol headers and data contained in these frames. The process implemented by the exchange of frames shown in Figure 8-4 establishes a **secure communication channel** between the primary domain controller, PCSV, and the workstation. From this time on, the workstation trusts the domain controller to authenticate domain users who will have access to the workstation's resources.

When there is more than one domain in the network, trust relationships among domains can be established. There are **trusted** domains and **trusting** domains, and the trust can be in one or both directions. For example, if there are two domains, one trusted and the other trusting, computers on the trusting domain will trust users authenticated on the trusted domain to access resources on the trusting domain. Thus, with one logon, a user on the trusted domain may be able to access resources on all domains with which trust relationships have been established. Secure communication channels between domains are established through the same communication mechanisms, described previously, that establish a secure communication channel between an NT workstation and an NT domain controller on the same domain.

8

DOMAIN CONTROLLERS

As you saw in Chapter 2, "Windows NT 4.0 Installation," Windows NT Server can be installed as a primary domain controller (PDC), a backup domain controller (BDC), or a member server. A member server does not participate in domain security, and it maintains its own user accounts. The PDC maintains the **master domain directory** of domain computers and user accounts. This database is synchronized with those of backup domain controllers every 5 minutes, or as specified in the Registry. The PDC sends notices to the BDCs asking them to request changes that have been made to the master domain directory. These changes are kept in a **change log**. Thus, typically, only the contents of the change log need to be transmitted to the BDCs. This is called **partial synchronization**. There may be circumstances when full synchronization of a BDC is necessary, such as when the BDC has been off-line. In a **full synchronization**, the entire master domain directory is transmitted to the BDC. Both PDCs and BDCs participate in the authentication of domain users when a user logs on to a domain.

USER MANAGER FOR DOMAINS

Figure 8-5 shows User Manager for Domains on a primary domain controller. The domain has the name Raleigh.

Under Username in the upper panel of the figure are listed the user names for the built-in accounts Administrator and Guest, which were automatically created when the domain controller was installed. The Administrator account can be used to log on to the domain controller to create domain user accounts. If you assigned a password to the Administrator account during the installation process, you must know this password in order to access the domain controller as Administrator. The Guest account allows a user to log on to the domain without a password but with limited rights.

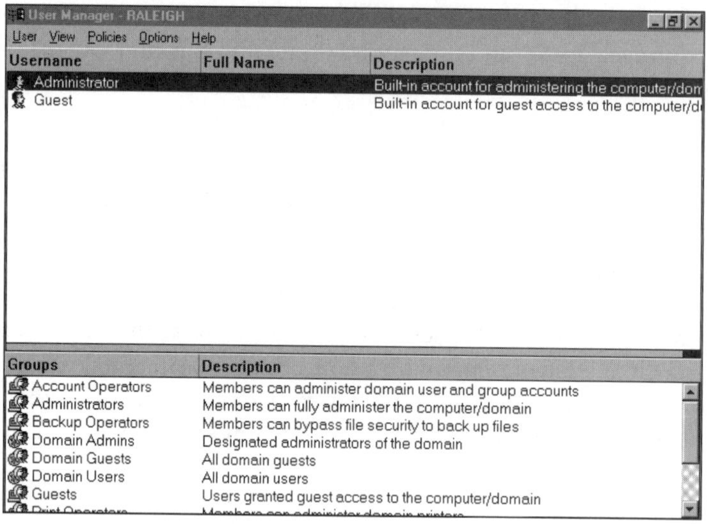

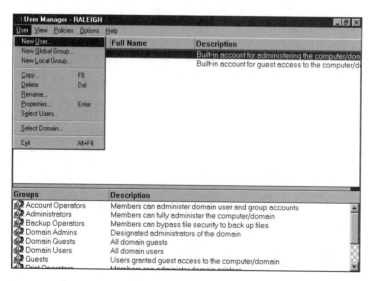

Figure 8-5   User Manager for the domain Raleigh

The bottom panel is the list of groups to which domain users can be assigned. Each of these group accounts has default rights that are inherited by user accounts that are assigned to those groups. For example, if a user account is assigned to the Administrators group, the user can fully administer the domain.

Figure 8-6 shows the User menu of User Manager for Domains.

Figure 8-6   User menu of User Manager for Domains

This menu is used to add a new User, Global Group, or Local Group account after you use Select Domain to select the domain to which they will be added. To see the properties of a domain user, you highlight the user on the screen shown in Figure 8-5 and you select Properties in Figure 8-6 to obtain the User Properties screen, shown in Figure 8-7.

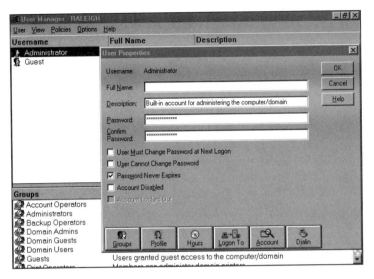

Figure 8-7   Properties of domain user Administrator

In Figure 8-7 you see the properties of domain user "Administrator." If the Groups button is clicked, the groups that Administrator belongs to are shown, as in Figure 8-8.

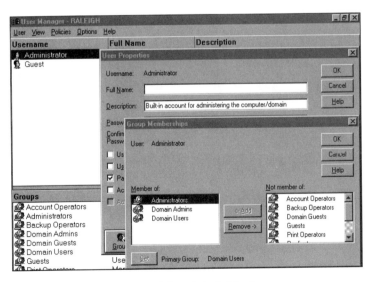

Figure 8-8   Groups containing Administrator

Figure 8-8 shows that Administrator is a member of the Administrators, Domain Admins, and Domain Users groups. Membership in the Administrators group means that the user

Administrator has the same domain rights as the Administrators group, that is, full administration of the domain.

Figure 8-9 shows the Policies menu of User Manager for Domains.

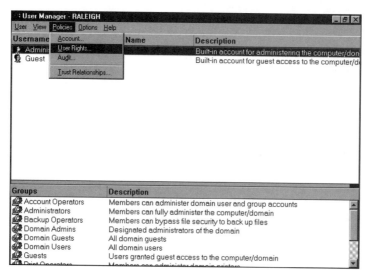

Figure 8-9   Policies menu of User Manager for Domains

Clicking User Rights on the Policies menu produces the screen shown in Figure 8-10.

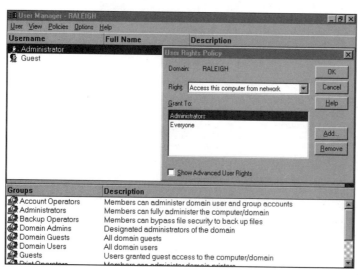

Figure 8-10   User Rights Policy dialog box

The right selected, "Access this computer from network," gives members of the groups Administrators and Everyone the right to access the domain controller from other computers on the network. Figure 8-11 shows that there are many other rights that can be assigned to members of these groups.

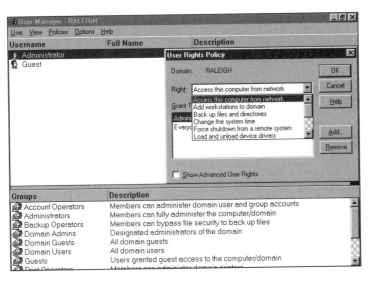

Figure 8-11   User Rights Policy dialog box

Clicking Account in the Policies menu opens the screen shown in Figure 8-12.

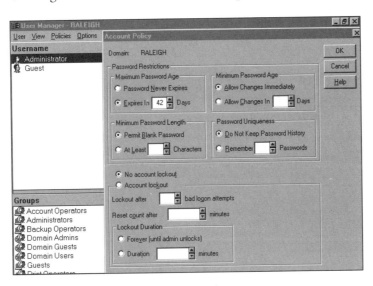

Figure 8-12   Account Policy dialog box

Figure 8-12 shows the many properties that can be associated with a user's password.

Earlier in this section, trust relationships between domains were discussed. Clicking Trust Relationships in the Policies menu opens the screen shown in Figure 8-13, the dialog box where those relationships can be defined.

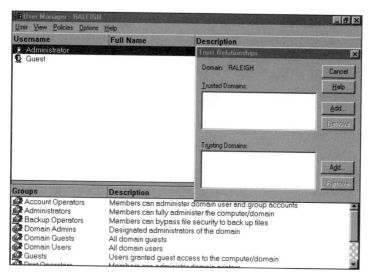

Figure 8-13   Trust Relationships dialog box

If the corporate network has more than one domain, as is the case for the example shown in Figure 8-1, it is necessary to define the trust relationships between the domains. Clicking on Help in this dialog box opens the User Manager Help screen shown on the right of Figure 8-14. This screen provides a good explanation of how to establish trust relationships once you have decided what they should be.

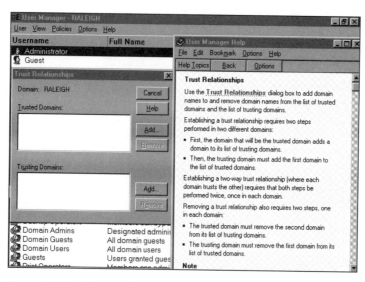

Figure 8-14   Trust Relationships Help

In a case in which the corporation would like all users to have equivalent access to the resources on each domain, two-way trust relationships would be established among Domains A, B, and C. These relationships are depicted for three domains in Figure 8-15.

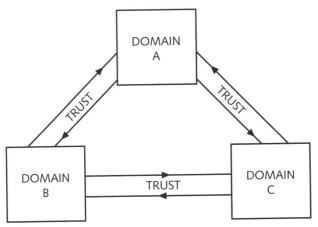

Figure 8-15 Two-way trust relationships among the domains shown in Figure 8-1

A final menu of interest in User Manager for Domains is the Options menu shown in Figure 8-16.

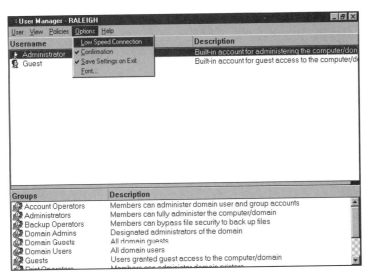

Figure 8-16 The Options menu

The menu item highlighted is Low Speed Connection. When a remote computer is connecting to a domain over a low-speed connection, such as when a modem is used, checking the Low Speed Connection menu item reduces the number of database queries to what is necessary for the active thread. A **thread** is the smallest set of instructions that is considered an entity of which processes are composed. This capability could be useful for the network shown in Figure 8-1, depending on how the router is connected to the Internet. Checking Low Speed Connection produces the screen in Figure 8-17.

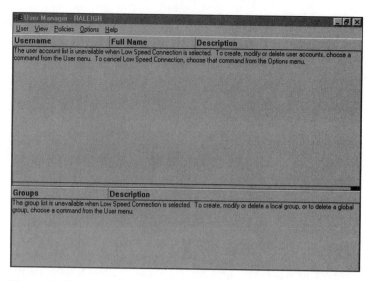

Figure 8-17   User Manager for Domains Low Speed Connection option screen

On a large network, removing all the users and group names from the display reduces the traffic required to produce and refresh the display at the remote user site, while still giving the remote user the same control.

Now that you have seen how user and group accounts can be added to a domain and how the properties of those accounts can be managed, let's examine how the domain is created. In other words, how are resources, such as workstations, backup domain controllers, and primary domain controllers, assigned to a domain? This subject is treated in the next section.

SERVER MANAGER

 You can select a file for sharing in Windows NT Explorer or in Shared Directories on the domain controller Computer menu.

You first saw some of the capabilities of Server Manager in Chapter 3, "Windows NT 4.0 Utilities." Figure 8-18 shows a Server Manager screen for the domain Raleigh, in which three computer accounts have been created: IBMWK, NCSU, and PCSV. Domains have computer accounts just as they have user accounts.

The Computer menu in Server Manager is analogous to the User menu in User Manager for Domains. Both of these menus are used to manage a domain entity, that is, the computer or the user. Figure 8-19 shows the Computer menu of Server Manager.

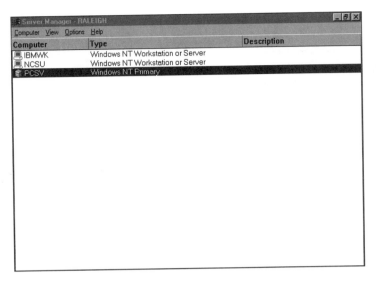

Figure 8-18   Server Manager

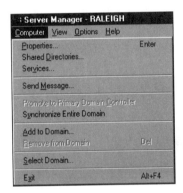

Figure 8-19   Server Manager Computer menu

Highlighting PCSV, the primary domain controller, in Figure 8-18 and clicking Properties on the Computer menu opens the screen shown in Figure 8-20.

The Usage Summary area lists the number of Sessions in which the PDC is participating, the number of Open Files on the PDC, the number of File Locks that prevent access to files, and the number of Open Named Pipes, which are processes that implement interprocess communications. Notice that PCSV is participating in one session and that there is one Open Named Pipe.

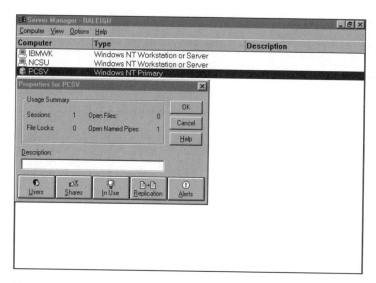

Figure 8-20   Computer menu Properties for PCSV

Clicking Users opens the screen shown in Figure 8-21, which indicates that the partner in this session is IBMWK, that the connection is implemented by the process IPC$, an Interprocess Communication process, and that IBMWK has not opened any resources on PCSV.

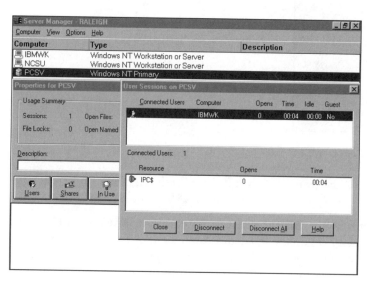

Figure 8-21   User Sessions on PCSV

The buttons at the bottom of the screen allow you to close the screen, disconnect a session, disconnect all sessions, or get online help.

The dialog box on the right of Figure 8-22 opens when you click the Shares button in the dialog box on the left.

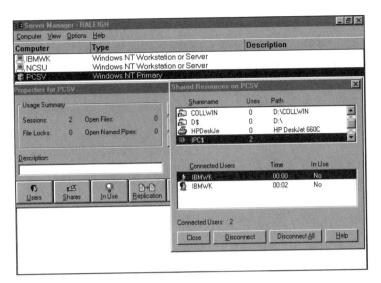

Figure 8-22   Shared Resources on PCSV

The top box in the Shared Resources on PCSV dialog box shows the names of files that are being shared by PCSV and paths for those files. PCSV is sharing the drive D (share name D$), an HP DeskJet printer driver, an IPC$ file, and a directory with the name Collwin. As seen in the bottom panel, IBMWK has established two sessions using the shared resource IPC$ on PCSV.

Clicking the In Use button in the Properties for PCSV screen on the left of Figure 8-22 tells you which resources are actually open and which user has opened them. The Replication and Alerts buttons will be discussed later in this section.

In Figure 8-19 you saw the item Synchronize Entire Domain on the Computer menu. If this is selected, the entire master domain directory will be copied to the backup domain controllers on the domain. Two other items on Computer menu are Add to Domain and Select Domain. Choosing Add to Domain allows you to add a computer to the local domain. Choosing Select Domain allows you to select any domain or computer for management.

The final step in the creation of the Raleigh domain is for the two workstations, IBMWK and NCSU, to join the domain. (Actually these workstations have been members of the domain so that you could see some of the screens that have been presented.) In Figure 8-18, you see the names IBMWK and NCSU because their accounts were created on PCSV using Add to Domain on Computer menu. This is a necessary condition, but not a sufficient condition, for them to become domain members. In addition, a user who has Administrator or Domain Administrator rights must log on to the workstations and add them to the domain. The steps for doing this for IBMWK are:

1. From the Start menu, Click **Control Panel**.

2. Double-click **Network** in Control Panel to obtain the screen shown in Figure 8-23.

3. Click **Change** to obtain the dialog box shown on the right in Figure 8-24.

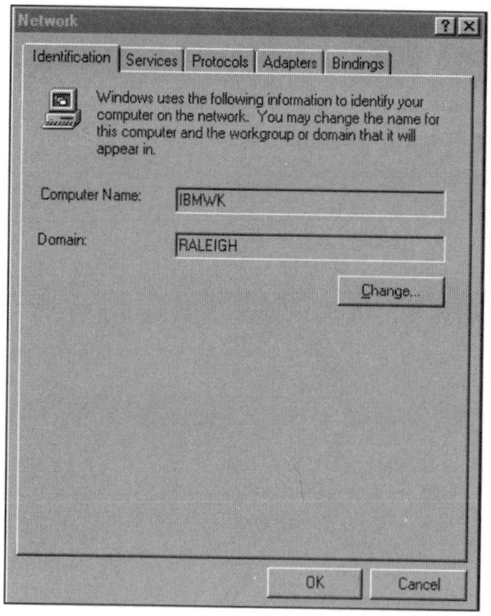

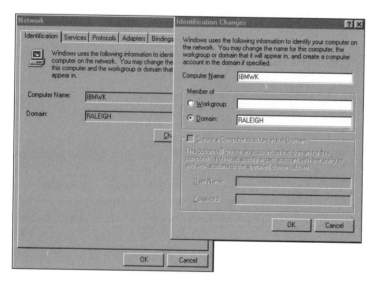

Figure 8-23   Network dialog box

Figure 8-24   Network Identification Changes

As expected, Figure 8-23 shows that the Computer Name is IBMWK and that it is a member of the RALEIGH domain. Thus nothing needs to be changed. If a change were needed, you would make it using the dialog box on the right of Figure 8-24 and click OK. You would then restart the computer for this change to be recognized by the domain controller. IBMWK is now a member of the Raleigh domain.

As promised, let's return to the Replication button in Figure 8-20. Directory Replication is a service that automatically exports updated subdirectories to other computers. This is a very useful service for keeping files and databases current throughout a domain or network.

Setting up Directory Replication is a complex operation the first time you do it, but the steps are quite straightforward.

Clicking Replication opens the screen shown in Figure 8-25, from which you begin to configure a domain controller for automatic directory export or import.

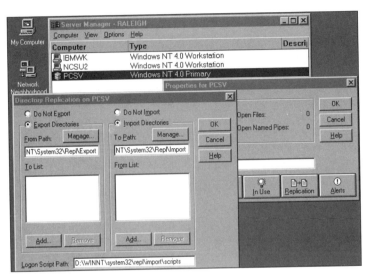

Figure 8-25 Directory Replication on PCSV

Tables 8-2 and 8-3 provide a step-by-step approach to Directory Replication configuration.

Table 8-2 Setting Up Directory Replication

Step Number	Step	Notes
1	Check **Export Directories** to enable subdirectory export. The default From Path is: C:\WINNT\System32\Repl\Export	a. Subdirectories to be exported are placed in the Export directory using Windows Explorer. b. The To List is blank, but the default entry is the domain of this domain controller, which is RALEIGH. If additions are made to list, the default entry is lost. If you still want to export to the default domain, explicitly include its name in the list. c. If you are exporting to a domain that contains computers that are connected to the export server by a WAN, you may have to explicitly specify those computers in the To List. d. Click the **Add** button to obtain a screen in which you can add domain or computer names. If you add a computer name, precede it by two backslashes (\\).

8

Table 8-2   Setting Up Directory Replication (continued)

Step Number	Step	Notes
2	**Click** Manage to open the screen shown in Figure 8-26. *You do not have to add subdirectories to this list, and doing so does not take the place of adding them to the Export Directory.*	a. Click **Add** to add export subdirectories to this list. b. Click **Add Lock** to stop the export of a subdirectory. c. Click **Wait Until Stabilized** to delay export for two minutes after an update occurs, in case other updates are imminent. d. Click **Entire Subtree** to export all subdirectories in a subdirectory tree. Click **OK**.
3	Click **Import Directories** in Figure 8-25 if you want this domain controller to import from other domain controllers.	a. In the From List the default domain is RALEIGH. Imports can be received from other domain controllers on this domain. b. Click **Add** to specify other domains or computers from which imports will be allowed and placed in the default directory C:\WINNT\System32\Repl\Imports
4	Logon Script Path C:\WINNT\System32\repl\import\scripts	a. The subdirectory where a copy of domain user logon scripts are stored. b. A logon script is a file that is assigned to a user's account and is executed when the user logs on to the domain.
5	In Server Manager highlight a workstation, domain, or server to receive exported directories.	In Figure 8-18, for example, IBMWK is highlighted.
6	Click Properties on Computer menu.	
7	Click the **Replication** button on the Properties for IBMWK screen.	a. As shown in Figure 8-27, the Directory Replication on IBMWK screen opens. b. A workstation can only import directories
8	Click **Import Directories**.	a. The From List is blank, but the default entry is the domain RALEIGH. b. Click **Add** to obtain a screen in which you can add other domains or domain controllers from which imports will be received.
9	Click **Manage**.	See Step 2 and Figure 8-26 for configuration of this screen.

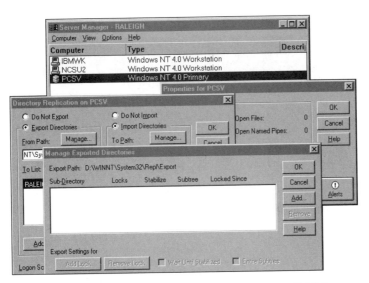

Figure 8-26   Manage Exported Subdirectories on PCSV

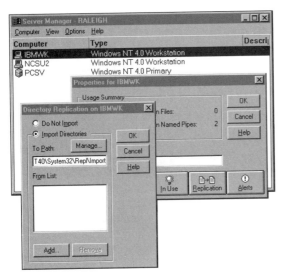

Figure 8-27   Configuring Directory Replication on IBMWK

Because Directory Replication is a service, it must have an account in order to log on to the domain. This service requires its own account just as a user does. Table 8-3 provides the steps for configuring the account.

Table 8-3   Configuring the Directory Replication Service Account

Step Number	Step	Notes
1	Open **User Manager for Domains** on the Administrative Tools (Common) menu.	a. See Figure 8-28, where the Username **Copy** has been created for the Directory Replication account. b. Copy was created by using the screen that opens when you click **New User** on the User menu.
2	With the Directory Replication Service Username (Copy) highlighted, click **Properties** on the User menu.	a. The screen on the left of Figure 8-29 is the User Properties screen. b. Enter a password and confirm the password. c. Check **Password Never Expires**. d. Click the **Hours** button and make sure that all hours are available, as shown in the screen on the right of Figure 8-29. Click **OK**.
3	In Control Panel, click **Services**.	a. See Figure 8-30. b. Highlight **Directory Replicator**. c. Click **Startup** to open the screen, Service, shown in Figure 8-31. Here you assign to the Directory Replicator service the account that it is to use to log on to the domain. d. Click **Automatic**. e. Under Log On As: Click **This Account**, where you configure the Directory Replicator account parameters. *Here, Account and Password must be identical to those created in User Manager for Domains.* f. Click **OK** to return to the Services screen shown in Figure 8-30. g. Click **Start** to start the Directory Replicator service.

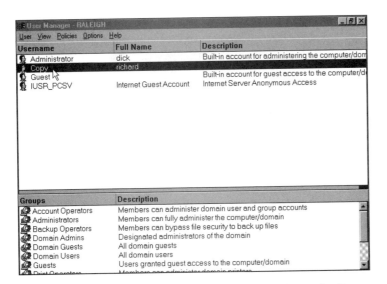

Figure 8-28 Creating a domain user account, Copy, for the Directory Replication service

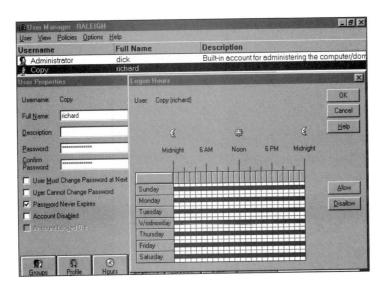

Figure 8-29 User Manager for Domains User Properties screen (left) and Logon Hours screen (right)

8

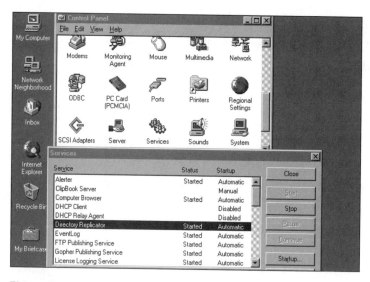

Figure 8-30   Services screen on IBMWK

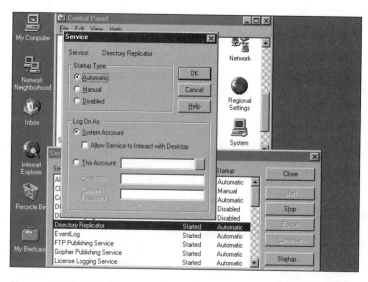

Figure 8-31   Directory Replicator service Startup Configuration screen for IBMWK

This completes configuration of directory export from one domain controller and directory import to one workstation. Only some of these steps will need to be repeated when configuring other workstations for import from the same domain controller.

The last button in Figure 8-20 to discuss is the Alerts button. Clicking this button gives you a screen in which you can enter the name of a computer or user that should receive administrative alerts generated by the operating system. If you choose to implement Alerts, open Services in Control Panel and start the Alerts and Messenger services on the computers between which alert messages will be sent.

In the next section, we will discuss how to set up directories for sharing on the network and techniques for accessing those directories from any computer in the domain. Network Neighborhood browser will be used to explore domain resources.

SHARING DOMAIN RESOURCES

Let's say that a domain user on the PCSV would like to access files on another domain computer. One of the advantages of Windows NT Domains is that directories and files on workstations, not just on servers, are accessible to all users with domain accounts. To make a directory and its files accessible, the directory containing the files must be made sharable on the computer by a user with the appropriate permissions. Figure 8-32 shows how to do this.

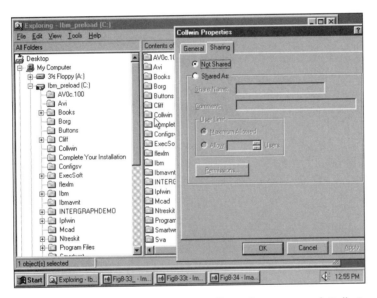

Figure 8-32   Windows Explorer, Collwin directory, and Collwin
Properties on IBMWK

The pointer in Windows Explorer is pointing to the Collwin directory, which is to be made sharable. The user on IBMWK highlights Collwin, selects Properties on the File menu, and then clicks the Sharing tab on the Properties screen. To make Collwin sharable, Shared As: and then Apply are clicked. As the dialog box on the right of Figure 8-33 shows, the Share Name appears.

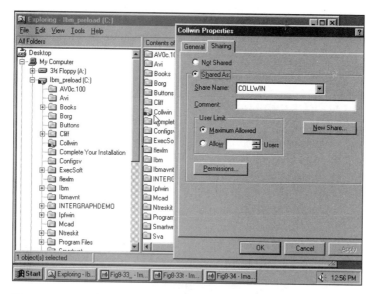

Figure 8-33   Sharing the Collwin directory

This name must be used to refer to the directory. You also see in Windows Explorer on the left of Figure 8-33, that a hand now supports Collwin, indicating that it is sharable. You then click Network Neighborhood on the PCSV desktop. This action initiates a call to the Master Domain Browser on PCSV to provide a list of domain resources. Figure 8-34 shows a graphical representation of that list on the screen in the background. Clicking Ibmwk initiates a call to the Backup Browser on ibmwk to transfer the list of shared directories to PCSV. Collwin is included.

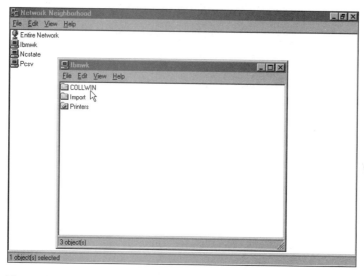

Figure 8-34   Using Network Neighborhood on PCSV to access the COLLWIN directory on Ibmwk

Another approach to sharing on a domain is to map a local drive letter to a remote drive or directory on another computer. This mapped drive will then appear in Windows Explorer as if it were a local drive. For example, let's say you want to map drive C on a workstation named NCSTATE, shown in Figure 8-35, to a drive on PCSV.

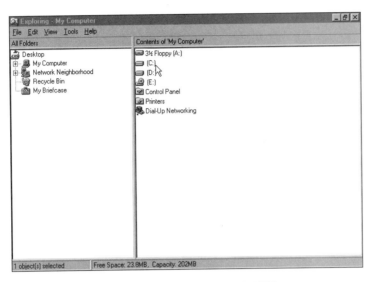

Figure 8-35   Drive C on workstation NCSTATE

You follow the steps described previously for the Collwin directory to make drive C sharable. Then, on PCSV, select **Map Network Drive** on the Tools menu of Windows Explorer, as shown in Figure 8-36.

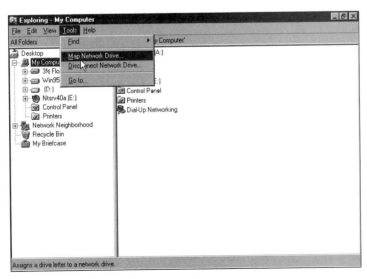

Figure 8-36   Map Network Drive on the Tools menu on PCSV

Selecting Map Network Drive initiates a call to the Master Domain Browser and opens the dialog box shown in Figure 8-37.

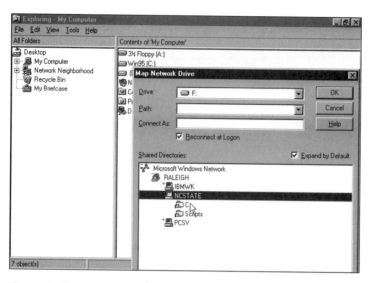

Figure 8-37   Mapping drive C on NCSTATE to drive F on PCSV

The Drive text box shows that drive C will be mapped to the local drive F. You could type in the path to C as **\\NCSTATE\C** and then click OK. It is easier, however, to click the C folder. This will cause the Backup Browser on NCSTATE to create the path and the mapping automatically. As you can see in Figure 8-38, drive C on NCSTATE is mapped to drive F on PCSV, and the contents of C are shown in the right panel.

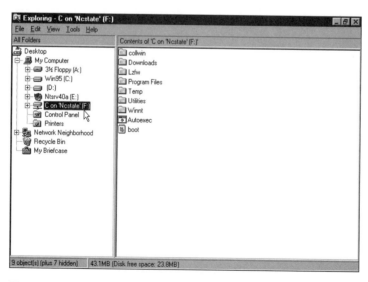

Figure 8-38   Drive C on NCSTATE mapped to drive F on PCSV

In this section you have seen how to manage a domain and access its resources from a primary domain controller, PCSV. It is also possible to manage a domain from a client workstation. You will configure the domain to make this possible, using the Network Client Administrator utility, in one of the Case Project exercises at the end of this chapter.

NETWORK MANAGEMENT

Network Management protocols enable a **network management utility** on a host to monitor the performance of a network device, to change the values of configuration variables and to receive event notifications. The utility on the managed device that implements these functions for the manager is called an **Agent**. Thus a network management system provides information that supplements that which is obtained from the Server Manager utility.

THE AGENT

In the language of the client/server model, the Agent is a server and the network manager is a client. The databases of information that are collected by the agent for the manager are called **MIBs**, where MIB stands for Management Information Base. There are standard MIBs and proprietary MIBs that are used to store device-specific information. As you saw in Chapter 4, " The TCP/IP Protocol Suite," the Simple Network Management Protocol (SNMP) is the protocol used for management communications on networks that use the TCP/IP protocol stack. Windows NT 4.0 includes SNMP and an SNMP Agent. It does not include a network manager. We will now configure an agent, install a third party network manager and use the manager to monitor a device.

To load the SNMP agent on a Windows NT 4.0 server or workstation, you open Network from Control Panel, click the Services tab, click Add and then Add SNMP Service. To configure the SNMP agent, you click SNMP Services in the Network dialog box and then Properties to open the screen shown in Figure 8-39.

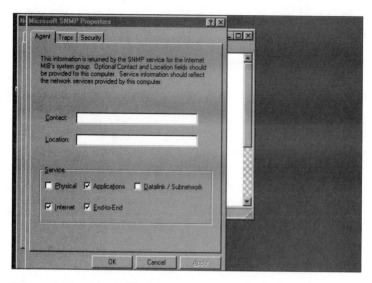

Figure 8-39   Microsoft SNMP Properties

The text at the top of the Agent tab says " This information is returned by the SNMP service for the Internet MIB's system group." The **Internet MIB** is a standard MIB and **system group** is one of the sets of data that are stored in this MIB. In Contact, you specify the person who uses this computer. In Location, specify the physical location of the computer. In Service, click the types of network capabilities that the computer provides so that information about those capabilities will be available to the network manager.

Next, click the Security tab to open the dialog box shown in Figure 8-40.

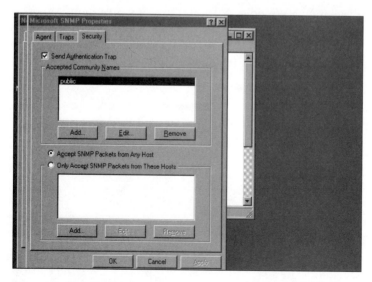

Figure 8-40   SNMP Security

Accepted Community Names is a list of strings. Figure 8-40 shows the string "public." This the default **community name**. If a device uses this community name and the message from the network manager contains the same community name, then the network manager is authenticated to obtain information about the device. The community string also has associated with it an **access mode** that is either read-write or read-only. The community string **public** usually has the access mode read-only associated with it. The community string **private** usually has the access mode read-write associated with it. When you click the lower of the two buttons in the middle of the screen, you can specify the IP addresses of those network managers from which the device will accept management queries. Clicking the Traps tab opens the screen shown in Figure 8-41.

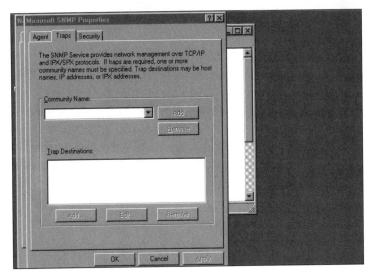

Figure 8-41   SNMP Trap configuration

In Community name, you specify the name of the community that should receive Trap messages. A **Trap** message is a notification of an event that has occurred on the device. It will be processed by any device that is a member of Community Name and whose IP address is listed in the Trap Destinations list.

THE NETWORK MANAGER

An excellent third party network manager is available from Technically Elite, Inc. It is called MeterWare for Windows NT/95. Figure 8-42 shows the Meterware for Windows window, the Network Map window and the Network Devices Palette.

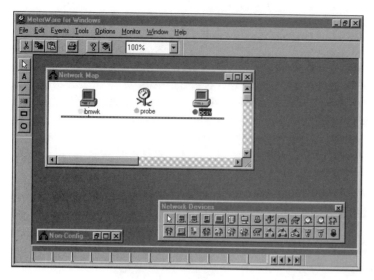

Figure 8-42   Meterware for Windows

The Netware Map shows three devices on an Ethernet segment. One is the workstation ibmwk, another is the server pcsv and the third is a remote network probe. The icons for these devices and the segment to which they are connected were taken from the Network Devices palette. Notice that each device has a color dot associated with it. The yellow dot indicates that ibmwk sent a trap message to the network manager. The green dot indicates that the network manager is successfully polling the agent on the probe. The red dot indicates that there is no communication between the manager and pcsv. A **network probe** is a device that can be attached to any segment to collect frames on that segment for analysis by the network manager.

Let's say you want to get information about ibmwk. You click ibmwk and then click SNMP utility on the Tools menu. This opens Figure 8-43.

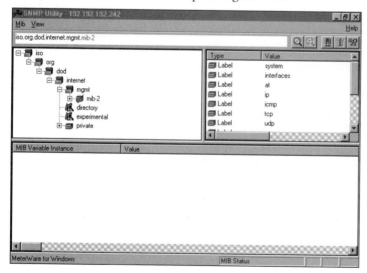

Figure 8-43   Network Manager screen for mib-2

In the upper left panel of the screen you see the tree that represents how SNMP management information is organized. The node **mib-2** is a standard MIB which contains objects managed on all SNMP devices. This is the MIB that is included with Windows NT 4.0. In the right panel of the screen you see the groups of objects that are included in mib-2. The bottom panel is where you will see mib-2 variables and their values for host 192.192.192.242 (ibmwk) if the agent on ibmwk is queried by the network manager. Let's say that you just want to know the values of the variables in the System group. You select system and click Get MIB on the mib menu. The network manager sends a **Get** frame to the agent on ibmwk and the agent returns the values of the system group variables shown in the bottom panel of the screen in Figure 8-44.

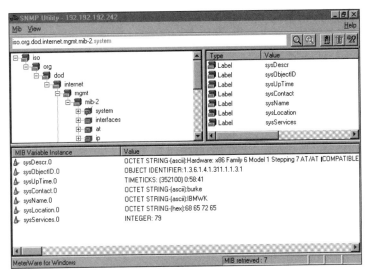

Figure 8-44   Values of the mib-2 system group variables on ibmwk

The topic of network management is extremely important in today's large networking environments. What has been described in this section is an introduction to the topic using the widely implemented SNMP, an SNMP Agent and an SNMP Manager.

HETEROGENEOUS NETWORK ENVIRONMENTS

Windows NT 4.0 makes major strides toward the implementation of a "global network" consisting of the seamless integration of networks using different operating systems. The goal is for the user to log on to any network and be authenticated to access resources on all networks.

Windows NT 4.0 ships with the utilities Gateway Services for Netware (GSNW), Client Services for Netware (CSNW) and Services for Macintosh that integrate computers on Netware and Macintosh networks into the Windows NT environment. Third party software currently is needed to provide this integration for UNIX and Banyon networks. There is also third party software that enables the X/Windows graphical user interface on a Windows NT computer. In this section, we will show one of the approaches for implementing communication between computers on UNIX networks and the Windows NT environment.

UNIX CLIENTS AUTHENTICATING TO WINDOWS NT SERVERS

Third party software from Intergraph, Inc. is recommended by Microsoft for providing the integration of UNIX networks into the Windows NT environment. This software, called DiskShare, can be downloaded free from Intergraph for a limited-time-period test drive. To do this, or to order the product, contact Intergraph at http://www.intergraph.com.

The UNIX operating system supports the Network File System (NFS). DiskShare software lets a computer running Microsoft Windows NT Workstation or Windows NT Server act as a NFS server. Users on systems running NFS software (called client systems) can gain access to files (called sharing) on the emulated NFS server by connecting those files to their systems. These files become indistinguishable from files on the user's system.

DiskShare lets the administrator map UNIX users and groups to Windows NT users and groups to control file access on Windows NT computers. You can map either to the server or more broadly to the domain. To specify file permissions for users on the UNIX client computers, the administrator must create the mapping from scratch or import the UNIX password file from the /etc directory on the UNIX computer. The /etc/group file can be imported as well. Figure 8-45 shows the screen that opens when you click DiskShare User Manager in the DiskShare Program Group.

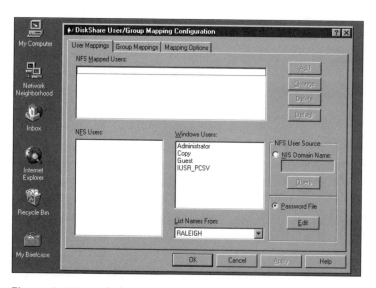

Figure 8-45   DiskShare User/Group Mapping Configuration

Since no files have been imported, the windows in the screen are blank. If NFS users are created or the password file is imported, the NFS Users window will list those UNIX client users. The administrator creates users, under Password File, Edit is clicked to get a screen where UNIX user IDs and passwords are defined. The Windows Users window shows the authenticated users on the Windows NT domain, Raleigh. To allow the users on the UNIX client computer to access files on the Windows NT domain computers, NFS User names must be mapped to Windows NT user names. This is done by selecting the UNIX user and clicking the Windows User. The mapping then appears in the NFS Mapped Users window. That NFS user on the UNIX client now has access to files on the Windows NT domain with the permissions and rights assigned to the Windows User used for the mapping. Group mappings are done in the same way. Figure 8-46 shows the screen where you can create and configure permissions for shares on Windows NT that will be accessible to the UNIX users.

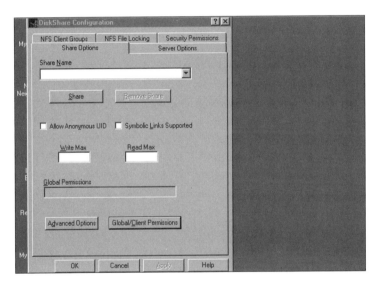

Figure 8-46   DiskShare Configuration

CHAPTER SUMMARY

This chapter described and discussed the following steps involved in configuring and using a Windows NT domain:

- Workstation logon
- Domain logon
- The Local Security Authority (LSA)
- Logon discovery packets
- Logon challenge packets
- Pass-through authentication
- Creating secure communication channels
- Creating domain computer accounts
- Creating domain user accounts
- Creating domain user accounts for services
- Directory Replication
- Managing domain computers
- Managing domain users
- Domain browsing
- Directory sharing between domain computers
- Domain management by clients
- Network Management using SNMP
- Heterogenous networking environments

REVIEW QUESTIONS

1. Which of the following is true about a Windows NT domain?

   a. Authenticated domain users can access shares on any domain workstation.

   b. A domain can have more than one primary domain controller.

   c. Domain member servers do not participate in domain user authentication.

2. What is the name of the security program that maintains the user and group accounts database?

   a. The Local Security Authority (LSA)

   b. The Security Account Manager (SAM)

   c. The Security Reference Monitor

3. What is a Windows domain security token?

   a. A frame used on a Token Ring network to control network access

   b. An index to the record of user credentials

   c. A record of user SIDs and rights

4. What is the purpose of Net Logon Service challenge packets?

   a. To find a PDC on the domain

   b. To find a BDC on the domain

   c. To verify that the computer logging on has an account on the domain

5. Which of the following groups has the right to manage other users on the domain?

   a. Administrators group

   b. Domain Users group

   c. Administrators group and Domain Admins groups

6. What is a trusted domain?

   a. One on which a PDC or BDC is trusted to authenticate user domain logons for a trusting domain

   b. One on which only a PDC is allowed to authenticate user logons on the domain

   c. One on which the PDC or a BDC can authenticate user logons for a non-trusting domain

7. What is a trusting domain?

   a. One on which users can be authenticated by the SAM on the workstation on which they log on

   b. One which allows the PDC or BDC on any domain to authenticate users who log on to the domain of which the PDC or BDC are members

   c. One which allows a user of its resources to be authenticated by a PDC or BDC on a trusted domain

8

8. What is the name of the utility that is used to manage local workstation user accounts?

   a. User Manager for Domains

   b. User Manager

   c. Network Client Administrator

9. Which menu do you use in User Manager for Domains to set password properties for a user?

   a. User menu

   b. Options menu

   c. Policies menu

10. Can the password of a user be configured to never expire?

   a. Yes

   b. No

   c. Depends on the user

11. What menu in User Manager for Domains do you use to configure domain trust relationships?

   a. Policies menu

   b. Options menu

   c. User menu

12. Which utility do you use to see and manage the properties of a computer on the domain?

   a. Server Manager

   b. User Manager for Domains

   c. Network Monitor

13. How do you monitor user connections to a computer on a domain?

   a. Use the Properties item on the Computer menu of Server Manager

   b. Use the Shared Directories item in the Computer menu of Server Manager

   c. Use the Workstations item on the View menu of Server Manager

14. The Server Manager Computer menu has an item called Properties, which opens a screen that has a Replication button. Which of the following does clicking this button allow you to do?

   a. Synchronize a PDC user account database with a BDC user account database

   b. Configure a computer to automatically export or import directories

   c. Configure a workstation to export directories

15. Which of the following actions is required to enable a workstation on a domain?

a. Adding the name of the workstation to the list of domain computers in Server Manager on a domain PDC or BDC

b. Entering the workstation name and domain name on the Network screen of the workstation

c. Adding the name of the workstation to the list of domain computers in Server Manager on a domain PDC or BDC *and* entering the workstation name and domain name on the Network screen of the workstation

16. In order to have a subdirectory exported automatically to other computers on the domain, which of the following must you do?

a. Add the computer name to the To List on the Directory Replication screen

b. Add the subdirectory to the Export directory of a PDC or BDC

c. Add the subdirectory to the Manage list obtained from the Directory Replication screen

17. Which of the following do you use to make a directory on one computer on the domain sharable to other computers on the domain?

a. Properties on the File menu in Windows Explorer

b. The Users screen of Server Manager

c. The Replication screen of Server Manager Properties

18. How does one computer on a domain establish a permanent link to a drive on another computer on the domain?

a. By using Map Network Drive on the Tools menu in Windows Explorer

b. By using Sharing on the File menu of Windows Explorer

c. By using Go To on the Tool menu in Windows Explorer

19. What submenu of the Windows Start menu contains the Network Client Administrator utility?

a. The Programs submenu

b. The Administrative Tools (common) submenu

c. The Accessories submenu

20. In addition to providing tools for client management of a domain, the Network Client Administrator utility also allows you to do which of the following?

a. Make a network installation startup disk

b. Make a copy of Windows NT Workstation

c. Make a copy of the Windows NT Server CD-ROM

CASE PROJECT

The status of the Case Project after Chapter 7, "Dynamic Host Configuration Protocol (DHCP)," is shown in Figure 8-47.

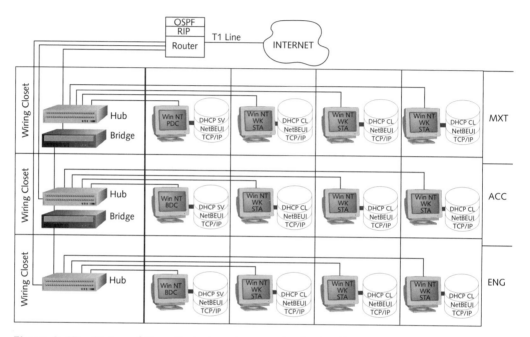

Figure 8-47   Status of Case Project environment prior to Chapter 8

In the Chapter 7 exercises, you established dynamic IP configuration for all the workstations on the networks in the three divisions of the company. Workstations in each division had the resources to communicate with each other and with servers using the NetBEUI or TCP/IP protocols, and they could communicate, using TCP/IP applications. However, workstations could not access resources on the servers or on other workstations because they were not authenticated domain members.

In this chapter you have learned about Windows NT domains, which provide the mechanisms that allow you to create a secure corporate network and to manage and access the resources on that network by logging on to any computer on the network. In the exercises that follow, you will create a domain for each of the divisions and establish trust relationships among those domains.

EXERCISE 1—USING SERVER MANAGER TO CREATE DOMAIN COMPUTER ACCOUNTS

In Server Manager, create four computer accounts, one for a PDC, one for a BDC, and two for workstations.

EXERCISE 2—USING USER MANAGER FOR DOMAINS

1. Name the two built-in domain user accounts that were created during installation of Windows NT 4.0 Server.

2. What is the default maximum password age for each of those accounts?

3. Using the User and Policies menus, in User Manager for Domains, add three new users and their passwords to the domain. Using Account on the Policy menu, set (1) Maximum Password Age, (2) Minimum Password Length, and (3) Lockout After parameters. List your choices below.

Username: _____ _____ _____

Password: _____ _____ _____

Max Pswd Age: _____ _____ _____

Min Pswd Length: _____ _____ _____

Lockout After: _____ _____ _____

4. Make two of the users listed previously members of the group Domain Users, and one a member of the Domain Admins group. List your choices below.

Members of Domain Users Group: _____ _____

Member of Domain Admins Group: _____ _____

5. Use the Policies menu to create *two-way* trust relationships among the Raleigh, Boston, and Chicago domains of the company. Use the User Manager Trust Relationships Help screen in Figure 8-14 or Help in the Trust Relationships dialog box to guide you in this effort. The advantage of *two-way* trust relationships is that a user is able to access resources in any domain regardless of where the user logs on.

EXERCISE 3—CHECKING COMMUNICATION BETWEEN THE PDC AND A WORKSTATION BEFORE DOMAIN MEMBERSHIP IS ENABLED FOR THE WORKSTATION

1. Highlight a workstation on Server Manager.

2. Click **Properties** on Computer menu.

3. Write down the message you see on the screen.

8

EXERCISE 4—ESTABLISHING WORKSTATION DOMAIN MEMBERSHIP

1. Use Control Panel at each workstation to include the workstation in the domain.
2. Write down the domain name and the workstation names that you chose.
3. Restart each workstation.

EXERCISE 5—EXAMINE PROPERTIES OF A WORKSTATION FROM THE PDC

1. In Server Manager, highlight the same workstation that you highlighted in Exercise 4.
2. Click **Properties** in Computer menu.
3. What do you see on the screen now that you included the workstation in the domain?

EXERCISE 6—DOMAIN BROWSING

1. In Server Manager highlight the PDC.
2. On the Computer menu, click **Shared Directories**.
3. Click **New Share** and add a new share.
4. Check that the Share Name that you created is shown in the Shared Directories dialog box.
5. From a workstation, double-click **Network Neighborhood**.
6. Double-click the PDC icon.
7. Write down the name of any directories that are being shared by the PDC.
8. Is the sharable directory you created on the PDC one of the above? If the answer is No, you have not made the directory sharable.

EXERCISE 7—DIRECTORY REPLICATION

In this exercise, you will create a subdirectory for export from a PDC to a workstation and confirm that replication is occurring.

1. Add a subdirectory to the Export directory on a PDC.

2. Use Services in Control Panel to check the status of the Directory Replicator service on the PDC and workstation.

3. Use Startup to configure the user account for the service on both the PDC and the workstation.

4. Check the Import directory on the workstation to see if the directory that you created has been imported.

EXERCISE 8—USE THE NETWORK CLIENT ADMINISTRATOR UTILITY TO ENABLE CLIENT DOMAIN MANAGEMENT

1. Access the Network Client Administrator utility on the server as indicated in Figure 8-48.

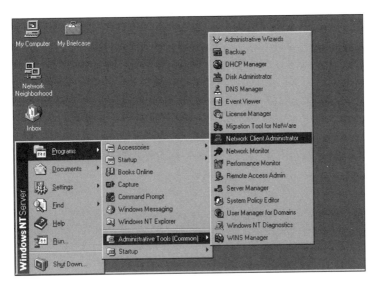

Figure 8-48   Network Client Administrator utility on Windows NT Server

2. Click **Network Client Administrator** to open the screen shown in Figure 8-49.

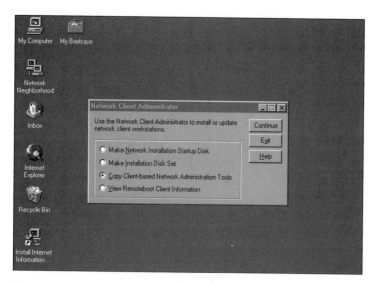

Figure 8-49   Network Client Administrator

3. Select **Copy Client-based Network Administration Tools** and click **Continue** to open the screen shown in Figure 8-50.

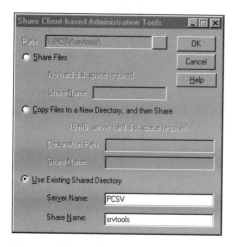

Figure 8-50   Share Client-based Administration Tools

4. As shown, there are three ways for a workstation to gain access to these tools. Use the third choice, Use Existing Shared Directory. This choice allows you to access the tools where they are on the hard drive on the server. Enter the server name and the share name of the tools directory, which is srvtools, and then click **OK**.

5. Open the Server Manager utility on the server, highlight the PDC, and click **Shared Directories** on Computer menu to open the screen shown in Figure 8-51 for PCSV in this case.

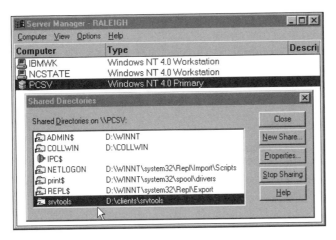

Figure 8-51   Shared Directories on PCSV

There you see that the directory srvtools is shared and is located in D:\clients which, in this case, is the on drive D, the partition where Windows NT Server resides.

6. From a workstation, (1) Click **Network Neighborhood** on the Desktop, (2) Click **PCSV** (in this case), (3) open **svrtools**, (4) open **Winnt**, (5) open **I386**, and then (6) open **srvmgr**. You will see the Server Manager screen, from which you can manage computers on the domain from your workstation.

Figure 8-52 shows the Case Project environment after completion of these exercises.

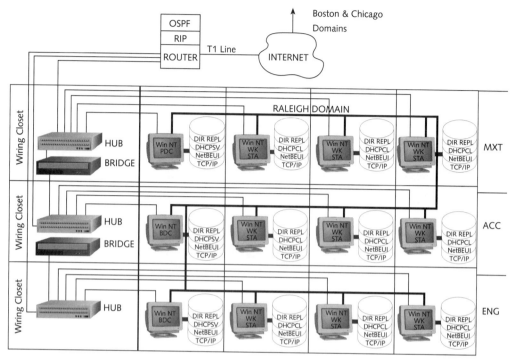

Figure 8-52   Case Project environment after completing Chapter 8

NAME SERVICES

The purpose of this chapter is to provide an integrated overview of TCP/IP name resolution methods. Name resolution is needed because human beings prefer to reference computers and other entities by names that are easily remembered. Using easily recognizable names works fine on Microsoft networks that use the NetBIOS application interface and the NetBEUI protocol stack, where the names are the actual addresses of the computers. However, on TCP/IP networks and others, communication between machines requires a numerical address for the machines. Thus for Microsoft networks to be routed to other networks, it is necessary to have an automatic mechanism for translating from a NetBIOS or domain name to an IP or other numerical address. This chapter discusses the mechanisms that are available for translating names to TCP/IP addresses and from TCP/IP addresses to names, and how these mechanisms work.

IN THIS CHAPTER YOU WILL:

LEARN HOW TO CREATE AN LMHOSTS FILE

LEARN HOW TO CREATE A HOSTS FILE

LEARN HOW TO SET UP A WINDOWS INTERNET NAME SERVICE (WINS) SERVER

LEARN HOW TO USE A WINS SERVER TO ENABLE TCP/IP COMMUNICATION

LEARN HOW TO SET UP A DOMAIN NAME SYSTEM (DNS) SERVER

LEARN HOW TO USE A DNS SERVER TO ENABLE TCP/IP COMMUNICATION

LEARN HOW TO USE NETWORK MONITOR TO ANALYZE NAME SERVICE FRAMES

NAME RESOLUTION MECHANISMS

Windows NT uses a hierarchy of name mechanisms that can all be available for name resolution if you choose to configure them. These mechanisms query name databases, such as a NetBIOS name cache, WINS, DNS, LMHOSTS, and HOSTS, as well as broadcast name queries over the local subnet. Each of these mechanisms may be able to provide the NetBIOS name to IP address translation that is needed. If one mechanism cannot provide the IP address, the computer will send a query to the next active mechanism in the hierarchy. The configuration of a computer determines the order in which these mechanisms are used. Windows-based computers can be configured as one of four NetBIOS node (computer on a network) types that are labeled b-node, p-node, m-node, and h-node. **b-node** is broadcast node, **p-node** is point-to-point node, **m-node** is mixed node, and **h-node** is hybrid node. Windows NT computers default to b-node when WINS is not enabled and to h-node otherwise. The way each node type functions when mapping NetBIOS names to IP addresses is described in Table 9-1. Name resolution mechanisms used are bolded to call attention to their order of execution.

Table 9-1   NetBIOS Node Types and their Functions

NetBIOS Node Types	Description
b-node	a. Query the NetBIOS name **cache** on the node. If the IP address is not found, b. **Broadcast** a message on the local subnet (broadcasts are not routed). If another computer has the NetBIOS name in the broadcast message stored in its NetBIOS cache, it returns the name and corresponding IP address. If not, c. Query **LMHOSTS** if enabled. If not found, d. Query **HOSTS** if enabled. If not found, e. Query **DNS** if enabled.
p-node	a. Query the NetBIOS name **cache**. b. Query **WINS** if enabled. c. Query **LMHOSTS** if enabled. d. Query **HOSTS** if enabled. e. Query **DNS** if enabled.
m-node	a. Query the NetBIOS name **cache**. b. **Broadcast** on the local subnet. c. Query **WINS** if enabled. d. Query **LMHOSTS** if enabled. e. Query **HOSTS** if enabled. f. Query **DNS** if enabled
h-node	a. Query the NetBIOS name **cache**. b. Query **WINS** if enabled. c. **Broadcast** on the local subnet. d. Query **LMHOSTS** if enabled. e. Query **HOSTS** if enabled. f. Query **DNS** if enabled.

Each node type begins the name resolution process by checking the NetBIOS name cache. If LMHOSTS is enabled, up to 100 name/IP address mappings can be loaded into this cache. The advantage of p-node and h-node configurations is that the WINS database will be accessed before broadcast is used. This reduces network traffic. The advantage of h-node over p-node is that h-node provides the broadcast mechanism if needed.

Discussion of the name resolution mechanisms in this chapter will refer to Figure 9-1.

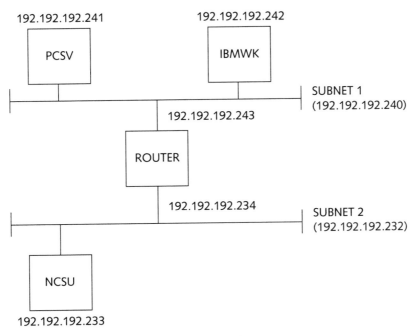

Figure 9-1   Raleigh domain with two subnets

Because our purpose for using name resolution is to obtain the IP address of a computer that is not on the local Microsoft network, one of the computers in the Raleigh domain, NCSU, has been moved across a router to create another subnet, as shown in Figure 9-1. The IP addresses of the interfaces shown in Figure 9-1 are listed in Table 9-2. These IP addresses have been chosen so that the domain will still be the Class C network that has been used in previous chapters. To create subnet addresses, part of the IP host address space (the last byte) has been divided into a subnet space and a host space.

Let's first examine the two static, local name resolution services—LMHOSTS and HOSTS—that can be used to map computer names to IP addresses. We will start with LMHOSTS.

Table 9-2   IP Addresses of the Devices on the Raleigh Domain Shown in Figure 9-1

Machine	IP Addresses	Description
PCSV	192.192.192.241	Primary domain controller (PDC)
IBMWK	192.192.192.242	NT workstation
Router	192.192.192.243 192.192.192.234	CISCO router providing default gateways for the subnets
NCSU	192.192.192.233	NT workstation
Subnet 1	192.192.192.240	Address of subnet with the nodes pcsv, ibmwk, and the router
Subnet 2	192.192.192.232	Address of subnet with the nodes ncsu and the router

THE LMHOSTS FILE

 There are three subtle points to remember if you use an LMHOSTS file: End the file with a carriage return; do not include DHCP addresses; and put each entry on a separate line.

A sample LMHOSTS file, which can be used for guidance in constructing one that you can use, is located in the default directory C:\Winnt\system32\drivers\etc. The MS-DOS name is **Lmhosts.sam**, where the extension "sam" stands for sample. The LMHOSTS file that you create will have the MS-DOS name **LMHOSTS**. It should be placed in the **etc** directory.

Figure 9-2 shows a simple LMHOSTS file for the domain in Figure 9-1. It was created using the WordPad utility available in Windows NT.

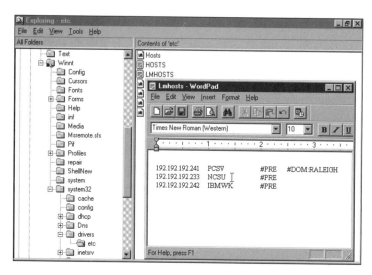

Figure 9-2   LMHOSTS file for the Raleigh domain

This file is the LMHOSTS file for the primary domain controller, PCSV. Each line must contain the IP address first, separated by at least one space from the NetBIOS name of the computer. The first line is the entry for PCSV. The keyword **#PRE** has been used so that the NetBIOS name/IP address mapping will be preloaded into the NetBIOS name cache when the computer starts. #PRE can be used with any entry for up to 100 entries. If you desire, you can have more than 100 entries in the name cache by modifying the Registry. The keyword **#DOM** is also used with the PCSV entry. DOM: RALEIGH specifies that PCSV is a domain controller on the Raleigh domain, and will result in PCSV being included in a domain group that can be referred to by one NetBIOS name. A message to this NetBIOS name will be multicast to all members in the group on the subnet to which the PDC is attached.

This LMHOSTS file can be made even simpler than in our example. It is only necessary for the file to contain an entry for remote computers, such as NCSU in this example. Since PCSV and IBMWK are on the same subnet, they can communicate using their NetBIOS names and the NetBEUI protocol stack. If either one of them needs the IP address of the other, they can use the broadcast mechanism to obtain it, as long as they are not configured as p-nodes, which do not use broadcast, as you have seen in Table 9-1.

You can also perform script-like functions with the LMHOSTS file. Such functions enable you to have LMHOSTS files on other computers read by your computer. You could use this approach to keep a central LMHOSTS file on one computer that could be read by all others. For example, you could force IBMWK to read the LMHOSTS file on NCSU by adding the following statements to the IBMWK LMHOSTS file:

```
192.192.192.233  NCSU    #PRE

#INCLUDE   \\NCSU\PUBLIC\LMHOSTS
```

You must include the #PRE keyword with the NCSU entry so that the INCLUDE statement will not be ignored. The PUBLIC directory is the default directory in which the LMHOSTS file must be placed unless you reconfigure the Registry. You can configure an LMHOSTS file to be replicated automatically by placing it in the Export directory, as you saw in Chapter 8, "Windows NT Domains."

As indicated in Table 9-1, the LMHOSTS file must be enabled. This procedure will be discussed when we examine WINS. First, however, let's look at the other static, local, name resolution database—HOSTS.

THE HOSTS FILE

The HOSTS file has long been used by many TCP/IP utilities, such as Ping and Finger, to find the IP address of an Internet domain name. A sample HOSTS file can be found in the directory C:\Winnt\system32\drivers\etc. A HOSTS file for PCSV on the domain shown in Figure 9-1 is shown in Figure 9-3. This file was created using the Word Pad utility.

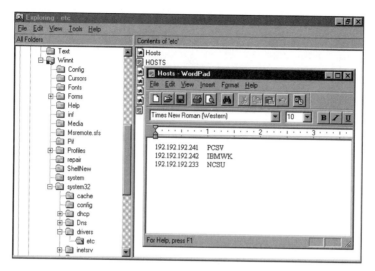

Figure 9-3   HOSTS file for PCSV

The HOSTS file is similar in format to the LMHOSTS file, but does not have all the configuration options. A primary difference is that the host name is written in domain name format. A domain name is a hierarchical name that can have a number of parts. For example, if we call the domain in Figure 9-1 Raleigh, and this domain is part of a company that has the name Innovation, the domain name of PCSV would be pcsv.raleigh.innovation.com.

Com stands for commercial, and is one of the authorized subdirectories in the root directory of the Domain Name System (DNS) tree. You will examine these names in detail when DNS is discussed later in this chapter.

The problem with LMHOSTS and HOSTS files is that they are static and local, and therefore must be managed manually and locally. It is difficult to maintain a consistent set of mappings this way on large networks. WINS provides dynamic databases of NetBIOS names/IP addressing mappings that can be updated with DHCP. DNS databases are static, but the maintenance is distributed. Let's look first at WINS.

WINDOWS INTERNET NAME SERVICE (WINS) CONCEPTS

For further information about the protocols on which WINS implementation is based, see NetBIOS over TCP/IP RFCs 1001 and 1002.

WINS is based on the NetBIOS over TCP/IP protocol described in the RFCs 1001 and 1002. NetBIOS is the API to DOS that many legacy applications use. NetBIOS over NetBEUI extended the resources available to NetBIOS applications to those on other computers on the local network. The NetBIOS over TCP/IP protocol was developed to extend the range of available resources to networks on which TCP/IP is the communication protocol stack. WINS is the Microsoft implementation of the NetBIOS Name Server (NBNS) described in RFC 1001. In the Windows NT environment shown in Figure 4-3 of Chapter 4, the Windows NT implementation of NetBIOS over TCP/IP (**NetBT** or **NBT**), is the interface between the TDI layer and the TCP/IP protocol stack. NBT implements NetBIOS name registration and NetBIOS name to IP address resolution, using one of the name resolution sequences described in Table 9-1, and establishes and terminates NBT sessions between clients and servers.

When a WINS client starts, it uses the file netbt.sys to send a name registration request message to a WINS server. (NetBIOS over TCP/IP). A **name registration request** is a packet, containing a NetBIOS name and the IP address of the WINS client that is sent to the IP address of the WINS server. The client's IP address can be a static address or one that has been obtained from a DHCP server. The NetBIOS name to be registered may be the name of the computer, the name of the logged-on user, or the name of a process running on the computer. Each of these unique clients will have a NetBIOS name that differs in the 16th byte of its 16-byte name. You can see the NetBIOS names that have been registered by your computer as well as other computers on the network by using the monitoring utility nbtstat.exe at the command prompt. Table 9-3 describes this command and its primary arguments.

Table 9-3   Nbtstat Command Arguments and Functions

Argument	Function
- n	Lists registered NetBIOS names on your computer
- c	Lists registered NetBIOS name/IP address mappings in the NetBIOS name cache. These are mappings for any computer on the network that this computer knows.
- a <remotename>	Lists the NetBIOS names registered by computer <remotename>
- A <IP address>	Lists the NetBIOS names registered by a computer with <IP address>

If there is no NetBIOS name in the WINS server database that is identical to the one sent in the name registration request, the server responds with a **positive name registration response**. This response includes a time-to-live (TTL) that indicates how long the client can own the NetBIOS name that was sent in the name registration request. If there is a NetBIOS name in the WINS server database that is identical to that requested, the WINS server will confirm the status of that name with the computer(s) that have registered the name. If the name is still claimed, a negative name registration response is sent to the client, the client marks the requested name with a conflict mark, and a session is not established. Similarly, when a WINS client needs to know the IP address of a computer for which it knows the NetBIOS name, it uses NBT to send a **name query request** to the WINS server. The server responds with either a **positive query response** containing the requested IP address or a **negative query response** if the name/IP address mapping is not contained in the WINS server database.

When a WINS client uses a controlled shutdown from the Start menu, it sends a **name release request** to the WINS server. Under normal circumstances, the server sends a **name release response** and marks the name for release after the TTL that was configured by the WINS server based on the TTL that was negotiated when the name was registered. When the client logs on again, if the TTL has not expired, a new TTL will be negotiated for the same name. If the TTL has expired, the client must send a name registration request.

A WINS server database is automatically replicated to other WINS servers with which it has pull and push agreements. This is a valuable feature of WINS because it distributes network traffic between clients and servers and provides backup WINS servers. A **pull partner** of a WINS server is a server that periodically requests that the WINS server send database entries that have a higher **version** number than entries that existed at the previous replication. A **push partner** of a WINS server is a server that is "pushed" to send a replication request to the WINS server when the number of changes in the database reaches the configured value.

WINS MANAGER

Let's now explore the WINS Manager utility to see how this graphical interface enables management of the capabilities discussed. WINS manager is a Windows NT Server utility. Before we open this utility, we should first examine the state of the network interface of PCSV, the Windows NT Server. This is done by typing the TCP/IP utility, **ipconfig**, and its switch **/all** at the command prompt. The screen in Figure 9-4 shows the current configuration of PCSV.

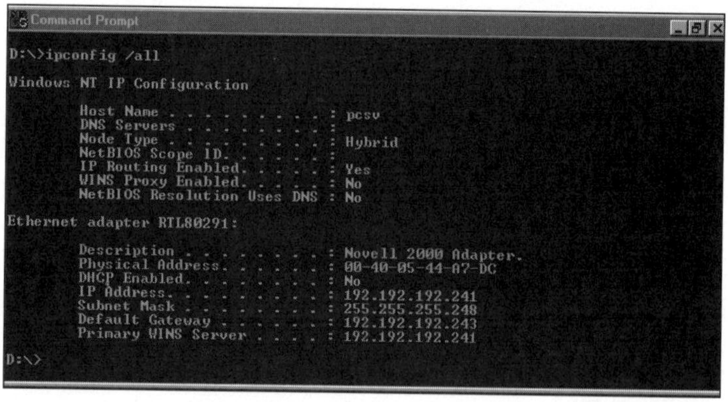

```
Command Prompt                                                      _ & X
D:\>ipconfig /all

Windows NT IP Configuration

        Host Name . . . . . . . . . . . : pcsv
        DNS Servers . . . . . . . . . . :
        Node Type . . . . . . . . . . . : Hybrid
        NetBIOS Scope ID. . . . . . . . :
        IP Routing Enabled. . . . . . . : Yes
        WINS Proxy Enabled. . . . . . . : No
        NetBIOS Resolution Uses DNS : No

Ethernet adapter RTL80291:

        Description . . . . . . . . . . : Novell 2000 Adapter.
        Physical Address. . . . . . . . : 00-40-05-44-A7-DC
        DHCP Enabled. . . . . . . . . . : No
        IP Address. . . . . . . . . . . : 192.192.192.241
        Subnet Mask . . . . . . . . . . : 255.255.255.248
        Default Gateway . . . . . . . . : 192.192.192.243
        Primary WINS Server . . . . . : 192.192.192.241

D:\>
```

Figure 9-4   Configuration of PCSV

First you see that the Node Type is **Hybrid**, that is, it is configured as an h-node. This configuration is an automatic consequence of configuring PCSV to be a WINS server. (Refer back to Table 9-1 to review the operation of an h-node.) IP routing is enabled on PCSV, but PCSV is not being used as a router in the example network in Figure 9-1. WINS Proxy will be discussed later in the chapter. DNS has not been enabled. Static IP addresses are being used, so DHCP is not enabled. You have already seen the IP address, Subnet Mask, and Default Gateway in Table 9-2. And, as just mentioned, PCSV is configured as a Primary WINS Server with the IP address 192.192.192.241. There are no other WINS servers in the Raleigh domain.

WINS Manager is accessed from the Administrative Tools (Common) menu, as indicated in Figure 9-5.

Figure 9-5   Accessing the WINS Manager utility

Clicking WINS Manager produces the screen shown in Figure 9-6.

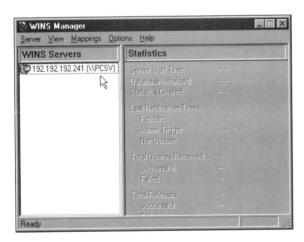

Figure 9-6   WINS Manager screen

Figure 9-6 shows a fresh WINS Manager screen. The WINS server has no static mappings registered, and it has received no dynamic mappings from the other two computers on the network, IBMWK and NCSU. The Mappings menu provides access to any static mappings that are registered and to the complete WINS database. Clicking Static Mappings on the Mappings menu produces a screen like the one shown in Figure 9-7.

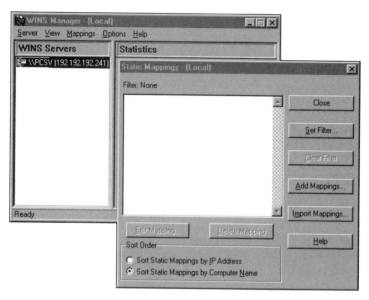

Figure 9-7   Static Mappings (local)

You would click the Add Mappings button to open the screen shown in Figure 9-8, where you can add static mappings consisting of IP address/NetBIOS name pairs that will remain in the WINS database. The types of mappings (unique, group, etc.) will be explained in Table 9-4.

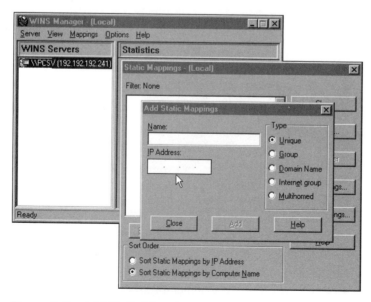

Figure 9-8   Add Static Mappings

Figure 9-9 shows a Static Mappings dialog box in which static mappings have been entered for two computers, IBMWK and NCSU, in the domain shown in Figure 9-1.

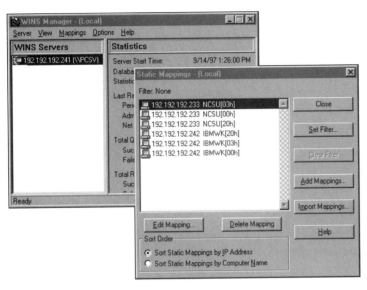

Figure 9-9   Static Mappings for IBMWK and NCSU

As you can see, there are more than two mappings. Although only one static mapping was entered for each computer, other mappings were registered automatically by the WINS server. Table 9-4 shows examples of NetBIOS names, including the NetBIOS names, shown in Figure 9-9, and describes their meaning.

By clicking Import Mappings, you can browse files on this computer or on other computers throughout the network. You can then import mappings from text files having the LMHOSTS format. The Set Filter button opens a screen on which you can specify how to filter the Static Mappings and Database displays so that you see only entries in which you are currently interested. The function of the Sort Order buttons is self-explanatory.

Table 9-4   NetBIOS Names

Number	NetBIOS Name		Description
	First 15 bytes	**16th byte (hex)**	
1	NCSU	[00]	The computer name. More specifically, the name of the **Workstation Service** that provides the interface between the user request and local or remote file systems.
2	NCSU	[03]	The name of the Messenger Service that sends and receives Administrator messages and messages from the **Alerter Service**. This code is also attached to the logged-on user or service.

Table 9-4   NetBIOS Names (continued)

Number	NetBIOS Name		Description
	First 15 bytes	16th byte (hex)	
3	NCSU	[20]	The Internet Group name. Identifies the IP addresses of a group of devices such as printers or Internet servers.
4	RALEIGH	[1B]	The name of the domain **master browser**—the primary domain controller. Maintains a list of domains and browsers that maintain a list of network resources.
5	IBMWK ††††††††††††	[BE]	The name used by a Network Monitor agent on the IBMWK computer
6	PCSV ††††††††††††	[BF]	The name used by the Network Monitor utility on the PDC
7	PCSV	[1D]	The name used by clients when accessing the master browser on a subnet
8	RALEIGH	[1C]	The name of the **domain name group**. It contains a list of addresses of computers that have registered the domain name. Used for pass through authentication.
9	_MSBROWSE_	[01]	Appended to a domain name and broadcast on the local subnet by the PDC to announce the domain to master browsers on the subnet.
10	RALEIGH	[1E]	A group name that browsers on the Raleigh domain use to elect a subnet master browser

Names 1, 2, 4, 5, 6, and 7 in the table are examples of **unique names**—names claimed by only one entity. The others are examples of **group names**—names that can be claimed by any number of clients or names that, when used as destination addresses, cause the message to be sent to all computers that have registered the group name.

Figure 9-10 is an example of the dynamic WINS database, for the domain shown in Figure 9-1, which is obtained by clicking Show Database on the Mappings menu.

This screen shows only mappings that have been registered by the WINS server with the IP address 192.192.192.241 that is installed on PCSV because the Show Only Mappings from Selected Owner button was selected under Owner and because this address was highlighted. If there were other WINS servers that are partners with this WINS server, their IP addresses would appear in the Select Owner list also. If you click Show All Mappings, mappings registered by other WINS servers will be displayed. These mappings were obtained by replication. There are no other WINS servers in the domain of Figure 9-1. In the panel Sort Order, you can select how you want the mappings to be displayed. In this example, they are sorted by IP address.

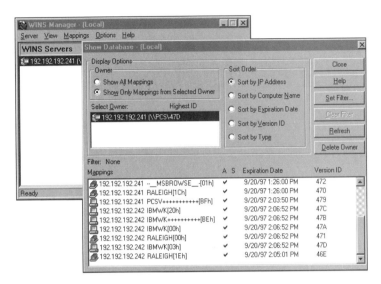

Figure 9-10   WINS database

The labels A and S at the top of the Mappings window indicate whether the mappings are Active or Static, respectively. **Active** implies dynamic mappings, which may change with time. Notice that none of the mappings is static because all static mappings shown in Figure 9-9 were removed. **Expiration Date** is the date and time when the WINS server will begin the process of removing the mapping from the database. This date is determined by the TTL, which can be set on a screen that you will see shortly, and is negotiated with the client when the mapping is registered by the client.

If the computer wishes to retain the mapping, it will send a **name refresh request** before the TTL expires. **Version ID** is a hexadecimal number that is an index of the time when a mapping was registered relative to the other mappings on the list. The higher the hexadecimal number the later the registration. WINS partner servers use this number to determine if they have the latest mapping list. The highest number and the last registration in this example are 47D, which corresponds to a registration by IBMWK[03], the messenger service process running on IBMWK.

Now let's return to the WINS Manager screen in Figure 9-6 and click Configuration on the Server menu to obtain the screen shown in Figure 9-11.

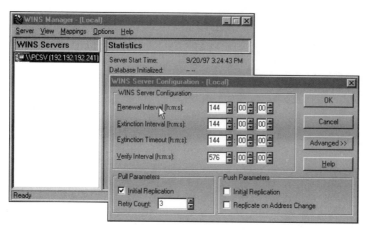

Figure 9-11   WINS Server Configuration

This is the screen, mentioned previously, where you can set the times that control the dynamic characteristics of the WINS server. The renewal interval is the TTL that has been discussed. The **renewal interval** is the time between the registration of the entry in the WINS database and the point at which it will be **released**, or marked for deletion. The **extinction interval** is the time interval from the point when the entry is marked released to the point when it is marked **extinct** or deleted. The **extinction timeout** is the time interval from the point when the entry is marked extinct to the point when it is **scavenged** from the database. The **verify interval** is the time interval from the point when the local WINS server registers a mapping obtained from a partner server to the point when the local WINS server must verify that the mapping is still active. These times are dependent on the value of the renewal interval and on that of the replication interval (discussed following).

The extinction interval, for example, is useful in the following way. After a name is marked Released, if a new registration arrives using that name but a different address, the name can be assigned to the requesting client. This might happen, for example, if the old client moves a laptop to another subnet. Also, if the old client reconnects after an orderly shutdown before the name is marked Extinct, the name will be reassigned without challenge. The extinction time-out is used to make allowances for the differences between replication intervals of different WINS servers in different time zones.

Now let's look at WINS database replication. **Replication** produces replicas of the local WINS database on other WINS servers on the network. These replicas serve three purposes: (1) ensure that each WINS server on the network has the same database, (2) provide backup in case of failure of a WINS server(s), and (3) distribute asynchronous name registration among WINS servers, and thus reduce intranetwork or Internetwork traffic. Clicking Preferences on the Options menu of WINS Manager and then Partners on the Preferences screen produces the screen shown in Figure 9-12.

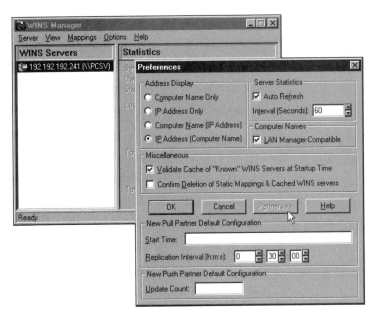

Figure 9-12   WINS Server Preferences and Partners

At the bottom of this screen you see two dialog boxes—one for a push partner and one for a pull partner. As described previously, a pull partner is a WINS server on the network that will automatically request database updates from the local WINS server on a periodic basis. A push partner is a WINS server on the network that will be "pushed" to request updates of the local WINS server database whenever a configured number of changes in the local WINS server database has occurred. WINS servers can be both pull and push partners of other WINS servers, and this is recommended in order to minimize delays in having consistent databases in all WINS servers.

For a pull partner, you can set the Start Time of the first "pull" and how often thereafter (that is, the **replication interval**) the pull partner will ask for an updated replica. For a push partner, you can specify the **Update Count**. This is the number of changes to the local WINS server database that will cause the local WINS server to send a message to the push partner requesting that that partner request an update of the local server's database.

You further configure the replication partners on the screen shown in Figure 9-13, which is obtained by clicking Replication Partners on the Server menu of WINS Manager.

The WINS Server dialog box provides a listing of the IP Addresses of the WINS servers on the network. What is shown in this list can be controlled by what you check in the WINS Servers To List check boxes—that is, you can list only Push Partners, only Pull Partners or WINS servers that are neither push nor pull partners. In Replication Options, you can configure the push and pull partners that you highlight in the WINS Server list.

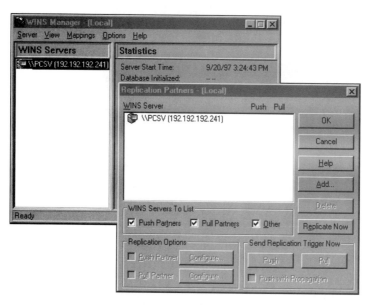

Figure 9-13   Replication Partners

Finally, in the Mappings menu of WINS Manager, you can click Initiate Scavenging if you want to clear the WINS database of names that have been marked released or old entries obtained by replication. Scavenging is then initiated automatically at a time determined by the renewal and extinction intervals. Also, you should click Backup to open a screen where you select a directory to receive a backup copy of the database.

Now let's look at the last of the name services—Domain Name System (DNS). You will see how it can be combined with WINS to provide a powerful method for resolution of either NetBIOS or DNS names into IP addresses.

DOMAIN NAME SYSTEM (DNS)

As you saw when examining LMHOSTS and WINS, both use **flat** names—that is, names without structure. Each host has a name that is not related to its location in the network. As the network grows, the local network administrator has to make sure that each name is unique and that there is no way to distribute the authority for creating unique names. In contrast, DNS uses a **hierarchical,** tree-like name structure in which the names used in any part of the tree (and related organizational structure) can be independently created by the network administrator for that part of the organization. Thus, name authority can be unique and distributed and can grow without limit. DNS is the name service used on the Internet.

DNS Concepts

 Information about InterNIC is available at http:// www.internic.net. To register a domain name, you can use http:// rs.internic.net For further information on DNS see RFCs 0881,0882,0883,1034,1035, and 2137.

Figure 9-14 shows the DNS hierarchy that is used in the United States. and managed by InterNIC, the Internet Network Information Center.

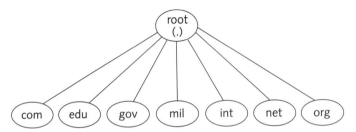

Figure 9-14   InterNIC Domain Name System (DNS) hierarchy

At the top of the hierarchy is the root, which has the domain label **n-ull**. It is represented by the dot (.) which ends a domain name. InterNIC distributes the **domain name space** among seven organizational domains: com., edu., gov., mil., int., net., and org., which are attached to the root. The names of these organizational domains are indicative of the types of organizations that will be assigned domain name space under that name. Commercial organizations register domain names and are assigned address space under the com. domain. Educational institution domains are included in the edu. domain. Under the gov. domain are domains for agencies of the federal government, such as the Department of Labor. Military agency domains, such as ARPA, come under the mil. domain. International organizations, such as the North Atlantic Treaty Organization (NATO), are assigned portions of the int. domain. Organizations that develop or manage major networks, such as NSF and the InterNIC itself, are included in the net. domain. The domain org. includes other organizations, such as nonprofit organizations, that are not included in one of the other domain classes. The following are examples of domains:

```
microsoft.com.

ncsu.edu.

whitehouse.gov.

nsf.net.
```

As mentioned previously, the dot (.) refers to the root of the tree. Its location in DNS names indicates how DNS names are constructed. The domain name of a node in the tree is constructed by climbing the tree from that node to the root of the tree (this is an upside-down tree). If you add the name of a computer in the domain to the domain name, you have what is called a **fully qualified domain name (FQDN)**, such as:

```
mycomputer.microsoft.com.
```

Microsoft can choose to divide up its domain name space (microsoft.com.) into other domains, or **zones**. There must be at least one **primary zone** in a domain. If there is only one zone, that zone and the domain encompass the same domain name space. Each zone can have one or more DNS servers that handle domain name queries for the zone, thus distributing the name query load. A DNS server can play one of three roles: primary, secondary, or caching-only. A **primary** server sends a copy of the zone file to a **secondary** server in a process called a zone transfer. A **caching-only** server stores results of queries it makes to primary or secondary servers.

Let's say that Innovation is the name of a company that is made up of the three divisions used in the Case Project: Raleigh, Boston, and Chicago. The name Innovation would have to be registered with the InterNIC to become authoritative. **Authoritative** means that the domain name innovation.com. would become part of the InterNIC tree and could be accessed by any Internet computer. The Innovation Chief Information Officer (CIO) can now create other domains within innovation.com. and register them with the InterNIC. He or she decides to create the following domains in innovation.com.:

```
boston.innovation.com.
raleigh.innovation.com.
chicago.innovation.com.
```

as indicated in Figure 9-15.

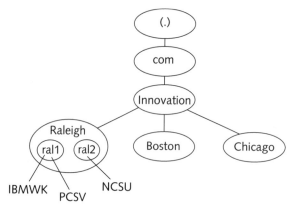

Figure 9-15   The domain innovation.com

The network administrator in Raleigh decides to divide the Raleigh domain into two zones: ral1 and ral2. There are two computers in ral1—IBMWK and PCSV—and one computer in ral2—NCSU. Thus the FQDNs of the computers in the domain raleigh.innovation.com. are:

```
pcsv.ral1.raleigh.innovation.com.
ibmwk.ral1.raleigh.innovation.com.
ncsu.ral2.raleigh.innovation.com.
```

There is only one DNS server available on the network in Figure 9-1, and its host is the computer pcsv. This host will provide DNS name service to both ral1 and ral2 zones.

It may help at this point to draw a more extensive diagram of a DNS to see how a request for a domain name to IP address mapping is typically handled. Figure 9-16 shows such a diagram.

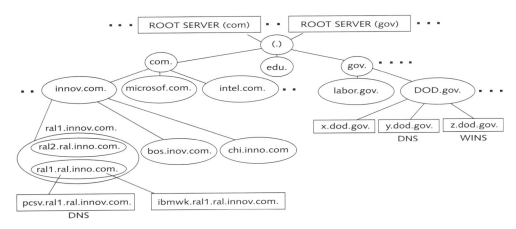

Figure 9-16   Network of DNS domain servers

The workstation IBMWK gives a command containing the domain name x.dod.gov. Table 9–5 describes the steps that are taken to resolve this domain name into the IP address of x.dod.gov.

9

Table 9-5   Resolution of a DNS Domain Name Request from Ibmwk

Step	Path Segment	Description
1	ibmwk.ral1.ral.innov.com. to pcsv.ral1.ral.innov.com.	This is a recursive request to the DNS server on PCSV for a mapping of the domain name x.dod.gov. to an IP address. A **recursive** request is one in which the requester does not participate in the resolution.
2	DNS server on PCSV to the ROOT-SERVERS in (.)	Iterative request for resolution of x.dod.gov. ROOT-SERVER authoritative for gov. receives the request. An **iterative** request is one in which the requester participates in the resolution.
3	ROOT-SERVER for gov. to DNS server on PCSV	Reply includes the IP address of DNS server y.dod.gov.
4	DNS server on PCSV to DNS server y.dod.gov.	Iterative request for resolution of x.dod.gov.
5	DNS server y.dod.gov. to WINS server z.dod.gov.	Iterative request for resolution of x.dod.gov. Since the WINS database is dynamic, it will contain the most recent mapping of x to IP address.
6	WINS server z.dod.gov to DNS server y.dod.gov.	Return the IP address of x.dod.gov. to y.dod.gov.
7	DNS server y.dod.gov. to DNS server on PCSV	Return the IP address of x.dod.gov. to PCSV.
8	DNS server on PCSV to ibmwk.ral1.ral.innov.com.	Return the IP address of x.dod.gov. to IBMWK.

Windows NT 4.0 contains the utility DNS Manager, which provides a graphical interface for the management of files and records of domain and zone resources. The next section discusses DNS Manager.

DNS Manager

 In DNS Manager, you use the right mouse button to click icons in the DNS server list to obtain menus that let you manage the resources associated with those icons. You select from the menus using the left mouse button.

Figure 9-17 shows the Windows NT menus that provide access to DNS Manager.

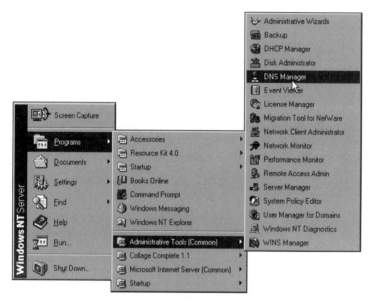

Figure 9-17   Access to DNS Manager

Clicking DNS Manager produces the screen shown in Figure 9-18.

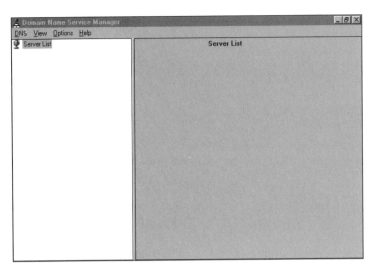

Figure 9-18   DNS Manager

From this screen, you can manage local DNS servers as well as DNS servers on other subnets or networks. No servers have been identified in Figure 9-18, so both panels are blank. (The right panel is labeled Server List but servers are never listed there.) To add a DNS server, you would click the DNS menu to open the screen shown in Figure 9-19, and then click New Server to open the screen shown in Figure 9-20.

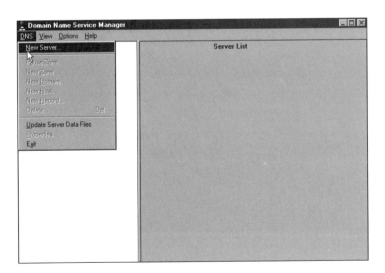

Figure 9-19   DNS menu

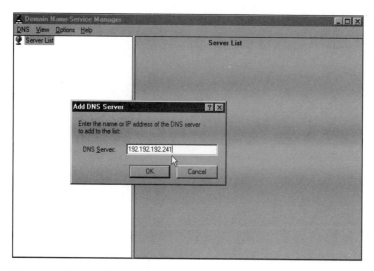

Figure 9-20   Add DNS Server

In Figure 9-20, the IP address of the DNS server has already been entered. After you click **OK**, a server icon and the name of the server host appear in the Server List in the left panel, and Server statistics appear in the right panel, as shown in Figure 9-21.

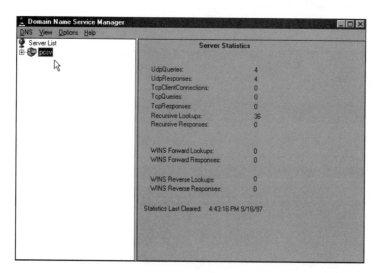

Figure 9-21   pcsv DNS Server

The statistics in Server Statistics are cumulative from the time the DNS server starts. Under Server Statistics, you see that 36 recursive lookups have accumulated and that there have been 4 queries of and 4 responses from the database over the network using the TCP/IP UDP transport protocol.

DNS ZONES

Figure 9-22 displays a Cache file and zones that were created either manually or automatically created by DNS Manager, for pcsv.

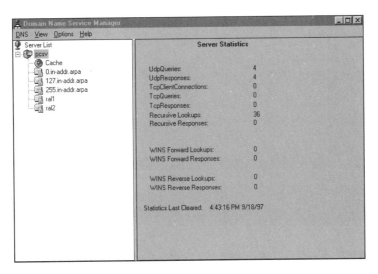

Figure 9-22   pcsv zones

The two zones at the bottom of the list, ral1 and ral2, are those that were manually created.

Normal zones

Zones ral1 and ral2 are examples of normal zones. You see the resources in the ral1 zone by clicking ral1. This opens the screen shown in Figure 9-23.

There are two resource records of type **A** – the ones with the names ibmwk and pcsv that are the names of the hosts that were added to ral1. A **resource record of type A** is one that maps the name of a computer to its IP address. There are 20 types of resource records that can be included in a zone file. Two other types are Name Server (NS) and Start of Authority (SOA). NS and SOA are automatically included in the file by DNS Manager when the zone is created. The data in the **NS** record identifies the name of a DNS server host. This data says that the DNS server host is pcsv and that pcsv is in the Raleigh domain. The data in the **SOA** record states that pcsv is the authoritative source for DNS mappings in zone ral1.

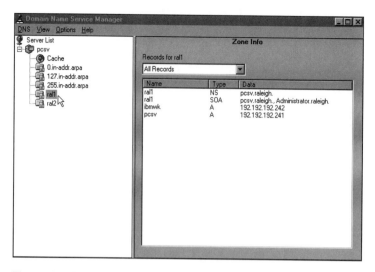

Figure 9-23 Resource records for zone ral1

Figure 9-24 shows the resource records for zone ral2.

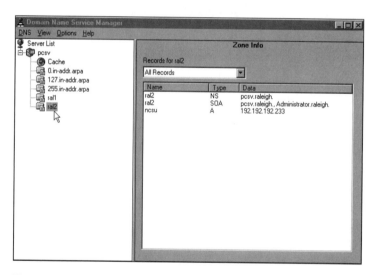

Figure 9-24 Resource records for zone ral2

There is one record of type A in the file for zone ral2—that for the ncsu host.

To manage the DNS server on pcsv, you right click the pcsv icon to open the screen shown in Figure 9-25.

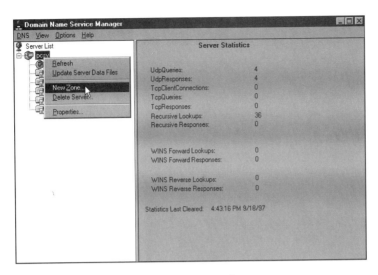

Figure 9-25   DNS server management menu

Using this menu you could, for example, add a New Zone for which pcsv would be the authoritative source for DNS mappings, Delete the Server, change server Properties and Update Server Data Files to include changes you have made to files. An important server property that you can configure is the requirement that the server use the service of another DNS server to obtain mappings that require the use of a WAN.

Right clicking a zone in Figure 9–24 opens a menu of items that can be used to manage the zone. Figure 9–26 shows such a menu for ral2.

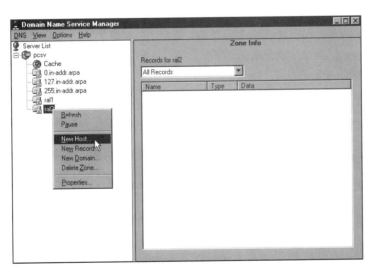

Figure 9-26   Zone management menu

Here, for example, you can add a new host to the zone, add a new record to the zone file, add a new domain to the zone, or delete the zone.

Let's now examine the zones and files that were automatically created by DNS Manager. (You will notice that all resources are now in the one primary zone, Raleigh, which is also the domain.)

In Figure 9-27, Cache has been opened to display the folders it contains.

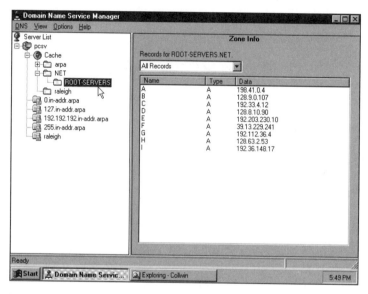

Figure 9-27   Cache file folders

 Updates to the list of ROOT-SERVERS is obtained from ftp://rs.internic.net/ domain/named.cache

The NET folder contains the ROOT-SERVERS folder and the ROOT-SERVERS folder contains server name to IP address mappings that are listed in the right panel of the screen. These servers are authoritative for the mappings of domain names to IP addresses in the top-level domains com., edu., gov., and others. You saw two examples of these servers, ROOT-SERVER (com.) and ROOT-SERVER (gov.), at the top of Figure 9-16.

Reverse zones

The other zones in Figure 9-27 are called **reverse lookup zones**. These are zones that contain IP address to host name mappings, the reverse of the mappings contained in the normal zones described in the previous section. Reverse lookup zones are accessed when one host knows the IP address of another host but does not know its name. Local DNS servers may contain a reverse lookup zone for hosts on the local subnet, but if they do, it will not contain all possible mappings for the Internet. To address this generically, a reverse lookup domain, labeled in-addr.arpa, (In = Internet, addr = address, and arpa is the Advanced Research Projects Agency) was created by the InterNIC. Nodes in this domain contain records of IP address/host name mappings for the domain. **In-addr.arpa** is the top level reverse lookup domain. Figure 9-28 shows the part of the in-addr.arpa. reverse lookup domain that is relevant to the discussion here. In what follows, we will first explain reverse lookup zones and then describe how you can create them.

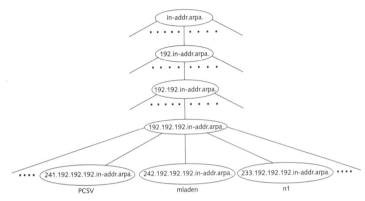

Figure 9-28   Part of in-addr.arpa. reverse lookup domain

Nodes in a reverse lookup domain are named by using a concatenation of the IP address with the text "in-addr.arpa." The order in which the IP address is written is reversed from the normal order to be consistent with the order of domain names. Figure 9-29 shows records for reverse lookup zone 192.192.192.in-addr.arpa.

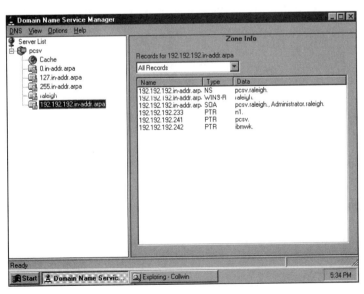

Figure 9-29   Records for reverse lookup zone 192.192.192.in-addr.arpa

The first record in Zone Info is 192.192.192.in-addr.arpa. The Type field says that this node is a Name Server (NS) and the Data field says that the NS is pcsv in the raleigh domain. Raleigh is a normal domain. The node 192.192.192.in-addr.arpa is authoritative for all reverse lookup nodes with addresses xxxx.192.192.192.in-addr.arpa. In the bottom 3 records, you see three examples of such reverse look up nodes. The IP addresses are written in normal order. Notice, however, that the IP address is written first and the host name is written last. This indicates that this is a mapping of IP address to host name, that is, it is a reverse mapping. Records of this type have the label PTR where PTR stands for pointer. Another record of interest here is the one having Type WINS-R. This record makes it possible for the DNS server host pcsv to use the WINS database to do a reverse lookup to get a host name from an IP mapping.

To create a reverse lookup zone, you take the following steps:

1. Right-click the DNS server icon (pcsv in this case) to open the menu shown in Figure 9-25.

2. Click New Zone.

3. Follow the instructions on the screens provided by the Windows NT wizard. These screens provide dialog boxes for:

   - Selecting to create a primary or secondary zone. A secondary zone is one to which a primary zone periodically replicates (transfers) its records. You want to create a primary zone.

   - Entering the name of the reverse lookup zone. As you have seen in Figure 9-28, this name is entered in the format xxxx.xxxx.xxxx.xxxx.in-addr.arpa.

   - Entering the name of the reverse lookup zone database file. A default file name is automatically created when you click that text box.

   - When you finish this screen, the reverse lookup zone name is added to the list under the DNS server name as shown in the left panel of Figure 9-29 for the example we have been discussing.

The other reverse lookup nodes automatically created by DNS Manager are 0.in-addr.arpa, 127.in-addr.arpa, and 255.in-addr.arpa. Their job is to block reverse lookup requests, for reverse lookup nodes that have the names

```
0.in-addr.arpa
127.in-addr.arpa
255.in-addr.arpa
```

from traversing to the top of the reverse lookup tree. You saw in Chapter 5, "IP Addressing," that an IP address of all zeros means that a host is referring to itself, an IP address beginning with 127 is a loopback address, and an IP address beginning with all ones (decimal 255) is a broadcast. These IP addresses should not used for reverse lookups. This can be assured for the node 127.in-addr.arpa, for example, by making pcsv authoritative for that zone. Then the search for any node with an address xxxx.xxxx.xxxx.127.in-addr.arpa will traverse the tree no further than the DNS server PCSV.

DNS Clients

Now that DNS server pcsv and its zone have been configured, the hosts IBMWK and N1 must become enabled DNS clients. This is done from Control Panel by clicking the Network icon, selecting TCP/IP Protocol, clicking Properties, and then clicking DNS to obtain the screen on the right of Figure 9-30.

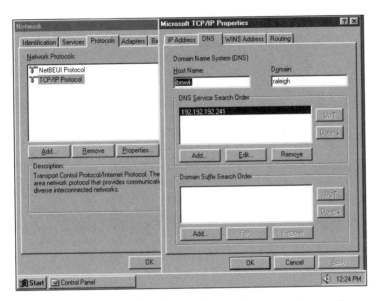

Figure 9-30   DNS dialog box in Microsoft TCP/IP Properties

The Host Name is ibmwk, and the domain name is raleigh. The DNS Service Search Order specifies 192.192.192.241, the IP address of the DNS server on PCSV. If there were other DNS servers in the domain, you could specify the order in which they would be searched for a domain name/IP address mapping request by IBMWK. In the middle text box it is specified that the DNS server with IP address 192.192.192.241 should be examined for domain-name-to-IP-address mappings. In the text box at the bottom of the screen you can include the domain suffix of your server that will be used to search the domain name tree for the address of your server. A **domain suffix** specifies the path from the root (.) to the domain that includes your server. OK is then clicked to enable the DNS client, ibmwk.

DNS-enabled WINS resolution

Windows NT 4.0 makes it possible for DNS and WINS servers to collaborate. This collaboration serves two purposes: (1) the DNS server can pass the resolution of the NetBIOS name part of the DNS domain name to the WINS server. (2) DNS is a static database, while WINS is a dynamic database. Thus, by passing host name resolution to the WINS server, the DNS service will have access to the most current IP addresses. This is especially useful in an environment where DHCP provides IP addresses. The combination of DNS, WINS, and DHCP is a powerful name resolution engine.

The screen in Figure 9-30 shows that you enable DNS for Windows resolution by checking the associated box. In the text box at the bottom of the screen, you can enter a scope ID. A scope ID adds a second label to a NetBIOS name. If used, only computers in the same scope can communicate. It is recommended that a scope ID not be used if DNS is used.

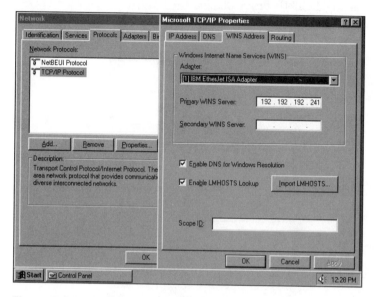

Figure 9-31   Enabling DNS for WINS resolution

Having been enabled for ibmwk, both WINS and DNS are then enabled on N1.

CHAPTER SUMMARY

This chapter explained the name services that are currently available for resolving host names to IP addresses and IP address to host names. You learned about:

- NetBIOS name types
- The InterNIC DNS hierarchy
- The syntax of LMHOSTS files and their use for the resolution of NetBIOS names to IP addresses
- The syntax of HOSTS files and their use for the resolution of DNS names to IP addresses
- NetBIOS over TCP/IP (NBT) node types
- The different name resolution methodologies used by different node types
- Using WINS Manager to configure a WINS server
- Installing static mappings in the WINS database
- Examining the dynamic mappings that are created by WINS clients

- The protocols implemented by a WINS client and server to register, renew, and release NetBIOS names and to request NetBIOS-to-IP-address resolution

- Replication of WINS databases between WINS servers

- Enabling a WINS client to use the services of a WINS server

- The meaning of fully qualified domain names

- The use of zones to divide up the administration of a domain

- Using the DNS Manager to configure the DNS server and its operation

- DNS domain and zone files

- Resource records in domain and zone files

- Reverse lookup zones that contain IP address to host name mappings

- Root servers of the InterNIC organizations

- Configuring a DNS client

- Configuring DNS and WINS domain name resolution collaboration

9

REVIEW QUESTIONS

1. What addresses are used by computers on a Microsoft network?

   a. Domain names

   b. NetBIOS names

   c. IP addresses

2. What is the name of the default protocol stack on a Microsoft network?

   a. NetBIOS over TCP/IP

   b. TCP/IP

   c. NetBEUI

3. Windows-based computers can be configured as one of four NBT node types. Which node type does not use WINS?

   a. h-node

   b. b-node

   c. p-node

4. Which is the only node type that does not use the broadcast mechanism for name resolution?

   a. h-node

   b. p-node

   c. b-node

5. What is one disadvantage of the b-node configuration?
  a. It uses the broadcast mechanism first.
  b. It does not use the HOSTS file.
  c. It does not use DNS.

6. What is the disadvantage of the p-node type?
  a. It uses the WINS database first.
  b. It does not use the broadcast mechanism.
  c. It does not use DNS.

7. What TCP/IP utility can you use to show you the node type of your computer?
  a. Nbtstat
  b. Ping
  c. Ipconfig

8. What is the subnet mask that is used for the network shown in Figure 9-1?
  a. 192.192.192.255
  b. 255.255.255.248
  c. 255.255.255.232

9. How many hosts can you have on subnet 1 in Figure 9-1?
  a. 8
  b. 6
  c. 7

10. How many hosts can you have on subnet 2 in Figure 9-1?
  a. 6
  b. 8
  c. 5

11. What is the purpose of the #PRE keyword in the LMHOSTS file?
  a. To label a primary domain controller computer
  b. To indicate which mapping should be read by the system first
  c. To indicate which mappings should be loaded into the NetBIOS cache

12. What types of host names are entered into the HOSTS file?
  a. Any TCP/IP host name
  b. A DNS domain name only
  c. NetBIOS names only

13. Where do you make static entries for computers in the WINS database?
  a. On the Server menu of the WINS Manager on the WINS server host
  b. In the Microsoft TCP/IP Properties screen of the WINS client host
  c. On the Mappings menu of the WINS Manager on the WINS server host

14. Where do you make dynamic entries in the WINS database?

    a. On the Mappings menu of WINS Manager

    b. On the WINS client

    c. You don't make them; the WINS client registers them automatically.

15. What is the only action you need to take to enable a WINS client to communicate with a WINS server?

    a. Provide the WINS client computer with the NetBIOS name of the WINS server host

    b. Provide the WINS client with the IP address of the WINS server host

    c. Provide the WINS server with the IP address of the WINS client host

16. What is the main distinction between a NetBIOS name and a DNS name?

    a. A NetBIOS name is composed of one label. A DNS name may be composed of many labels.

    b. A NetBIOS name is a structured name, while a DNS name is a flat name.

    c. A NetBIOS name cannot be used in the Hosts file.

17. A fully qualified domain name is defined as:

    a. A name specified by the path from the host to the root of the DNS tree

    b. A name that is assigned by the InterNIC

    c. A name that is assigned by your network administrator

18. DNS Manager is used to build the files of DNS domain-name-to-IP-address mappings. This file contains:

    a. Static mappings only

    b. Dynamic mappings only

    c. Both static and dynamic mappings

19. You enable the DNS client to access the DNS server:

    a. On the DNS menu of DNS Manager

    b. On the Microsoft TCP/IP Properties screen on the DNS client host

    c. On the DNS Manager Zone menu for the zone that contains the DNS client

20. You can enable DNS server and WINS server collaboration on the DNS client. How many of the following are true statements about the benefits of this collaboration?

    a. The DNS server can pass the host part of the resolution of the DNS name to the WINS server.

    b. If a DNS client host is moved to another subnet, DNS will get the correct IP address from the WINS server database.

    c. The WINS server will automatically update the DNS database with IP addresses that it receives from DHCP.

CASE PROJECT

The status of the Case Project after Chapter 8, "Windows NT Domains," is indicated in Figure 9-32.

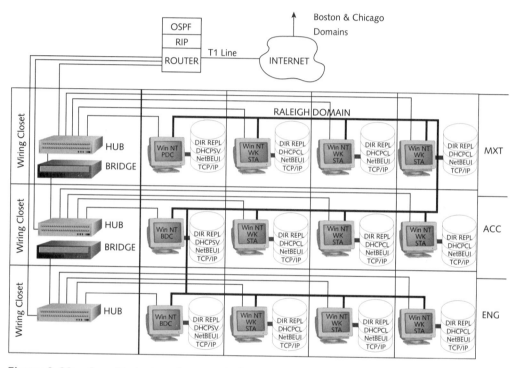

Figure 9-32   Case Project environment after completing Chapter 9

In Chapter 9 you learned about, and took the steps necessary to create, a Windows NT Raleigh domain, and in principle, you learned to establish domains at the Boston and Chicago divisions of your company. This involved using Server Manager to create computer accounts, and using User Manager for Domains to create client accounts. A client could then log on to the domain and access any of its resources according to the rights and permissions assigned to the client account. You then established trust relationships among the domains in the company so that a user on one domain could be authorized to access resources throughout the company.

Accessing a resource on another subnet of a domain or on another domain that is accessed over the Internet requires that the name of the resource be translated into an IP address. The name resolution mechanisms available to address this requirement were the subject of this chapter. In the exercises that follow, you will establish WINS and DNS name services for the computers on the Raleigh domain, so that users of this domain can access resources on the other domains that make up the company network.

EXERCISE 1—TESTING DNS ON THE NETWORK IN FIGURE 9-1

Testing will be done from the host NCSU, which has the zone name ncsu.ral2. We will attempt to ping IBMWK, which has the zone name ibmwk.ral1. This will be a good test of DNS because NCSU and IBMWK are on different subnets, and the destination IP address for IBMWK must be obtained from the DNS server on PCSV in order for NCSU to communicate with IBMWK. (Refer back to Figure 9-1.)

Figure 9-33 shows the Command Prompt screen on NCSU.

```
C:\>ping ibmwk.ral1

Pinging ibmwk.ral1 [192.192.192.242] with 32 bytes of data:

Reply from 192.192.192.242: bytes=32 time=10ms TTL=127
Reply from 192.192.192.242: bytes=32 time<10ms TTL=127
Reply from 192.192.192.242: bytes=32 time<10ms TTL=127
Reply from 192.192.192.242: bytes=32 time<10ms TTL=127

C:\>ping ibmwk.ral1

Pinging ibmwk.ral1 [192.192.192.242] with 32 bytes of data:

Reply from 192.192.192.242: bytes=32 time=10ms TTL=127
Reply from 192.192.192.242: bytes=32 time<10ms TTL=127
Reply from 192.192.192.242: bytes=32 time<10ms TTL=127
Reply from 192.192.192.242: bytes=32 time<10ms TTL=127

C:\>
```

Figure 9-33   Pinging ibmwk.ral1 from ncsu.ral2

The TCP/IP Ping command has the argument ibmwk.ral1. The results shown on the screen indicate that replies to the ping were received from ibmwk.ral1. (Four reply frames are received because Ping is currently configured to send four request frames.) Let's examine Network Monitor to see the summary of frames that were generated by execution of the Ping command. Figure 9-34 shows the 16 frames that were captured by Network Monitor.

Frame	Time	Src MAC Addr	Dst MAC Addr	Protocol	Description
1	13.655	Cisco 00ED6E	PCSV	DNS	0x1:Std Qry for ibmwk.ral1. of type Host
2	13.656	PCSV	*BROADCAST	ARP_RARP	ARP: Request, Target IP: 192.192.192.243
3	13.657	Cisco 00ED6E	PCSV	ARP_RARP	ARP: Reply, Target IP: 192.192.192.241 1
4	13.657	PCSV	Cisco 00ED6E	DNS	0x1:Std Qry Resp. for ibmwk.ral1. of typ
5	17.408	PCSV	002035E41D2B	ARP_RARP	ARP: Reply, Target IP: 192.192.192.242 T
6	17.408	002035E41D2B	PCSV	SMB	C tree disconnect
7	17.409	PCSV	002035E41D2B	SMB	R tree disconnect
8	17.409	002035E41D2B	PCSV	SMB	C logoff & X
9	17.409	PCSV	002035E41D2B	SMB	R logoff & X
10	17.410	002035E41D2B	PCSV	TCP	.A...F, len: 0, seq: 5837295-583729
11	17.410	PCSV	002035E41D2B	TCP	.A...F, len: 0, seq: 6057597-605759
12	17.410	002035E41D2B	PCSV	TCP	.A...., len: 0, seq: 5837296-583729
13	21.737	002035E41D2B	PCSV	LLC	RR DSAP=0xF0 SSAP=0xF1 C N(R) = 0x05 POL
14	21.737	PCSV	002035E41D2B	LLC	RR DSAP=0xF0 SSAP=0xF1 R N(R) = 0x06 FIN
15	22.621	PCSV	002035E41D2B	LLC	RR DSAP=0xF0 SSAP=0xF1 C N(R) = 0x06 POL
16	22.621	002035E41D2B	PCSV	LLC	RR DSAP=0xF0 SSAP=0xF1 R N(R) = 0x05 FIN
17	0.000	000000000000	000000000000	STATS	Number of Frames Captured = 16

Figure 9-34   Network Monitor summary of captured frames

You see that the source of Frame 1 is a device with the MAC address (hardware address) Cisco 00ED6E. This is the interface of the Cisco router on subnet ral1. The destination of this frame is the DNS server pcsv.ral1. You can also see in the frame Description that the frame is a DNS query for ibmwk.ral1 (that is, a query for the IP address of ibmwk.ral1). Now let's look at the decode of Frame 1 by double-clicking Frame 1. The Capture (Detail) screen, shown in Figure 9-35, opens.

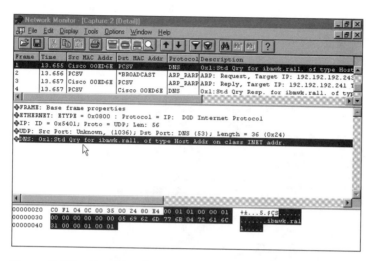

Figure 9-35   Decode of Frame 1 in the Network Monitor summary

In the top panel of this window, you see the first four frames from the Summary screen in Figure 9-34. (You can click any of these frames to see their decode in the middle panel.) The middle panel is the decode of the hexadecimal data shown in the bottom panel. (You can click on the + sign next to any line in the middle panel to open the details of that line.) Answer the questions in Table 9-6 using the information contained in Figure 9-35.

Table 9-6   Information in Decode of DNS Request Frame 1 shown in Figure 9-34

Question	Answer
Which type of Ethernet frame was used to send the query?	
Which protocol encapsulated the DNS query?	
Is IBMWK using a reliable or unreliable link to the DNS server process on PCSV?	
What is the well-known-port number of the DNS process on PCSV?	
Why is the Ethernet frame source address that of the Cisco router?	

Figure 9-36 shows the detail that opens when you click (+) next to DNS in Figure 9-35.

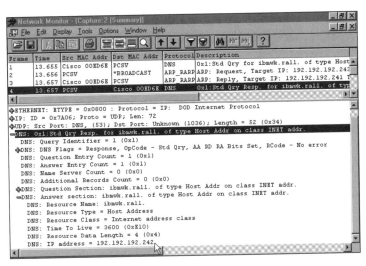

Figure 9-36   DNS server response to ibmwk.ral1 DNS name query

Using the information in Figure 9-36, complete Table 9-7.

Table 9-7   Information in Decode of DNS Reply Frame 4 Shown in Figure 9-36

Question	Answer
Why is the destination MAC address in frame 4 (upper panel) the Cisco router address?	
Is the destination port the same as the source port in Figure 9-34?	
Should it be, and if so, why?	
What IP address did the DNS server return to NCSU?	
How do you know if this is the correct IP address for IBMWK?	
Referring to Figure 9-16, why was it not necessary for the DNS server pcsv.ral1 to send an ibmwk.ral1 domain name resolution request to the root server (.)?	

The sequence of frames in the top panel of Figure 9-36 is instructive. Figure 9-37 diagrams the sequence.

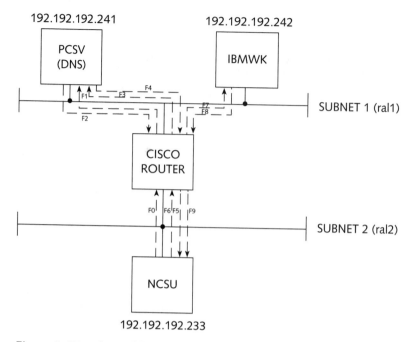

Figure 9-37 Flow of frames generated by the Ping command shown in Figure 9-33

The first frame sent is the DNS domain name resolution request from client NCSU. Let's label this frame F0. F0 is sent to the Cisco router and is therefore not detected by Network Monitor. F1 (Frame 1 in Figure 9-34) is the DNS request repackaged by the router and sent to the DNS server on PCSV. F2 is a broadcast frame from PCSV that contains the ARP_RARP protocol. This is an ARP request frame for the hardware address of the Cisco router on the ral1 interface. PCSV knows the ral1 IP address of the router but needs the hardware address in order to respond to F1. F3 from the router to PCSV is an ARP reply that contains the router's hardware address. F4 is the response from the DNS server to the router, which contains the IP address of ibmwk.ral1. The router repackages the IP address of ibmwk.ral1 and sends it to NCSU in F5. DNS has done its job. Now, the Ping command can be executed on NCSV.

The frames that result from the Ping command are not shown in Figure 9-35 because they are not captured by Network Monitor. F6 is an ICMP echo request from NCSU to 192.192.192.242 (IBMWK). The router repackages the echo request and sends it to IBMWK in F7. IBMWK sends an echo reply to the router in F8. The router repackages it and sends it to NCSU in F9. This is the first of the replies from 192.192.192.242 that you saw in Figure 9-33.

EXERCISE 2—USING WINS MANAGER TO CREATE A PDC WINS SERVER AND A BDC WINS SERVER

1. In WINS Manager, click **Add WINS Server** on the Server menu.
2. In the resulting dialog box, type in the IP address of the PDC, to add it to the WINS Servers list.
3. Click **Add WINS Server** again.
4. In the resulting dialog box, type in the IP address of a BDC, to add it to the WINS Servers list.

EXERCISE 3—USING WINS MANAGER TO CONFIGURE PDC AND BDC REPLICATION PARTNERS

To implement the steps in this exercise, you will need to have one WINS server on a PDC and one WINS server on another PDC or a BDC, as described in Exercise #1. The WINS servers can be on the same Microsoft network, on different subnets, or on different networks. If you do not have these resources, the steps in the exercise will show you what has to be done when the resources become available.

This exercise configures WINS pull and push partners. A pull partner of a WINS server automatically requests a replication of the WINS database of that WINS server at configured intervals. A push partner of a WINS server sends a message to that WINS server telling it to request entries that have been added to the push partner's database since the last replication. The push partner is configured with an update count that triggers the message when the number of updates reaches update count. In general, all WINS servers should be pull and push partners of each other in order to keep the database as current as possible. PDCs and BDCs *must* be both pull and push partners of each other to ensure consistency of primary and backup WINS databases.

1. Click **Replication Partners** on the Server menu to open the window shown in Figure 9-38.
2. Highlight the **BDC** WINS server in WINS Manager.
3. Check **Pull Partner** on the Replication Options panel.
4. Click **Configure**.
5. In the dialog box that opens, type in a Time Interval of 10 minutes, at which time the WINS Server on the BDC should send a request for a WINS database replication to the WINS server on the PDC.
6. Highlight the **PDC WINS server** in WINS Manager.

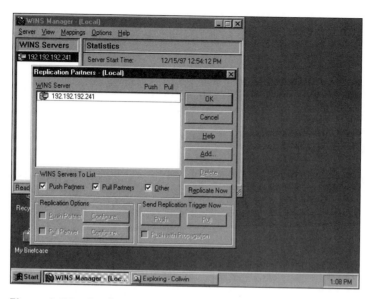

Figure 9-38   Replication Partners (Local)

7. Click **Static Mappings** on the Mappings menu.

8. Type in an IP address and click **Add** to add it to the WINS database.

9. After 10 minutes, highlight the **BDC WINS server**.

10. Click **Show Database** on the Mappings menu to view the WINS database. Was the WINS database on the PDC replicated to the WINS database on the BDC?

EXERCISE 4—CONFIGURATION OF A WINS CLIENT

1. On a workstation, in Control Panel double-click **Network**.

2. In Network, click **Protocols**.

3. Highlight **TCP/IP Protocol** and click **Properties**.

4. Click the **WINS Address** tab.

5. In the Primary WINS Server dialog box, type in the IP address of the PDC.

6. In the Secondary WINS Server dialog box, type in the IP address of the BDC.

7. Click **OK**.

8. Restart the workstation to enable the WINS client.

9. Click **Show Database** on the Mappings menu of the PDC WINS Manager to see the dynamic mappings that have been added by the client.

In the table that follows, write in the IP addresses, NetBIOS names, and the meaning of the 16th byte in the name (refer back to Table 9-4 for the meaning of the 16th byte).

Table 9-8   WINS Database on the PDC

IP Address	NetBIOS Name	Meaning of 16th Byte

EXERCISE 5—CREATING A DNS SERVER ON THE PDC

1. Click **DNS Manager** on the Administrative Tools (common) menu.
2. Right-click the **Server List**.
3. Click **New Server**.
4. Type in the IP address of the PDC.
5. Click **DNS** on DNS Manager.
6. Click **New Zone** on the DNS menu.
7. Check **Primary Zone**. Every DNS domain must have at least one Primary Zone.
8. Click **Next**.
9. Type in a Zone Name for the Primary Zone. Click the Zone File box and accept the file name for the zone that appears.
10. Click **Next** to enter the zone in the list of zones covered by the PDC. The zone that you entered is now part of the PDC's domain.
11. Right-click the zone name.
12. Left-click Refresh.
13. Complete the following table with the information you see in the Zone Info box.

Table 9-9   Zone information for the PDC Zone

Name	Type	Data

EXERCISE 6—ENABLING A DNS CLIENT

1. In Control Panel on a workstation, double-click **Network**.

2. In Network, click the **Protocols** tab.

3. Highlight **TCP/IP Protocol**.

4. Click **Properties**.

5. Click the **DNS** tab.

6. Type in the name of the DNS server host (the PDC in this example).

7. Type in the DNS domain name.

8. Click **Add** to get a dialog box in which you can type the IP address of the DNS server on the PDC. Then click **Add** in this dialog box.

9. Repeat Step 8 if you have other DNS servers on the network. Mappings are examined starting with the DNS server at the top of the DNS Server Search Order box.

10. Click **Add** to add to the Domain Suffix dialog box. After typing in the suffix, click **Add**. A **domain suffix** is the DNS name of the domain to which a workstation belongs. These suffixes are searched in the order in which you add them for the requested IP address of a host.

11. Click **OK**.

12. Restart the workstation to enable the DNS client.

13. At the workstation, open the Command Prompt.

14. Use the Ping command to ping the DNS name of the BDC. Do you get an echo reply from the BDC? If so, DNS is working, because the DNS name has been translated to an IP address in the manner demonstrated in Exercise 1.

EXERCISE 7—ENABLING DNS FOR WINDOWS RESOLUTION

1. On the DNS client-enabled workstation, access Microsoft TCP/IP Properties.

2. Click the **WINS Address** tab.

3. Check the box **Enable DNS for Windows Resolution**.

4. Click **OK**.

5. Click **Close** on the Microsoft TCP/IP Properties window.

6. Restart the workstation to enable DNS and WINS servers collaboration.

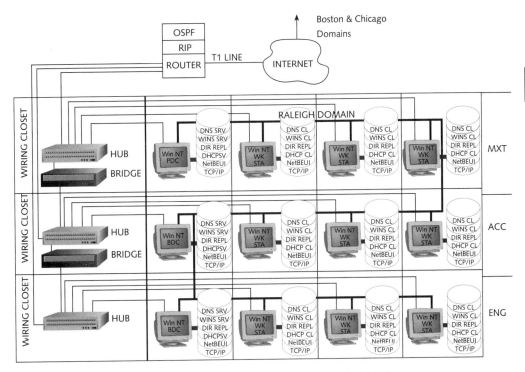

Figure 9-39   Case Project environment after completing Chapter 9

NETWORKING
SERVICES

In this chapter you will examine the features of Windows NT 4.0 that you can use to interface with the Internet and your company's intranet. These features include (1) electronic mail, (2) Remote Access Service (RAS) for dialing into and logging on to your company network and connecting to the Internet through your company network, (3) using Microsoft Internet Information Server to establish FTP, Gopher, and WWW publishing services, and (4) Internet Explorer for browsing the Internet. Implementations of these services depend on TCP/IP protocols that you have studied and on WAN protocols such as Point-to-Point Protocol (PPP) that you will examine in this chapter.

The goal of this chapter is to describe the networking fundamentals that make today's Internet resources accessible. To understand these fundamentals better, it is important to see how they are implemented. Therefore, in addition to the exercises at the end of the chapter, some experiments will be carried out to test the principles as they are being discussed.

IN THIS CHAPTER YOU WILL:

EXAMINE, CONFIGURE, AND USE ELECTRONIC MAIL PROTOCOLS

EXAMINE, CONFIGURE, AND USE RAS PROTOCOLS THAT CONNECT A REMOTE RAS CLIENT TO A RAS SERVER OVER THE PSTN

EXAMINE, CONFIGURE, AND USE MICROSOFT INTERNET INFORMATION SERVER TO SET UP INTERNET PUBLISHING SERVICES

EXAMINE, CONFIGURE, AND USE INTERNET EXPLORER TO BROWSE THE INTERNET

E-MAIL PROTOCOLS

E-mail applications used in the TCP/IP environment depend on the protocols Simple Mail Transport Protocol (SMTP), TCP, IP, Point-to-Point Protocol (PPP), and the Post Office Protocol (POP). A network using these protocols to make the connection between a computer and a remote mail server and between the mail server and the Internet is shown in Figure 10-1.

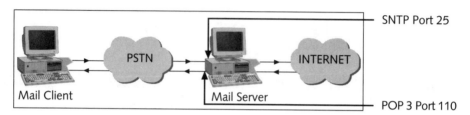

Figure 10-1 Network using PPP, SMTP, and POP 3 to access a remote mail server

Figure 10-1 shows a network configuration in which mail from the Internet is collected by a remote mail server. A **mail server** is a process that manages mailboxes in which received mail is stored and from which it is accessed by a mail client process. The mail client process may be running on the mail server computer, on another computer on the local network, or on a remote standalone computer, as indicated in Figure 10-1. Instead of using a mail server, you could have mail collected by your computer if you wanted to keep your computer on at all times. Most people prefer to use the mail server configuration.

Figure 10-1 also shows that the Public Switched Telephone Network (PSTN) is the WAN that is being used to make the connection between the mail client and the mail server. The connection to the PSTN could be a network modem adapter, an X.25 network PAD adapter, an ISDN network Basic Rate Interface (BRI) adapter, or a leased line.

Point-to-Point Protocol (PPP)

 For more information about PPP, see RFCs 1661 and 1662. A starting point for investigating HDLC is the ISO 3309 document.

The format of a PPP frame is shown in Figure 10-2.

Flag	Address	Control	Protocol	Information	FCS	Flag

Figure 10-2 PPP frame format

On a TCP/IP network, the PPP protocol is used to send and receive mail messages. When the PPP frame is used to send mail, its Information field includes IP, TCP, and SMTP headers and the mail message. **PPP** is a High-Level Data Link Control (HDLC)-type protocol. **HDLC** is the basis for a large number of such protocols, of which one is PPP. HDLC is defined by several ISO documents.

The **Flag** field in the PPP frame is analogous to the Preamble field in the Ethernet frame. It is used when synchronous transmission is employed to synchronize sending and receiving machine bit streams. The Address field is a source address consisting of all ones, the broadcast address. This is point-to-point communication, so there is no need to specify a destination address. The Control field is set to 03hex, which means, in HDLC language, that the frame is an Unnumbered Information (UI) frame. A **UI frame** carries information, and the frames are not numbered or tracked. That role is delegated to TCP. The Protocol field contains a number that identifies the network layer protocol that is being used. PPP can use network layer protocols other than IP. When the connection is established during the "handshaking" process, the Information field contains the Link Control Protocol. The **Link Control Protocol (LCP)** is used to open the connection, negotiate network layer protocols, and close the connection. After the connection is established, the Information field contains network layer and transport layer protocols and mail messages. **FCS** is the frame check sequence, which is used to check for transmission errors. The trailing flag is the same as the leading flag.

10

Simple Mail Transfer Protocol (SMTP)

 For more information about SMTP, see RFCs 821 and 822.

You can send mail to and access mail from a mail server by typing Telnet and the IP address of the mail server at the command prompt, and then typing SMTP or POP commands to send or receive mail, respectively. The descriptions that follow explain these commands in the order in which they occur. Of course, there is application software, such as Microsoft Windows Messaging, that executes these commands for you when you click menu items in the application window. Figure 10-3 shows the content of the PPP frame Information field for SMTP mail messages.

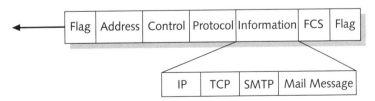

Figure 10-3   SMTP frame

The sequence of SMTP commands and arguments that are sent during the SMTP mail transfer process is described in Table 10-1.

Table 10-1   Description of SMTP Commands

Command	Code	Argument	Description
HELO		domain	This is the first SMTP command sent. HELO stands for Hello. The argument, domain, is the domain name of the host that is initiating the mail session.
OK	250		OK, usually accompanied by some text, is the response to the HELO command if the receiver can receive mail.
Mail From		e-mail address	e-mail address is the address of the sender in the form <sender ID>@<reverse path>. The **reverse path** is a list. The first entry in the list is the domain name of the host that is sending the message. Optional entries are the names of hosts through which the mail should be routed.
OK	250		This is the reply sent by the receiver if the Mail From command is accepted.
RCPT TO		e-mail address	The argument has the form <recipient ID>@<forward path> where **forward path** is an optional list of hosts through which a response should be sent.
OK or Failure	250 or 550	e-mail address	For each argument in the RCPT TO list that is known to the receiver, an OK message is returned. If a recipient is not known, a Failure message is returned.
Data			Indicates that what follows is the message.
	354		Response to Data command if accepted. All succeeding lines are considered to be part of the message.
To:		e-mail address	
From:		e-mail address	
Subject			Optional subject of e-mail.
cc			e-mail addresses of recipients that should receive copies.
bc			e-mail addresses of recipients that should receive copies but are not shown on the cc list.
Attachment		Path to attachment file	Absolute path to the file attachment in the sender's computer.
			Body of mail message.

Table 10-1   Description of SMTP Commands (continued)

Command	Code	Argument	Description
End of text	.		Period (.) signals end of mail message.
OK	250		Indicates that End of mail text was received.
Quit			Request to terminate the connection.
	221	Host name of recipient	Connection closed.

There are other SMTP commands in addition to those previously described. For an explanation of these more specialized commands, see the RFCs mentioned here.

Post Office Protocol (POP)

For more information about POP, see RFC 937 (POP version 2) and RFC 1725 (POP version 3).

POP is used by the mail client to send a request-for-delivery message to the mail server. There are two versions of POP in use, POP 2 and POP 3. Windows NT 4.0 uses POP 3. The commands used by POP 3 are distinct from the set used by POP 2, but the functions performed are much the same. POP 3 has additional security features. The mail application and the mail server support will determine which you should use. Figure 10-4 shows the content of the PPP Information field for a POP 3 mail message.

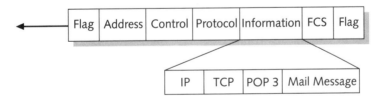

Figure 10-4   POP 3 frame

Table 10-2 describes the basic POP 3 commands.

Table 10-2   Description of POP 3 Commands (xxx = variable number of octets)

Command	Code	Argument	Description
User		user ID	User sends ID.
OK			Response, if user ID is recognized, and request for password.
pass		password	User sends password.

Table 10-2   Description of POP 3 Commands (xxx = variable number of octets) (continued)

Command	Code	Argument	Description
OK			Response if password is authenticated. Number of messages in mailbox folder is specified.
stat			Display the number of unread messages and the total number of bytes.
OK			Includes the number of messages and the total number of bytes.
retr 1			Retrieve message number 1.
OK		xxx octets	Number of octets in message 1 and text of message 1.
dele 1			Delete message 1. Optional.
OK		Message 1 deleted	
retr n			Retrieve message number n.
OK		xxx octets	Number of octets in message n and text of message n.
dele n			Delete message n. Optional.
OK		Message n deleted	
quit			Close the connection.
OK			Connection closed.

There are POP 3 commands in addition to those described in the table. See the RFCs mentioned previously for an explanation of these other commands.

In the next section you will see how dial-up networking is configured in Windows NT to provide access to remote resources. Such resources include mail servers in particular, but in general they are resources provided by server processes in client/server communications.

DIAL-UP NETWORKING

In this section you will examine two Windows NT utilities—Dial-Up Networking and Dial-Up Monitor. These utilities will be used to make and monitor a connection to a remote mail server.

DIAL-UP NETWORKING

Double-clicking My Computer on the desktop of Windows NT workstation ibmwk opens the window shown in Figure 10-5, which contains the Dial-Up Networking utility icon.

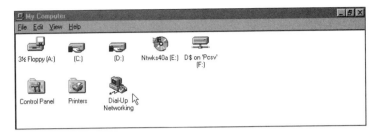

Figure 10-5   Dial-Up Networking utility

Double-clicking the Dial-Up Networking icon produces the screen shown in Figure 10-6, if Dial-Up Networking has been configured previously.

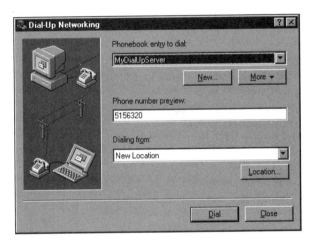

Figure 10-6   Dial-Up Networking

If Dial-Up Networking has not been configured previously, you are presented with Windows NT Wizard screens that walk you through setting up and configuring your modem and then configuring the connection to the remote computer. The configuration information that is saved is automatically labeled My DialUpServer. You can change this name to one that is more descriptive of how this connection profile will be used. The phone number that you see in Phone number preview and "New Location," which you see in Dialing from, were entered during a previous configuration of the remote connection by Windows NT Wizards. The New button provides a screen where you can create another "Phonebook Entry to dial" profile. The More button provides a list that is used to configure "Phonebook Entry to dial." The key item on the More menu is Edit entry and modem properties. Clicking this item opens the screen shown in Figure 10-7.

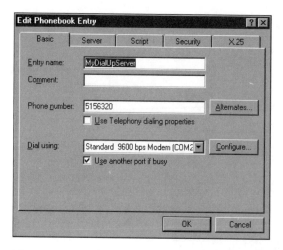

Figure 10-7   The Basic tab of Edit Phonebook Entry

The Entry name textbox contains the Phonebook Entry to dial name, My DialUpServer, seen previously in Figure 10-6. Phone number is also the same as that shown in Figure 10-6. Clicking **Alternates** would open a screen where you could enter alternate phone numbers for the connection specified by Entry name, in case one phone number is busy. "Dial using" specifies the interface that is being used. In this case it is a Standard Modem that is attached to COM2. The term Standard Modem means that this modem is one for which the Universal Modem (unimodem) driver can be used. Clicking Configure would open a screen like that shown in Figure 10-8, where you configure the port COM2, in this example.

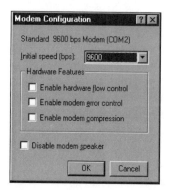

Figure 10-8   Modem Configuration

    You can also configure ports using the Ports utility in Control Panel.

Data compression software used by modems makes it possible to increase the information transfer rate of a modem beyond its maximum speed in bits per second. Data often contains redundant patterns that do not need to be transferred. The receiving modem uses compatible decompression software to expand the data to its original form.

Here you set the Initial speed in bits per second (bps) at which your modem will begin its speed negotiation with the remote modem. In this case an old modem that operates at a maximum speed of 9600 bps is being used. Today, you would typically be using a modem that can operate at speeds up to 33,600 bps. You can enable (1) hardware flow control, (2) modem error control, and (3) modem compression, if your modem supports these features. Modem compression compresses data sent between modems. (It is better to use software compression, which you can select in Figure 10-9. Software compression is an end-to-end compression. Do not use both.)

The Server tab in Figure 10-7 is clicked to open the screen shown in Figure 10-9, where you select and configure the network protocols that will provide the connection to the server for the Dial-Up Networking client.

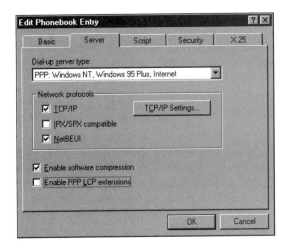

Figure 10-9   Selection of protocols for the connection
to the server

Dial-up server type shows the default WAN protocol PPP that is used by Windows NT, Windows 95, and the Internet. You select the check boxes adjacent to the network layer protocols that you wish the PPP Link Control Protocol (LCP) to negotiate using the handshaking messages between the client and server computers, as shown in Figure 10-9. NetBEUI will not be used if the Dial-Up Networking messages must traverse a router, because the NetBEUI protocol stack does not have a network layer. The Enable software compression option allows you to opt for software compression, as discussed previously. The Enable PPP LCP extensions option should be selected if these extensions are supported by the version of PPP used by the server computer. **PPP LCP extensions** allow

PPP to provide additional configuration status, for example, sending echo messages to test connectivity. Clicking TCP/IP Settings opens the screen shown in Figure 10-10.

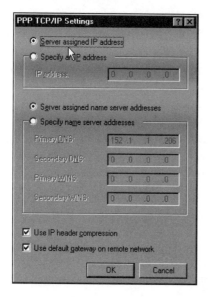

Figure 10-10   PPP TCP/IP Settings

Clicking the Server assigned IP address button means that the client will send a request to a DHCP server for an IP address lease. The Server assigned name server addresses button is clicked if you want the server to provide DNS and WINS server IP addresses that your computer can access for name resolution. As you can see in the example shown in Figure 10-10, the DHCP server returned an address of 152.1.1.206 for the DNS server. As you saw in Chapter 9, "Name Services," WINS and DNS databases contain host name to IP address mappings and domain name if enabled, to IP address mappings, respectively. The resolver on your computer would access one of these name server IP addresses to obtain the IP address for the host ibmwk2 in one of the following ways:

Name Service	Name Provided by Resolver	IP Address returned
WINS server	ibmwk2	192.192.192.242
DNS server	ibmwk2.raleigh.com.	192.192.192.242

Check Use IP header compression if you want this compression to be implemented. Check Use default gateway on remote network if your computer is attached to a LAN that has a router, but you want the router on the remote network to route packets. OK is clicked to return to Figure 10-9.

The Script tab in Figure 10-9 can be used to cause a terminal window to open after the connection is established, if the remote computer requires a user ID and password to be entered interactively. Also, you can create a script that will run after the connection is established.

The Security tab provides password encryption options that can be used, depending on the types supported by the server.

The X.25 tab is used to configure a network Packet Assembler/Dissassembler (**PAD**) adapter interface to a packet-switched network, as mentioned before.

The configuration of the Phonebook entry to dial is now complete, and OK would be clicked to return to Figure 10-6. At this point, you would click Dial to cause PPP to negotiate a connection with the remote server. If you are going to use e-mail, you then open Windows Messaging or another e-mail application, and create and send an e-mail message.

You will often want to know how Dial-Up Networking is performing. This can be done with Dial-Up Monitor, as explained in the next section.

DIAL-UP MONITOR

The Dial-Up Monitor utility collects port statistics and displays the configuration of the dial-up interface. Figure 10-11 shows how to access Dial-Up Monitor from Control Panel.

10

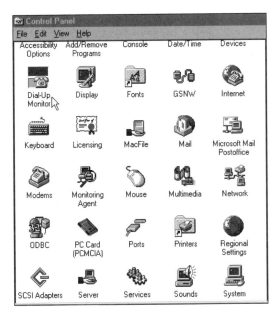

Figure 10-11   Control Panel and the Dial-Up Monitor icon

Double-clicking Dial-Up Monitor on PCSV opens the screen shown in Figure 10-12.

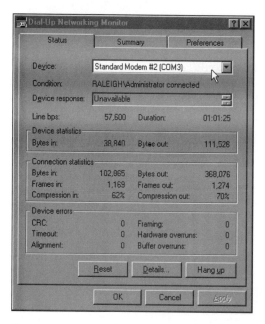

Figure 10-12   Dial-Up Networking Monitor Status tab

Device is the device Standard Modem #2 that is connected to COM3 on PCSV.
Condition indicates that Administrator on the Raleigh domain is logged on to the remote
computer. **Device response**, when provided, is the feedback from the modem that
describes the modem protocol that is being used, such as V.34bis. According to the Help text
provided when you click the question mark (?) at the top right of the screen and then click
on Line bps, **Line bps** is the speed in bits per second at which data is being transferred
between modems. (The value 57,600 that is being reported is actually the maximum speed
configured for this modem.) Under Device statistics, **Bytes in:** is the number of compressed
bytes that have been received during **Duration**, and **Bytes out:** is the number of decompressed bytes that were sent during **Duration**. Under Connection statistics, **Bytes in:** is the
number of decompressed bytes received during **Duration**, and **Bytes out:** is the number of
compressed bytes sent over the connection during **Duration**. **Compression in:** is the ratio
of bytes not sent to decompressed bytes received. The formula for Compression in is:

$$\text{Compression in} = \frac{\text{Connection statistics } \textbf{Bytes in} - \text{Device Statistics } \textbf{Bytes in}}{\text{Connection statistics } \textbf{Bytes in}}$$

For the numbers on the screen :

$$\text{Compression in} = \frac{102,865 - 38,840}{102,865} = 62\%$$

Under Device errors are listed the different types of errors that can occur over the connection and the number of times they have happened during Duration. The buttons at the bottom of the window allow you to Reset the statistics to zero, get network configuration Details, or Hang up the connection. The screen provided by clicking Details will be discussed when it is used later in this chapter. The Summary and Preferences tabs are of minor importance for the purposes of this discussion.

In the next section we will examine the principal screens provided by Windows Messaging that enable you to configure Windows Messaging, create messages, manage messages, and use Dial-Up Networking, PPP, SMTP, and POP 3 to send and access mail messages.

WINDOWS MESSAGING

Inbox is the icon on the Desktop that opens Windows Messaging. (You can also open Windows Messaging from the Programs menu.)

Figure 10-13   Desktop Inbox

Clicking Inbox twice produces the screen shown in Figure 10-14, where you start the process of configuring Windows Messaging.

10

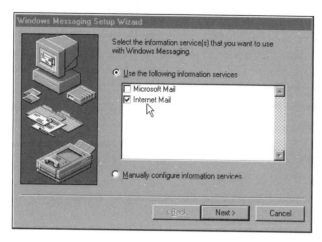

Figure 10-14   Windows Messaging Setup Wizard

From this screen, the Windows NT Wizard program opens a series of screens that walk you through the configuration of Windows Messaging. Most of the information that is requested was provided when Dial-Up Networking was configured in an earlier section of this chapter. However a couple of the screens in this series contain mail-server–specific information that is instructive. The first of these is shown in Figure 10-15.

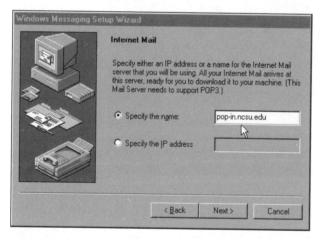

Figure 10-15   Internet Mail—mail server address

On this screen you specify either the DNS domain name or the IP address of your mail server. In this case the DNS domain name pop-in.ncsu.edu was entered. Pop-in is the mail server pop-in on the domain ncsu.edu. The screen shown in Figure 10-16 is a summary of Internet Mail configuration data that was entered in the sequence of Wizard screens mentioned previously.

Figure 10-16   Internet Mail—configuration summary

10

Clicking the Advanced Options button opens the screen shown in Figure 10-17.

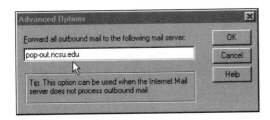

Figure 10-17   Advanced Options

If your mail system uses one mail server for inbound mail, for example pop-in.ncsu.edu, and another mail server for outbound mail, for example pop-out.ncsu.edu, this is the screen on which you enter the outbound mail server domain name.

After all configuration screens are completed, you arrive at the Windows Messaging Inbox screen, which is shown in Figure 10-18.

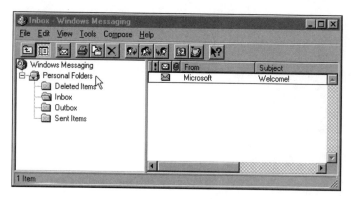

Figure 10-18   Windows Messaging Inbox

The left panel of this screen is a list of your Personal Folders in which mail is stored, and the right panel lists the mail that is in the folder that is open. The Compose menu provides access to a very convenient form on which messages can be composed, and the Tools menu contains the items (1) Remote Mail, which allows you to access a list of your mail messages stored on the mail server, and (2) Deliver Now, which sends and accesses your messages immediately. When you click on Remote Mail on the Tools menu and then click Connect on the Remote Mail Tools menu, you are executing the POP 3 command List. When you click Deliver Now on the Windows Messaging Tools menu, you are starting the series of SMTP and POP 3 commands described in Tables 10-1 and 10-2.

In the next section you examine the Windows NT Remote Access Service (RAS). RAS uses Dial-Up Networking to provide and authenticate remote access to Windows NT Domain resources.

REMOTE ACCESS SERVICE (RAS)

The Windows NT RAS server makes it possible for a RAS client to log on to a domain from a remote computer by using the Dial-Up Networking utility, PPP, a modem, and the PSTN. The remote client can use either NetBEUI, IPX, or TCP/IP transport over the PSTN. Only TCP/IP is used if the Internet is part of the connection, unless there is a gateway that translates other protocol stacks to TCP/IP for the Internet path. PPP is the WAN protocol used by RAS. If the RAS client wants to access the Internet, the client can dial in over the PSTN, use NetBEUI, log on to the domain, and then access the Internet through a NetBEUI-to-TCP/IP gateway on the domain. Figure 10-19 shows the connectivity that can be provided by RAS.

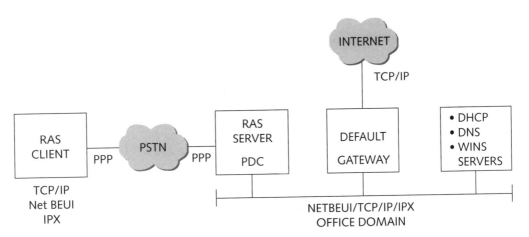

Figure 10-19   Connectivity provided by RAS

The RAS server is configured from Control Panel and the Network dialog box. Figure 10-20 shows the Services tab of Network on the Windows NT 4.0 Server PCSV. RAS has already been installed. If that were not the case, you would click Add to get a list of services from which you could install it.

10

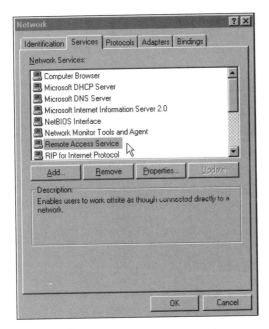

Figure 10-20   Network Services tab

To configure the RAS server, you highlight Remote Access Services and click Properties to obtain the screen shown in Figure 10-21, which shows that the RAS server interface is COM3 on the server PCSV.

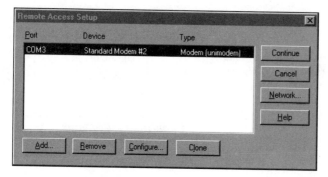

Figure 10-21 Remote Access Setup

Clicking Configure opens the screen shown in Figure10-22, where you specify how COM3 will be used by the RAS server. The button selected configures the port to Dial out and Receive calls.

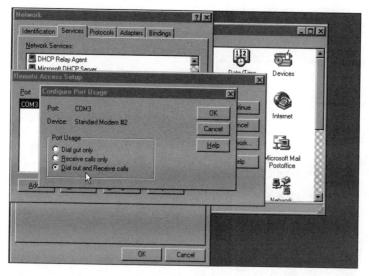

Figure 10-22 Configure Port Usage

Clicking OK returns you to the screen in Figure 10-21. This time you click Network to open the screen shown in Figure 10-23, where you configure the network protocols that RAS can use.

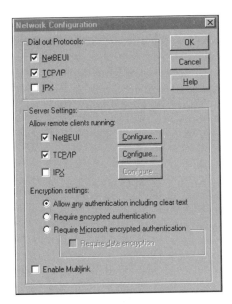

Figure 10-23   RAS Network Configuration

10

RAS client/server connectivity can be established by the three protocol stacks shown—NetBEUI, TCP/IP, and IPX. We have previously specified that clear text authentication is allowed. Thus that button is selected. To configure how each protocol will be used, you would click Configure next to that protocol. For example, clicking the Configure button next to TCP/IP opens the screen shown in Figure 10-24.

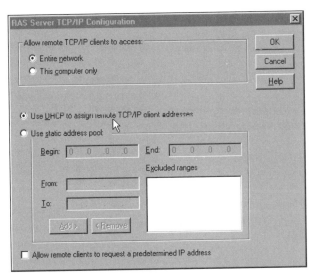

Figure 10-24   RAS Server TCP/IP Configuration

The top panel in Figure 10-24 shows that you can allow the RAS client to access all computers on the domain(s) for which the RAS client is authenticated, or just to access the computer that is hosting the RAS server. The middle panel gives you the option to have DHCP provide an IP address for the RAS client computer, or to configure the RAS server to assign IP addresses from an address pool that it maintains. At the bottom of the screen, you can check a box that will allow remote clients to request a predetermined IP address.

It is now time to try out the RAS client and server connection. Figure 10-25 shows the network that will be used to do that.

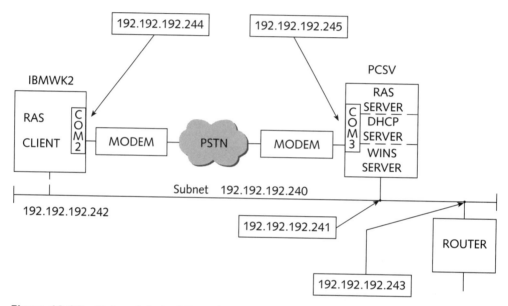

Figure 10-25   Network to test RAS client/server communications

IBMWK2 is the RAS client host. The IBMWK2 Ethernet interface 192.192.192.242 has been disconnected so that IBMWK2 will be sure to register its name using the WAN. PCSV is the RAS server host. The WAN connection between IBMWK2 and PCSV is made using the PSTN, two phone lines, and two modems. IBMWK2 will dial up on one of the lines and PCSV will answer on the other. Thus we are emulating a situation in which IBMWK2 is a remote computer dialing up the PDC on the office network to access resources on the office domain and other trusted domains.

On My Computer on the Desktop of IBMWK2, double-clicking Dial-Up Networking opens the screen shown in Figure 10-26. Notice that a new "Phonebook entry to dial" profile, with the name pcsv-ibmwk2, has been created.

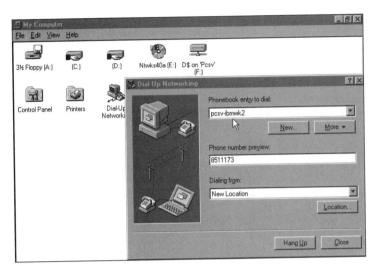

Figure 10-26   Dial-Up Networking phone book entry

Clicking Dial dials the number 8511173 of the RAS server, PCSV. You then see a window telling you that the number is being dialed and, if the connection is made, you see the screen shown in Figure 10-27. You can also "logon using dial-up networking," when you first start the remote computer, by clicking that check box.

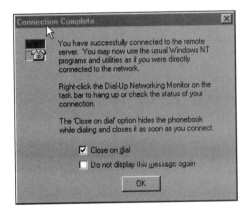

Figure 10-27   Connection Complete

To look at what is happening on the connection, you double-click Dial-Up Monitor on Control Panel to get the screen shown in Figure 10-28.

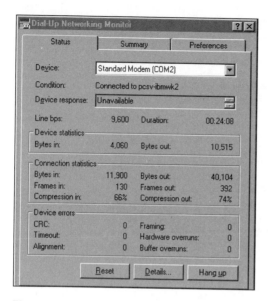

Figure 10-28   Dial-Up Networking Monitor—COM2

These are the connection statistics for the COM2 interface on IBMWK2 after the connection has been open for 24 minutes and 8 seconds. The screen shown in Figure 10-29 shows the statistics at almost the same time, 24 minutes and 12 seconds, for the COM3 interface on PCSV.

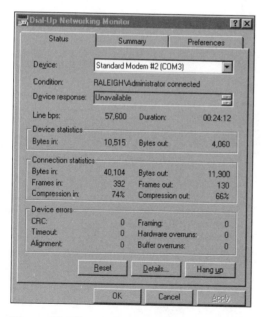

Figure 10-29   Dial-Up Networking Monitor—COM3

In Figures 10-28 and 10-29 you see, under Device Statistics for example, that Bytes in: for COM2 is the same as Bytes out: for COM3, and that Bytes in: for COM3 is the same as Bytes out: for COM2.

In order to make the dial-up connection work with TCP/IP, it was necessary to configure DHCP so that it would provide IP addresses to the dial-up interfaces COM2 and COM3. As was discussed in Chapter 7, "The Dynamic Host Configuration Protocol (DHCP)," you do this on the DHCP Manager screen, which can be accessed from the Administrative Tools (common) menu. To see how this was done, start with the DHCP Manager screen shown in Figure 10-30.

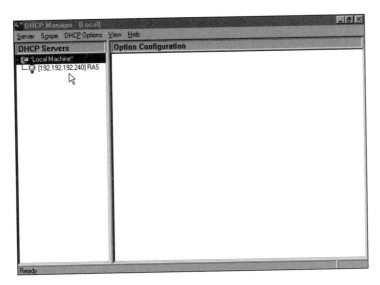

Figure 10-30   DHCP Manager

It is necessary to create a scope for the subnet to which IBMWK2 is connected by the dial-up connection. Local Machine in Figure 10-30 refers to PCSV, the computer that is hosting the DHCP server. 192.192.192.240 is the address of the subnet to which IBMWK2 is attached. You would create a scope for this subnet by clicking Create on the Scope menu. This produces the Scope Properties form shown in Figure 10-31, which has been completed with the numbers that are being used for the test.

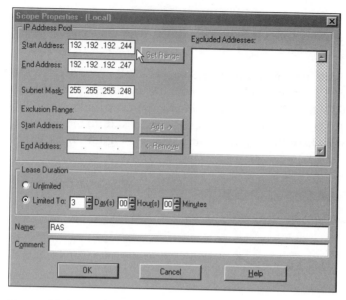

Figure 10-31   Scope Properties

The IP Address Pool, with a Start Address of 192.192.192.244 and an End Address of 192.192.192.247, has been made available to DHCP. No addresses in this range have been excluded. The following table lists the devices on the subnet 192.192.192.240.

Table 10-3   IP Addresses of the Devices on the
Subnet 192.192.192.240

Device	IP Address
PCSV on Ethernet	192.192.192.241
RAS server	192.192.192.241
DHCP server	192.192.192.241
Default Gateway on Ethernet	192.192.192.243
Subnet	192.192.192.240
Subnet Mask	255.255.255.248
PCSV COM 3 on WAN	Assigned by DHCP
IBMWK COM 2 on WAN	Assigned by DHCP

You can see what IP address assignments DHCP has made by using the Ipconfig command on the Command Prompt screen. Typing ipconfig /all | more at the command prompt on IBMWK2 produced the screen shown in Figure 10-32.

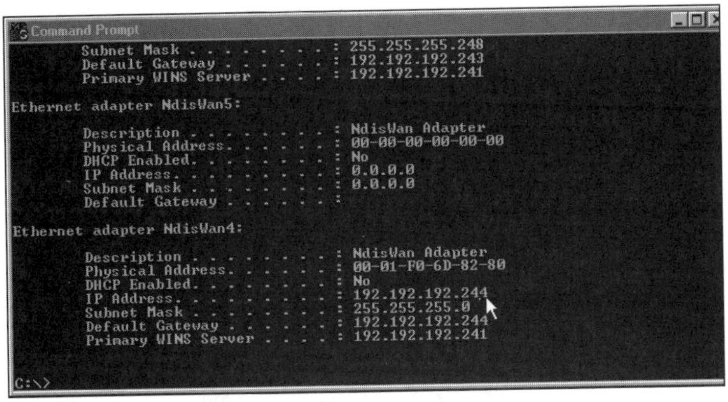

Figure 10-32   IP Configuration of Interfaces on IBMWK2

The last set of data shown indicates that the interface is an NdisWan adapter. **NDIS** is Network Device Interface Standard. NdisWan refers to a virtual WAN adapter that is a software interface to the physical interface labeled COM2. In this case, the physical adapter is connected to a modem that is using PPP to connect to the PSTN. The physical address of the adapter is 00-01-F0-6D-82-80. DHCP has assigned the IP Address 192.192.192.244 to COM2, which is one of the addresses in the IP Address Pool configured in Figure 10-31.

Figure 10-33 shows configuration data obtained when ipconfig /all | more was typed at the Command Prompt on PCSV.

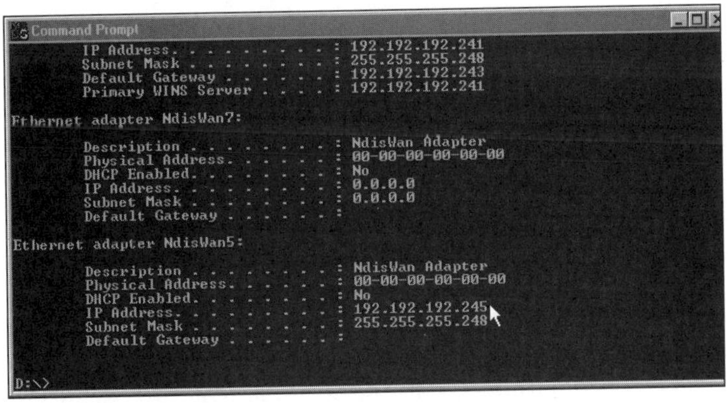

Figure 10-33   IP Configuration of Interfaces on PCSV

You see that the COM3 NdisWan Adapter was assigned the IP address 192.192.192.245 from the DHCP IP address pool. The physical address of COM3 was not provided.

Now that we have the RAS connection between the remote RAS client computer IBMWK2 and the RAS server computer PCSV on the domain, we should have access to files on the domain computers that have been shared. Let's see if we do. On IBMWK2, the domain browser Network Neighborhood is clicked, and then PCSV is double-clicked to produce the screens shown in Figure 10-34.

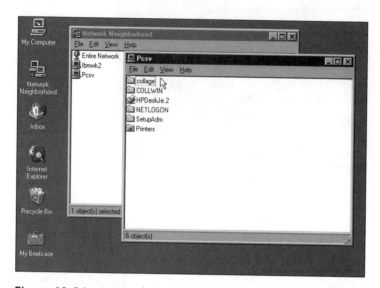

Figure 10-34   Network Neighborhood (left) and PCSV shared files (right)

The listing of shared files on PCSV has been transferred to IBMWK2. Thus RAS is work-ing and IBMWK2 can access all resources on the domain that are sharable and for which the remote account has the appropriate permissions. When you are finished with the remote connection, you can Hang Up either by clicking that button on Dial-Up Networking Monitor or by clicking it on Dial-Up Networking.

In the next section you will configure Microsoft Internet Information Server to provide FTP, Gopher, and WWW services to Internet users, and you will use the Internet browser to access these services using the PSTN, as you did to test the RAS configuration.

MICROSOFT INTERNET INFORMATION SERVER (IIS)

IIS is installed from Network on Control Panel. If it was installed at the same time as Windows NT Server, it will be listed under Network Services on the Services tab. If it does not appear on that list, click Add to obtain the list of all Network Services. You would then highlight Microsoft Internet Information Server 2.0 on that list and click OK. The screen shown in Figure 10-35 opens, and you specify where the installation files are to be located.

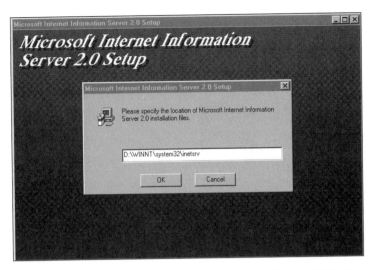

Figure 10-35   Microsoft Internet Information Server 2.0 Setup

Clicking OK opens the screen shown in Figure 10-36, where you select the Internet services you want to install.

10

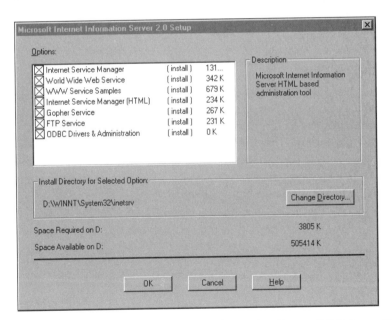

Figure 10-36   Microsoft Internet Information Server 2.0 Setup—Options

Before making selections, click Help to get an overview of what each service provides. Then check the boxes next to the services that you wish to install and click OK. The screen shown in Figure 10-37 opens and shows the default directories for the WWW, FTP, and Gopher publishing directories.

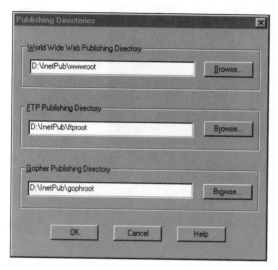

Figure 10-37   Default Publishing Directories for WWW, FTP, and Gopher Files

These are the home directories for the files that you make available to Internet clients. Clicking OK will show the services that you have selected being installed. A screen then opens where you can select Open Database Connection (ODBC) drivers for data sources. Only one driver, that for the SQL server, is available. Highlight that driver and then click OK on this screen and the one that follows. The Services tab in Network opens, and you should see Microsoft Internet Information Server 2.0 in the Network Services list. After clicking Close on the Network screen, you would access the Microsoft Internet Server (Common) menu, which is shown in Figure 10-38.

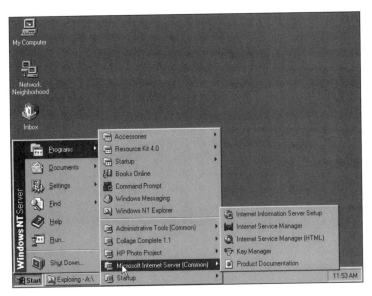

Figure 10-38   Microsoft Internet Server (Common) menu

Clicking Product Documentation will give you a thorough description of the many features
provided by Microsoft Internet Information Server. Then you click Internet Server Manager
to see the screen shown in Figure 10-39, where you start to set up the publishing services.

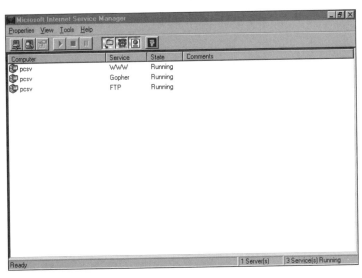

Figure 10-39   Microsoft Internet Server Manager

Figure 10-39 lists the three publishing services, WWW, Gopher, and FTP, that were installed.
Let's examine each in turn, beginning with the FTP service.

FTP SERVICE

Highlighting the FTP line and clicking Service Properties on the Properties menu opens the screen shown in Figure 10-40.

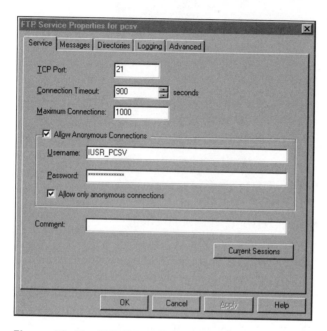

Figure 10-40   FTP Service Properties for PCSV

On the Service tab you see the well-known TCP Port 21, at which an FTP server listens for FTP client connection requests. In Connection Timeout you enter the amount of time that a client can keep the connection open. In Maximum Connections you limit the number of connections that can access this port simultaneously. If you check the box Allow Anonymous Connections, neither a user ID nor a password is required to access files from the home directory. However, the entries in the Username and Password text boxes that follow control anonymous user access. An anonymous user has only the rights and permissions assigned to the IUSR_PCSV account. This is typically what you want to do to protect your resources. Checking the lower check box means that *only* anonymous logons will be allowed. The Current Sessions button provides a screen where you can see who is connected to the service and for how long.

Clicking the Messages tab opens a screen where you can create a Welcome Message to be read by clients. Clicking Directories opens the screen shown in Figure 10-41.

Figure 10-41   Directories

The Directory D:\InetPub\ftproot is the default directory for FTP files. As mentioned previously, this is the home directory for published FTP files. You can also publish FTP files in other directories that are called **virtual directories**. They are called virtual because, to a browser application, they appear to be subdirectories of the home directory. To access these virtual directories, the Universal Resource Locator (URL) address must include the alias for the path to the virtual directory. Thus when the browser uses the URL ftp://ibmsv.ibm.com/money it is requesting that the real directory, for which /money is an alias, be opened. This real directory-to-alias mapping would appear on the screen shown in Figure 10-41. If instead the browser used the URL address ftp://ibmsv.ibm.com/, the home directory ftproot would be opened. To create a home (real) or virtual directory, click Add on the Directories tab to open the screen in Figure 10-42.

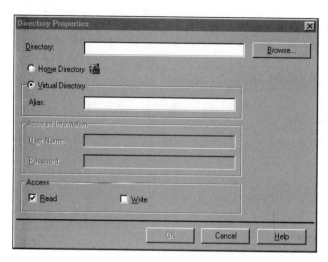

Figure 10-42 Directory Properties

You Browse for or type in the path to the Home Directory or the Virtual Directory in the Directory box, click either the Home Directory or Virtual Directory button, and enter the virtual alias if that was the type of directory created. The Account Information is added only if the Directory name is a Universal Naming Convention (UNC) name for a directory that is shared on the network. A **UNC** name has the form

//<computername>/<shared directory name>

where <computer name> is the name of the computer that is sharing <shared directory name>. You typically provide only Read access to your FTP directories, but you can check Write to allow files to be put into the publishing directories.

Returning to Figure 10-40, you see that there are two more tabs that have not been discussed. The Logging tab is used to create a log of FTP sessions and their users, and the Advanced tab is used to specify the IP address of computers that will not be allowed access to the FTP service. Now let's return to Figure 10-39 and examine the properties of the WWW service.

WWW SERVICE

In Figure 10-39, you highlight the WWW service, and on the Properties menu click Service Properties to open the screen shown in Figure 10-43.

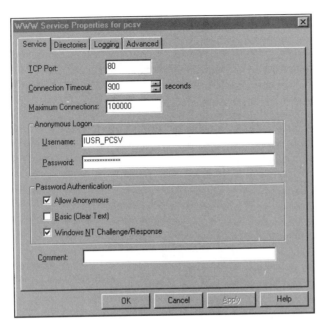

Figure 10-43   WWW Service Properties for PCSV

The primary differences between the WWW Service Properties for PCSV screen and the FTP Service Properties screen that you saw in Figure 10-40 are that the WWW TCP Port is 80 and Password Authentication is more extensive. If Allow Anonymous is not checked, the two access options are Basic (Clear Text) and Windows NT Challenge/Response.

Basic (Clear Text) Password Authentication

If used by itself, Basic (Clear Text) requires a user ID and password for access to the WWW service, but the user ID and password are not encrypted for transmission. When used with the Secure Sockets Layer (SSL), a Presentation layer protocol in the language of the OSI model, Basic (Clear Text) provides:

- Security handshaking that results in the client and server agreeing on a level of security.

- Encryption of the Application layer segment transmitted to the WWW server. This includes the URL, credit card numbers, user names, and passwords, for example.

- Encryption of the data returned from the server to the client.

Enabling SSL requires that encryption keys be created and that certification of those keys be obtained from an official body. Use Key Manager on the Microsoft Internet Server (Common) menu and its Help menu to learn how to obtain the keys necessary to implement SSL.

Windows NT Challenge/Response

This approach to authentication is the standard Microsoft Network authentication that was discussed in Chapter 8, "Windows NT Domains." It is currently supported only by Microsoft Internet Explorer 2.0 and later versions. Authentication is provided by requiring that the client user account be valid on the domain server computer that is running the WWW service.

Both Allow Anonymous and Windows NT Challenge/Response check boxes can be checked at the same time. If the client or server does not use Windows NT Challenge/Response, the connection will use Anonymous "authentication."

Clicking Directories on the screen shown in Figure 10-43 opens the screen shown in Figure 10-44.

Figure 10-44   Directories

Here you see that one home directory, D:\InetPub\wwwroot, and two virtual directories, /script and /iisadmin, were created automatically during the installation process. Enable Default Document is checked so that if these directories are accessed and they are empty, the client will see the Default.htm file. If Directory Browsing Allowed is checked and you have subdirectories in your home or virtual directories, the client will be shown a listing of subdirectories that can be browsed. To add more directories, click the Add button to obtain the Directory Properties screen. This Directory Properties screen is the same one you saw for FTP in Figure 10-42.

Now let's return to Figure 10-39 and examine the Gopher service.

Gopher Service

The Gopher service provides access to Gopher servers worldwide when you access any Gopher server. Clicking Service Properties on the Properties menu opens the Gopher Services screen shown in Figure 10-45.

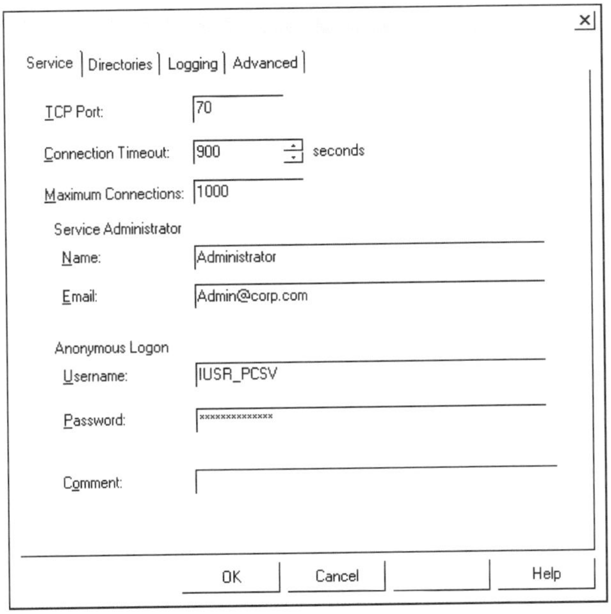

Figure 10-45   Gopher Service Properties for PCSV

The Gopher TCP Port is 70. The data under Service Administrator is what will be reported to the Gopher client, depending upon which Gopher server you access. The Administrator is the person responsible for the Gopher service at corp.com. Gopher allows only anonymous logons. Clicking the Directories tab opens a screen showing the Gopher directories that have been created. In this case, it is the home directory D:\InetPub\gophroot. Clicking Add on this screen opens a screen of the type you have seen for the FTP and WWW services, where Gopher directories can be added.

Now that you have seen how to manage the three services that are provided by IIS, let's go through the steps of actually implementing the WWW service.

WWW SERVICE IMPLEMENTATION

Figure 10-46 shows the experimental arrangement that will be used.

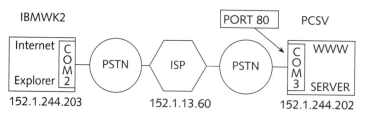

Figure 10-46   Network for testing the WWW service

As was done for the test of RAS, two telephone lines, two modems, and PPP are used to make the connection between the WWW service running on one computer and a Dial-Up Networking client running on another computer. Each computer uses Dial-Up Networking to make a circuit-switched connection through the PSTN to the Internet Service Provider (ISP). The ISP routes the request for the WWW service to the server and port that are running the WWW service, and routes the reply to the WWW client. In this experiment, the computers running the WWW service and the WWW client are in the same room. They could just as well be across the world from one another. In order for the client and the server computers to communicate, their interfaces must have IP addresses. We rely on the DHCP service being run by the ISP to lease temporary IP addresses to each of these interfaces and to provide a DNS server IP address. DHCP support is configured in Figure 10-47.

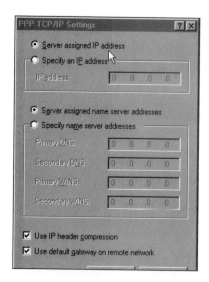

Figure 10-47   Dial-Up Networking DHCP IP configuration

The first button, Server assigned IP address, is selected so that the ISP DHCP server will assign an IP address to the serial interface to which the modem on the client is attached. Dial-Up Networking for the computer running the WWW service is likewise configured. When the button Server assigned name server addresses is selected, the ISP is being asked to send an IP address that can be accessed in case DNS resolution is needed. Then, on both computers, Dial is clicked on their Dial-Up Networking screens. PPP connections are made to the ISP and account IDs, and Passwords are verified. Clicking the Dial-Up Monitor on Control Panel for each computer allows you to see that connections have been made; then click Details to see the IP address leases provided by the DHCP server at the ISP. Figures 10-48 and 10-49 show the Dial-Up Networking configurations that were created by the DHCP server at the ISP for COM2 on WWW client IBMWK2 and for COM3 on WWW server PCSV. These IP addresses have been added to Figure 10-46 and included in Table 10-4.

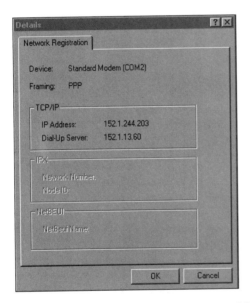

Figure 10-48   Network Registration—COM2

Table 10-4   IP Addresses of the Devices on the Network in Figure 10-45

Device	IP Address
COM2	152.1.244.203
COM3	152.1.244.202
ISP Dial-Up Server	152.1.13.60

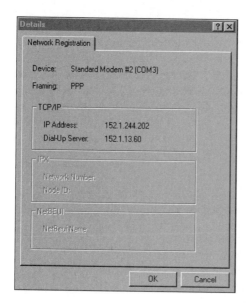

Figure 10-49   Network Registration—COM3

Now that a TCP/IP network has been established between the client and the server, we can use Internet Explorer on the client to access the WWW service on the server. We will attempt to access the WWW home directory because that directory contains WWW service samples that we can examine. We begin from the Windows NT desktop, which is shown in Figure 10-50.

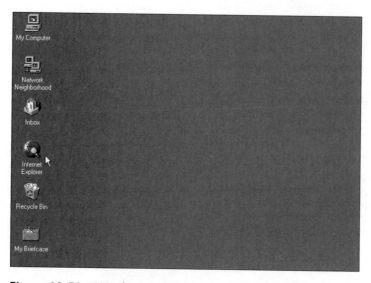

Figure 10-50   Windows NT Desktop—Internet Explorer

The pointer points to Internet Explorer, which is double-clicked to open the screen shown in Figure 10-51.

MICROSOFT INTERNET EXPLORER

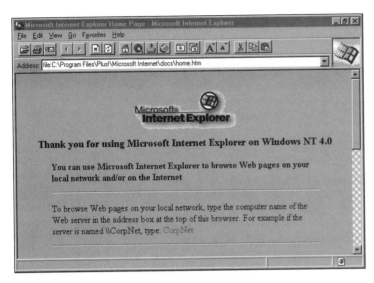

Figure 10-51   Microsoft Internet Explorer home page

The Address text box specifies the location of this file, home.htm, on IBMWK2. Although not shown in its entirety in Figure 10-51, this page discusses the resources you need to browse Web pages on the Internet and gives some useful Microsoft addresses from which you can get product and technical information. To begin the process of opening a file on the WWW server, the File menu in Figure 10-51 is clicked to open the screen shown in Figure 10-52.

10

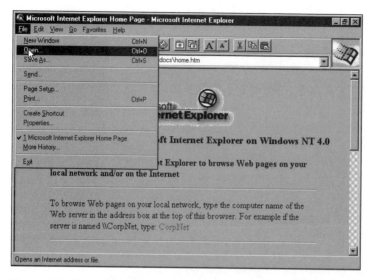

Figure 10-52 File menu on Microsoft Internet Explorer home page

Clicking Open opens the screen shown in Figure 10–53, where a WWW address is entered.

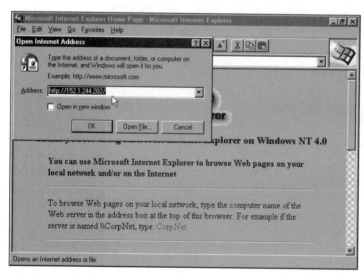

Figure 10-53 IP address of PCSV

This is the IP address of the serial interface of the computer PCSV, leased by a DHCP server on the ISP network, that is hosting the WWW server. Http is the Application layer protocol that is used. The address 152.1.244.202/ ensures us that the open request will open the home directory wwwroot. If the computer that is hosting the WWW server has a domain name authorized by the InterNIC, you will usually enter the domain name rather than the IP address. OK is clicked to open the wwwroot directory. In Figure 10-54, you see the default.htm file in the wwwroot directory that is opened and returned to the WWW client.

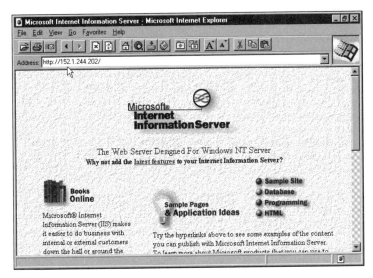

Figure 10-54   WWW home directory default.htm file

Notice, in the Address text box, that the IP address of the WWW server is the same as was requested by the WWW client. As was mentioned previously, default.htm is the file that is returned when there are no subdirectories in the home directory to browse, or when "Directory Browsing Allowed" is not checked on the Directories tab of the WWW Service Properties screen. Both are the case here.

Figure 10-55 shows the contents of home directory D:\InetPub\wwwroot.

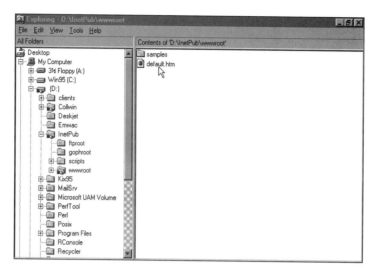

Figure 10-55   Contents of D:\InetPub\wwwroot

In Figure 10-55, you see that in addition to the default.htm file, wwwroot contains a samples folder. If the HTML button on the right of the screen shown in Figure 10-54 is clicked, you can access the sample HTML file in this folder. You can also explore other files in the samples folder to learn about how to construct HTML files that can be read by Internet browsers. A vivid snapshot of an animation, for which the HTML code is provided in the samples folder, is shown in Figure 10-56. Notice the 3D effects.

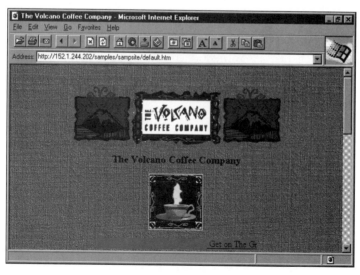

Figure 10-56   The Volcano Coffee Company

CHAPTER SUMMARY

- You learned about the format of the protocols PPP, SMTP, and POP 3 and how those protocols are used to establish an e-mail system that is based on the transport layers of the TCP/IP protocol stack.

- The typical method of implementing an e-mail system is to install a mail server service on a computer that is available at all times. This mail server service uses the Application layer protocol SMTP to transmit mail from you to the Internet, where it is routed to the recipient, and to receive mail for you from the Internet and store it in your mailbox folder.

- You access mail from your mailbox using the POP 3 protocol.

- The Microsoft Windows Messaging e-mail application program (Inbox) gives you the graphical tools to create, send, access, store, and manage e-mail messages.

- You learned how to set up the Microsoft Dial-Up Networking utility to provide a dial-up connection profile that includes the phone number of your mail server, alternate phone numbers, the serial port of your computer and its configuration, modem configuration, network protocols and their configuration, how the IP address of your computer is configured, and how to configure the IP addresses of name resolution services.

- The Dial-Up Monitor utility provides real-time information about traffic through the serial interface being monitored and the current IP address of your serial interface and that of the interface with which it is communicating.

- Remote Access Service (RAS), which is provided by Windows NT 4.0 Server, makes it possible for a remote RAS client to use the Dial-Up Networking utility and the PSTN to connect to a PDC or BDC computer and access domain resources as if the client were attached directly to a network in the domain.

- To test a RAS connection you can use one computer as a RAS client and another computer as a RAS server, connect them through two lines to the PSTN, dial using the Dial-Up Networking utility, use DHCP to provide dynamic IP addresses for the two serial ports from the DHCP scope that you created, monitor the serial ports of each computer using Dial-Up Monitor, and then use the Network Neighborhood domain browser to transfer a list of sharable files on the RAS server to the RAS client.

- You learned about Microsoft Internet Information Server (IIS) and how to use it to set up Internet FTP, WWW, and Gopher publishing directories.

- By applying networking security principles, the WWW service that you provide can be protected from intrusion. IIS Key Manager provides a mechanism by which you obtain a secret key that is used with a public key to encrypt your messages using the Rivest, Shamir, Adelman (RSA) Public Encryption algorithm.

- You can test your WWW publishing service using the PSTN, two phone lines, two modems, and an Internet Service Provider (ISP). After connecting the two

10

computers through the ISP using the Dial-Up Networking utility, Microsoft Internet Explorer browser was used on the WWW client computer to open the WWW home directory on the WWW server computer and to transfer the default.htm file from the home directory to the WWW client.

REVIEW QUESTIONS

1. SMTP is a TCP/IP protocol. To which layer in the TCP/IP protocol stack is it assigned?

   a. Transport

   b. Application

   c. Internet

2. Why do you typically place a mail server service on a computer other than your own?

   a. A computer running a mail service must have multiple NICs.

   b. A mail service server requires extremely high processor speed.

   c. I do not want to keep my computer on at all times to receive mail.

3. What security precautions are implemented on a mail server to ensure that only you can read your mail?

   a. A mailbox is assigned to your name.

   b. A mailbox account is established by assigning you a user ID and password.

   c. Your IP address in the POP frame is read to authenticate you.

4. Why is a PPP frame or equivalent used to encapsulate TCP/IP protocols when sending mail to and receiving mail from a remote mail server?

   a. Because it is a WAN protocol that is recognized by the devices used to make a point-to-point remote link

   b. Because it provides control of message flow

   c. Because it numbers frames that are sent

5. Which protocol provides your authentication ID and password to the mail server?

   a. SMTP

   b. POP 3

   c. PPP

6. During the handshaking process between serial devices at each end of a point-to-point WAN, PPP uses Link Control Protocols to negotiate communication configuration parameters such as modem speed. What field in the PPP frame contains the information that implements these protocols?

   a. Control

   b. Information

   c. Protocol

7. To what layer in the TCP/IP protocol stack does Windows Messaging belong?

   a. Not part of any layer

   b. Application layer

   c. TCP layer

8. Can a Windows RAS client that uses NetBEUI use the Internet?

   a. Yes

   b. No

   c. It depends on the modem installed in the RAS client.

9. What Windows NT utility can you use to determine if your RAS serial ports are receiving frames with errors?

   a. Network Monitor

   b. Windows Diagnostics

   c. Dial-Up Monitor

10. What utility can you use to determine the IP address that was assigned to a remote RAS client by a DHCP server?

    a. DHCP Manager

    b. Remote Access Administration

    c. Dial-Up Monitor

11. What network design, other than that shown in Figure 10-39, might you use to test RAS client/server connectivity?

    a. Connect a client and server on a LAN

    b. Connect a client and server using their modems and an RJ-11 cable

    c. Connect a client and server using their COM ports and an RS-235 cable

12. If the RAS client has only the TCP/IP protocol stack available, is it possible for the client to be authenticated on a Windows NT domain?

    a. Yes, using NBT

    b. No

    c. Yes, if the client only wants to access resources on the PDC or BDC

13. What are the three Internet publishing services provided by IIS hypertext transfer protocol (HTTP)?

14. What well-known port does the WWW service use?

    a. 21

    b. 70

    c. 80

15. To which layer of the TCP/IP protocol stack does HTTP belong?

    a. IP

    b. Application

    c. Network

16. What is the absolute address of the home directory of the Windows NT WWW service on drive D:?

    a. D:\Winnt\wwwroot

    b. D:\InetPub\wwwroot

    c. D:\Winnt\system32\wwwroot

17. If a virtual directory that has the absolute address C:\Winnt\system32\rfc on the computer ds.internic.net has the alias /rfc, which of the following provides a URL address with the correct format to access files in this virtual directory?

    a. http://ds.internic.net/rfc

    b. http://ds.internic.net/c:/Winnt/system32/rfc

    c. http://ds.internic.net/c:/Winnt/system32/

18. When a client uses the ID anonymous to access WWW, FTP, or Gopher services, what determines the permissions that the anonymous client has?

    a. Permissions assigned to the account anonymous

    b. Permissions assigned to the account IUSER_<computername>

    c. It depends on the password that the anonymous client uses.

19. What is the advantage of allowing only anonymous access to your Internet publishing services?

    a. The client does not have to remember a password.

    b. The client only has access permissions assigned to one account.

    c. The client can only access the service home directory.

20. What Windows NT 4.0 Server utility provides access to public encryption keys?

    a. Key Manager

    b. SSL

    c. Internet Service Manager

CASE PROJECT

The Case Project environment after Chapter 9, "Name Services," is shown in Figure 10-57.

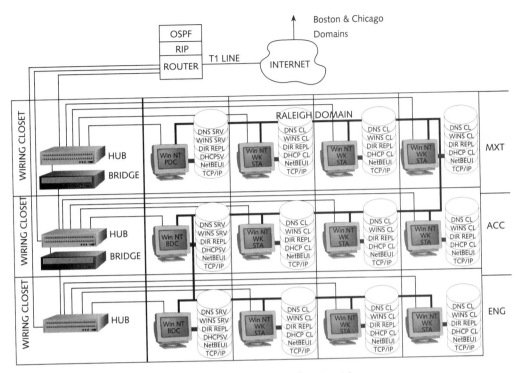

Figure 10-57 Case Project environment prior to Chapter 10

The focus of Chapter 9 was on the installation and configuration of the name resolution services that are available on Windows NT and how to use these services to translate NetBIOS names and domain names into IP addresses. This chapter, the last in the book, required all of the knowledge you obtained from previous chapters in order to establish a networking capability that included e-mail, remote access, and Internet publishing services. The exercises that follow will give you additional practice with using the networking service concepts that have been covered and will complete the installation of the resources necessary to provide the communications capability required by your company.

EXERCISE 1—WINDOWS MESSAGING

 For this exercise, your Windows Messaging connection profile should not be configured for Remote Mail. Use the first five steps following to check this configuration and to change it if necessary.

1. Click **Services** on the Tools menu in Windows Messaging.

2. Click **Properties** on the Services tab.

3. Click the **Connection** tab on the Internet Mail form.

4. Remove check (✔) from the "Work off-line and use Remote Mail" check box.

5. Click **OK** to return to the Inbox – Windows Messaging screen.

6. Click **Folders** on the View menu to get a list of your Personal Folders. There should be no files in your folders except the Welcome message from Microsoft in the Inbox folder.

7. Click **New Message** on the Compose menu and compose a message to yourself.

8. Click **Send** on the File menu to put New Message into your Outbox folder.

9. Click **Close** on the File menu to return to the Inbox – Windows Messaging screen.

10. Answer the following questions.

    a. Which Personal Folder contains the message you just created?

    b. Why does the message not appear in your Sent Items folder since you clicked Send on the File menu on the New Message form?

    c. Why does the message not appear in your Inbox folder since you "sent it" to yourself?

    d. What have you not done that is necessary in order to actually send your message?

    e. Perform this missing step and then describe what happens.

    f. What protocols are being used when you take the missing step?

EXERCISE 2—WINDOWS MESSAGING REMOTE MAIL

For this exercise, return to the Internet Mail form, click the **Connection** tab, and add the check (✔) to the check box next to "Work off-line and use Remote Mail."

1. Open Inbox – Windows Messaging.

2. If you do not have mail in your Inbox, ask a friend to send you a message.

3. Click **Remote Mail** on the **View** menu to open the Remote Mail screen.

4. Click **Connect** on the Tools menu of Remote Mail. If your mail server supports Remote Mail, the header of the message(s) should be listed on the screen. What POP 3 command displayed the header(s) when you clicked Connect?

5. Click **Mark to Retrieve** on the Edit menu and **Connect** on the Tools menu. When these commands are executed, your message(s) will be transferred to your Inbox Personal Folder and deleted from your mailbox on the mail server.

6. What happened to the message header in Remote Mail and why did it happen?

7. Open your Inbox Personal Folder to see if your message(s) are there.

EXERCISE 3—REMOTE ACCESS SERVICE

This is a good exercise to share with a friend, if both of you have either Windows NT Server operating system or Windows NT Workstation operating system. RAS is available with both systems. You might also do this exercise by dialing up your office or lab domain PDC, if that computer is always up and hosts the RAS server.

1. Arrange for your computer and yourself to have accounts on the primary domain controller that is hosting the RAS server. This is necessary so that the PDC can authenticate you and your computer when you dial up as a RAS client.

2. Obtain the telephone number that you should dial to connect to the computer that is hosting the RAS server.

3. Access the Dial-Up Networking utility screen on the RAS client and:

   a. Enter the telephone number to be dialed.

   b. Enter a name for the phone book entry that is going to be the name of your dial-up profile.

   c. Click **More** and then **Edit entry and modem properties**.

   d. Select and configure **Dial using** according to the compatibility of the modems on the RAS client computer and the RAS server computer.

   e. Click the **Server** tab and complete the form according to the compatibility of the protocols that the client and server can recognize.

   f. Click **TCP/IP Settings** and specify how the client and server are going to obtain IP addresses.

4. Return to the Dial-Up Networking utility screen and click **Dial**.

5. Use the Network Neighborhood browser on the Desktop of the RAS client to see if you have access to shared files on the computer hosting the RAS server and on other computers in the domain if you have accessed a RAS host in a domain. Double-click **Network Neighborhood** and then double-click the icon representing the computer hosting the RAS server. You should see a list of files shared by that computer.

6. Double-click a file to see if its contents are transferred to your computer.

7. If you have accessed a domain, double-click the icon of another domain computer to see if you are presented with a list of its sharable files.

10

EXERCISE 4—PUBLISHING A WWW PAGE

This is another exercise that will be fun to do with a friend. You can both create a simple WWW page using HTML and then use Internet Explorer to browse them. You may need to learn a little about HTML, but the samples provided in the Windows NT Server home directory, for example D:\InetPub\wwwroot\sample, may be sufficient.

1. Access the sample HTML files in the WWW Service home directory and study the HTML format.

2. Use Notepad to create a small HTML file.

3. Save the file in the WWW Service home directory wwwroot.

4. As was done in the test of the WWW service in the chapter, use Dial-Up Networking to call your Internet Service Provider (ISP), and use the DHCP server of the ISP to get a leased IP address for your computer.

5. Call your friend and tell her what your leased IP address is. You will find this on the Connection tab of your Dial-Up Monitor.

6. Your friend should now use her Internet Explorer browser and a URL address that includes your IP address to connect to your WWW page.

7. Reverse roles and browse her WWW page.

Figure 10-58 shows the status of the Case Project environment after completing this chapter.

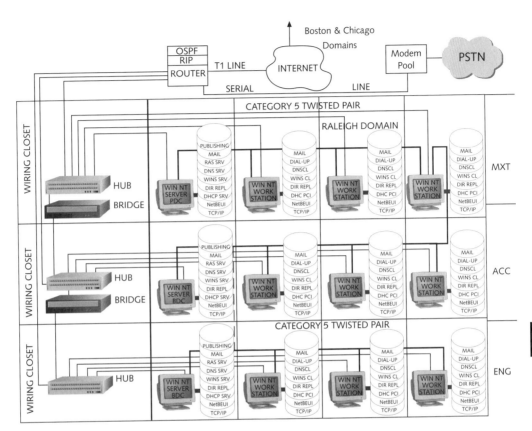

Figure 10-58   Case Project environment after completing Chapter 10
—= Raleigh domain 192.192.192.0

You have configured Dial-Up Networking, installed Windows Messaging, installed and configured Remote Access Service, and installed and configured Microsoft Internet Information Service publishing directories for FTP, Gopher, and WWW. With this chapter, therefore, you have completed the task of establishing the following communications capabilities required by your company. These include:

- Communication using both TCP/IP and NetBEUI

- Dynamic IP addressing using DHCP

- Name resolution using either WINS, DNS, or both

- Electronic Mail Service

- Intradepartment 10BASET LAN communication between computers running Windows NT 4.0 Workstation and a PDC or BDC running Windows NT 4.0 Server

- Interdepartment communication using bridges between departments

- Interdivision communication using a router and the Internet

- Interdivision (intranet) and remote communication using RAS and the PSTN

- Company-wide WWW, FTP, and Gopher publishing services

- An Internet browsing capability

SOME USEFUL WINDOWS NT TCP/IP DIAGNOSTIC UTILITIES

The following table describes utilities that were especially useful in implementing the intranet described in this book. There are many other commands that you can find by selecting Help on the Start menu and then selecting Windows NT Commands on the Help menu.

Command	Argument	Description
ping	destination	1) Verifies an IP connection between the host on which ping is executed and the argument <destination>. <Destination> can be either a host name or an IP address.
		2) Causes ICMP to send Echo Request packets (four by default).
		3) <Destination> sends Echo Reply packets (four by default) containing its IP address and the exact message in the Echo Request packet.
		4) Other command arguments that customize the command are available but are not usually needed.
Tracert	destination	1) Determines the route to <destination>. <Destination> can be either a host name or an IP address.
		2) Causes ICMP to send Echo Request packets in which the time-to-live (TTL) value is incremented by one in each packet.
		3) Each router along the path decrements TTL. The router at which TTL reaches zero in each Echo Request packet returns its IP address in an Echo Reply packet. Finally <destination> returns its IP address.
arp		1) Displays a list of switches and arguments available.
	-a	2) Displays current mappings in the arp cache of the local host.
	-a inet_addr	3) Displays current mappings in the arp cache of the interface specified by the IP address <inet_addr>.
	-s inet_addr ether_addr	4) Adds a permanent entry to the arp cache that maps the IP address <inet_addr> to the physical Ethernet address <ether_addr>.
		5) Arp cache entries that are not made permanent, for example by Step 4, are removed in a time specified in the arp configuration.

Command	Argument	Description
ipconfig		1) Displays IP address, subnet mask, and default gateway for all interfaces on the host on which it is executed.
	/all	2) In addition to interface configurations, displays host configurations such as Name Resolution services enabled on the host.
	/renew	3) If used by a DHCP client, renews the IP address lease.
	/release	4) Releases a leased IP address.
nbtstat		1) Displays current connections of registered users and processes of NetBIOS over TCP/IP as well as protocol statistics.
	-n	2) Displays the local NetBIOS name table.
	-a remotename	3) Displays the NetBIOS name table of a remote computer with the name remotename.
	-c	4) Displays the cached mappings of NetBIOS names to IP addresses.
		5) Other arguments are available to further customize the nbtstat display.
net view		1) Displays a list of Master Browsers and Back-up Browsers in the domain. One of these browsers sends the list of domain resources to nonbrowsers (browser clients) when the Network Neighborhood utility is used.
route	print	1) Displays the routing table of the host on which it is executed.
	print destination	2) Displays the routing table on the host specified by <destination>.
		3) Other arguments can be specified.
nslookup		1) Displays information maintained by DNS servers.
		2) There are two nslookup modes—interactive and noninteractive. Noninteractive is used when only one piece of information is needed.
	hostname server	3) <Hostname> is the name or IP address that is being requested. <Server> is the name or IP address of a DNS server. If <server> is not specified, the default DNS server is queried.
	- server	4) This argument is used if you want to use interactive mode to lookup DNS names or IP addresses for more than one host.
		5) The following is an example of using nslookup. If you want the IP address of a host with the name mladen, using the DNS server pcsv.raleigh.NET., you type the following at the command prompt: nslookup mladen pcsv.raleigh.NET.
		6) There are many <options> that can be used on the command line of nslookup.

GLOSSARY

10BASE2 cable Shorthand for thinnet coaxial cable that operates at a transmission rate of 10 Mbs and uses baseband; the maximum length of a segment without repeaters is 185 meters.

10BASET Shorthand for cable consisting of four twisted pairs of wire operating at 10 Mbs using baseband, that connects devices to a hub, to form a LAN.

A

Abstract syntax notation.1 (ASN.1) Generic format for representing information in a hierarchical structure.

ACK frame Acknowledgment frame sent by both sending and receiving computers in response to frames they receive.

Address Classes Five standard classes defined by the Internet Protocol standard to provide different numbers of networks and hosts on each network.

Address Resolution Protocol (ARP) Protocol used by a computer to obtain the hardware address of another computer on the network, when the IP address of that computer is known.

Adjacency Under OSPF protocol, this indicates that a group of two or more routers has agreed to let one of the group advertise the link status of each of them.

Administrative distance Rating of the reliability of a routing information source; can be between 0 and 255 (the higher the number, the lower the reliability).

Agent Software that accesses and stores information about the usage of a network device.

Alias Name that stands for a path.

API *Application Program Interface.* For example, a C function that provides a common access for application programs to an operating system process.

Application layer Layer of the OSI protocol stack that contains software that provides common services needed by application programs such as word processors, spreadsheets, and e-mail.

Area Under the OSPF protocol, a site can be partitioned into areas so that the routing topology in each area can be configured differently.

Area border router Under the OSPF protocol, a router that connects two or more areas.

ARP Reply Type of message that provides a destination hardware address so that the source computer can send a packet that has been stored awaiting this information.

ARPA *Advanced Research Projects Agency.* An agency of the U.S. Department of Defense.

ARPANET Network developed by the Advanced Research Projects Agency of the U.S. Department of Defense to connect academic institutions; served as the testing site for the TCP/IP protocol stack, and later expanded to become the Internet.

Authoritative Domain name that has been registered with the InterNIC, added to the InterNIC name hierarchy, and used by any computer on the Internet as the starting point for a domain name search.

Autonomous system Administrative entity consisting of a group of networks on the Internet; the Internet contains many autonomous systems.

B

Backbone area Under the OSPF protocol, an area that contains connected routers that connect other areas.

Backup designated router Under OSPF protocol, router assigned to take over as the designated router if the designated router fails.

Backup domain controller (BDC) Computer that maintains a copy of the database of domain computers and users' accounts that is synchronized with the database on the PDC.

Bandwidth Frequency range.

BER *Basic Encoding Rules.* Used with ASN.1 to format information for network communication.

b-node Broadcast node type; one of four NetBIOS node types in which a Windows-based computer can be configured. Determines the order in which name resolution mechanisms are used.

Boundary routers Under the OSPF protocol, routers that communicate reachability information about networks in one autonomous system to another autonomous system.

Bridge Connects two segments of a LAN, two LANs of the same media type, or two LANs of different media types; receives frames from one segment and forwards them to the segment.

Bridge groups Group of bridge network interfaces that are managed by a spanning tree protocol.

Bridge table In the operation of a bridge, records the source address of each frame received and the port through which it was received.

BSD *Berkeley Software Distribution.* A version of the UNIX operating system.

Bytes 8-bit units of data.

Bytes in Number of compressed bytes that have been received during the duration of a transfer of data.

Bytes out Number of decompressed bytes that were sent during the duration of a transfer of data.

C

Cache SRAM used to store data requiring fast access or a reserved section of DRAM.

Category Number A numeric classification of cable identifying thickness of wire, number of twists per foot, and other parameters.

Challenge packets Packets sent by the domain controller in response to discovery packets, verifying that the computer logging on has a valid account on the domain.

Change log List of changes made to the master domain directory on the primary domain controller since the last time it was synchronized with the directories maintained by backup domain controllers.

Circuit switching Type of switching that involves a permanent physical circuit between the caller and receiver.

Client/server communications architecture Network architecture on which central storage and resources are controlled by one or more server computers and are accessed by client computers.

Communications architecture A system of rules and practices that enable computers to share information over a network.

Compression in Ratio of bytes not sent to decompressed bytes received during a transfer of data.

Connectionless protocol Protocol that includes no mechanisms for providing reliability across a network, such as error checking, requests for transmission, or flow control.

Cost Under the OSPF protocol, a measure of the type of service that can be provided by a link.

CSMA/CD *Carrier Sense Multiple Access with Collision Detection.* Provides controlled access to an Ethernet LAN.

D

Data Link layer Layer of the OSI protocol stack that specifies the procedures that are followed in order to achieve reliable point-to-point transfer of information between two devices on a network.

De-encapsulation Refers to removing the series of layers that enclose a packet of data after it has been transported.

Default router Router used to forward ID packets destined for another network.

Designated router Under OSPF protocol, the router assigned to advertise the link status of each of the routers in a group of adjacent routers.

Device General networking term that encompasses hardware or software that implements network communication.

Device response Feedback from a modem that describes the modem protocol that is being used.

DHCP TCP/IP application layer protocol. The DHCP server process leases an IP address, from a range of IP addresses (the scope) managed by the DHCP server, for the network interface on the machine hosting the client process that makes the lease request using the interface.

DHCP options Options that are configured resulting in additional IP network information being provided to the DHCP client in the option fields of the DHCP packet.

DHCP relay Relays requests for DHCP service to a DHCP server, other subnets, or other networks.

DHCP scope Range of IP addresses from which an address is leased by the DHCP server to the DHCP client for a configured time interval, the TTL interval.

Dial-Up Monitor Utility used to monitor a dial-up connection.

Dial-Up Networking Using a dial-up connection to add a node to a network.

Discovery packets Packets sent by the Net Logon Service of a Windows NT workstation.

DNS *Domain Name System.* Hierarchy of Internet domain names and the protocol for accessing them.

DNS zone Division of a DNS domain that is assigned control over part of the domain's resources.

DNS reverse zone Zone that contains IP addresses to host name mappings.

Domain name Name of a device in the DNS hierarchy.

Domain name space Range of IP addresses assigned to a DNS domain.

Dotted decimal notation Format of IP addresses; consists of four fields, each containing a decimal number, separated by dots, with each field having a value in the range 0 to 255.

DRAM *Dynamic Random Access Memory.* RAM that must be electronically refreshed.

Driver Software extension of the operating system that controls the operation of devices on the system.

E

EIA/TIA *Electronic Industries Association/ Telecommunications Industries Association*

Encapsulation Refers to enclosing data within a series of protocol stack headers in order to transport it over a network.

Enterprise network Network that provides global connectivity for a company. Also called *intranets.*

Expiration date Date and time when a WINS server will begin the process of removing a registered mapping from the database.

Exterior Gateway Protocols (EGP) Category of routing protocols that manage communication among autonomous systems on the Internet.

Extinct IP address entry that is deleted from a WINS database.

Extinction interval Time interval from the point when the entry is marked released to the point when it is actually deleted.

F

FAT *File Allocation Table.* Contains location of first sector of a file on the hard drive.

File system server Translates between the Windows NT file system and the file systems understood by clients on the network.

File Transfer Protocol (FTP) A TCP/IP protocol used by client and server processes to request and transfer files.

Filtering (bridge) Discarding a frame containing a hardware destination address on the network from which the frame was received.

Flag Bits employed to synchronize the sending and receiving of machine bit streams.

Flag field Used when synchronous transmission is employed to synchronize sending and receiving machine bit streams.

Flat name Domain host name that does not have a hierarchical structure to determine its location on the network.

Forwarding (bridge) Receiving a frame and passing it to the next port on the way to its destination.

Frame Smallest unit of information sent over a network.

FTP *File Transfer Protocol*

Fully qualified domain name (FQDN) DNS name that specifies the path in the DNS tree from a host to the root of the tree.

G

Group name (NetBIOS) Name claimed by any number of clients on a Windows NT domain. When used as a destination address, causes the message to be sent to all computers that have registered the name.

GUI *Graphical User Interface*

H

HDLC *High-Level Data Link Control.* Data link layer protocol.

Header Additional information added to a packet that tells the peer layer in the destination computer how to process the packet.

Hello Under OSPF, a packet broadcast on directly connected networks to find neighboring routers.

Hierarchical name Domain host name with a tree-like structure related to its location on the network.

High Level Data Link Control (HDLC) Basis for a large number of mail transmission protocols, including PPP.

h-node Hybrid node type; one of four NetBIOS node types in which a Windows-based computer can be configured. Determines the order in which name resolution mechanisms are used.

Home Directory Default publishing directory that will be opened by a WWW, FTP, or Gopher client request unless an alias directory is specified in the URL.

Hops Number of the routers that must be traversed in order to reach the destination subnet; RIP uses this measure to determine the best route to take when routing information.

Host Computer that functions as a source of information or services.

Hosts file Text file in which the entries are mappings of host names to IP addresses.

Hub Multiport repeater; used in 10BASET networks.

Hybrid Default node configuration for a computer configured as a WINS server.

I

IAB *Internet Activities Board*

ICMP *Internet Control Message Protocol.* Protocol of the IP layer that generates packets which test and report the status of network connectivity and performance.

IIS *Microsoft Internet Information Service*

Interface Transition between two implementations of electronic communication enabled by a protocol.

Interior Gateway Protocols (IGP) Category of routing protocols used within an autonomous system on the Internet to manage communication within the system.

Internet Group Management Protocol (IGMP) Protocol used by multicast hosts and gateways to communicate group membership information.

InterNIC *Internet Network Information Center*

Interprocess communication Communication in which two active programs, also known as processes, send information to one another.

Interrupt Request (IRQ) Signal that informs the operating system as to which device needs its attention.

IP Connectionless protocol that provides the mechanisms for routing packets between networks without dependence on hardware implementation.

ISA *Industry Standard Architecture.* 8- and 16-bit bus architecture.

ISA bus *Industry Standard Architecture* bus. Basic 8-bit or 16-bit bus that connects computer system devices.

ISDN *Integrated Services Digital Network*

L

LAN *Local Area Network*

Legacy adapter Adapter that uses the ISA bus and must be configured by setting jumpers on the NIC or by using software to set the parameters.

Line bps Speed in bits per seconds at which data is being transferred between modems.

Link Control Protocol (LCP) Protocol used to open a mail session connection, negotiate network layer protocols, and close the connection.

Link state advertisement Under OSPF, a packet sent by a router advertising its connectivity.

Link state messages Routers using the OSPF protocol can send these, containing information about the links to which they are directly attached; routers can then use these instead of a static routing table to independently create a routing table consisting of a tree of routes to all destination networks.

LMHosts file Text files in which the entries are mappings of NetBIOS names to IP addresses.

Local area network Network that is typically implemented by directly connecting segments using bridges and routers.

Local bridge Used to make a direct connection between two LANs.

Logical link Conceptual rather than physical communication link between two processes.

Logical Link Control (LLC) Sublayer of the Data Link layer of the OSI protocol stack that ensures reliable transmission of information between two devices.

LSA *Local Security Authority.* Process that manages security implementation during the logon process.

M

Machine Computer or other network device.

Mail server Manages mailboxes in which received mail is stored and from which it is accessed by a mail client process.

Master domain directory Database of domain user accounts maintained by the primary domain controller on a Windows NT server.

Maximum hops (DHCP) Number of hops that a message from the DHCP Relay Agent may take in attempting to find a DHCP server before the message is discarded.

Medium Access Control (MAC) layer Sublayer of the Data Link layer of the OSI protocol stack that ensures orderly access to the network medium using the CSMA/CD method of access.

Medium access unit (MAU) Receives signals from the network and transmits signals onto the network.

Microsoft Fast Tips service Automated service that provides answers to common technical questions.

Microsoft Windows Network domain Network consisting of at least one computer using the Windows NT Server operating system and other computers that share resources with authorized users.

m-node Mixed node type; one of four NetBIOS node types in which a Windows based computer can be configured. Determinines the order in which name resolution mechanisms are used.

Modem Device that translates between digital pulses and audio signals.

MSDL *Microsoft Download Service*—offers direct modem access to a variety of technical information.

Multicasting Destination of an IP address recognized by a group of machines.

Multihomed system Workstation that is connected to more than one network interface.

N

NAK frame Negative acknowledgment frame sent in response to frames received in error.

Name query request Sent by a WINS client to the WINS server when it needs to know the IP address of a computer for which it knows only the NetBIOS name.

Name refresh request Message sent to a WINS client when half of the TTL has expired, to renew the TTL.

Name registration request Type of message sent by a WINS client to the WINS server when logging on in order to register NetBIOS name or service ID and its IP address.

NOIS Wrapper The software module Ndis.sys that provides a uniform interface between multiple protocol stacks and an Ndis NIC driver.

Negative query response Sent by a WINS server to a WINS client in response to a name query request, indicating that the information was not found in the server's database.

Neighbor Under OSPF protocol, a router directly connected to the same network.

Net Logon Service When a user logs on to a network domain from a workstation, this local service is activated to find a domain controller on that domain.

NetBIOS API function that originally provided a monolithic network communications protocol for DOS, and served as the basis of NetBEUI.

NetBIOS Extended User Interface (NetBEUI) Protocol that enables the use of NetBIOS names on a TCP/IP network.

NetBIOS over TCP/IP (NBT) Protocol that enables the use of NetBIOS names on a TCP/IP network.

Network address distance to network address pairs Under the RIP protocol, routers collect this information from previous RIP messages received from other routers connected to the same network.

Network layer Layer of the OSI protocol stack that provides the mechanisms for transporting a packet from the source network to the destination network.

NIC *Network Interface Card.* Also called an adapter.

Node Connection point for a network device.

NOS *Network Operating System*

NSF *National Science Foundation*

NTFS *NT File System*—Windows NT file system that is typically used on Windows NT 4.0 servers because it provides faster access to large volumes of data and contains enhanced security features.

O

Open Shortest Path First (OSPF) protocol IGP protocol that periodically advertises routing services it can provide.

Open System Interconnection Reference Model Seven-layer stack of protocols established by the International Organization for Standardization to guide the development of interoperable communication standards.

OSI *International Organization for Standardization*

Overhead Nonproductive part of a process that is nonetheless required in order to transmit data over a network.

P

Packet Message and headers that make up the data field of a frame.

Packet switching Type of switching whereby voice or data is converted into a stream of bytes that is divided into packets of a fixed size and then stored in the RAM of each network device along the path from sender to receiver, until the path to the next device is available.

Partial synchronization Transmission of only change log entries to a backup domain controller from a primary domain controller.

PCI *Peripheral Component Interface*

PCI bus Local bus that connects the processor with other high speed devices.

PCMCIA adaptor *PC Memory Card International Association.* Laptop NIC.

Peer-to-peer communications architectures Network communication whereby all PCs have the same hardware and software resources and the same level of responsibility.

Physical layer Layer of the OSI protocol stack that defines the electrical, mechanical, functional, and procedural specifications for the hardware that connects a device to the network.

p-node Point-to-point node; one of four NetBIOS node types in which a Windows-based computer can be configured, determining the order in which name resolution mechanisms are used.

Point-to-Point (PPP) High-level data link control type protocol used to send and receive mail messages.

Point-to-Point protocol (PPP) High-level Data Link Control type of protocol used on WANs.

POP *Post Office Protocol*

Port Set of memory locations used to store data being passed across an interface.

Positive name registration response Response sent by the WINS server to a WINS client logging in if the NetBIOS name it has attempted to register for the session is not in use.

Positive query response Sent by a WINS server to a WINS client to provide the IP address requested in the client's name query request.

Post Office Protocol (POP) Protocol used by a mail client to send a request-for-delivery message to a mail server.

PPP LCP extensions Software extensions that allow PPP to provide additional configuration status—for example, to send messages to test connectivity.

Preamble Field in a frame used to synchronize transmission between source and destination devices.

Presentation layer Layer of the OSI protocol stack that provides an interface between the Application layer and the layers below the Presentation layer.

Primary domain controller (PDC) Server on the domain that maintains the master list of authenticated domain accounts, files identified as sharable, and user permissions for file access.

Process Active program.

Promiscuous mode Feature of a protocol analyzer that enables the analyzer to capture all packets regardless of source and destination addresses.

Protocol Set of rules that must be followed in order for two devices in a communications architecture to exchange information.

Protocol stack Chain of protocols that together constitute the rules of a communications architecture.

Pull partner WINS server that periodically requests new WINS database entries from another WINS server.

Push partner WINS server that sends a message to another WINS server to notify it to request a database replication.

R

RARP *Reverse Address Resolution Protocol.* Protocol used by a computer, that knows its hardware address, to obtain its IP address from a RARP server on the network to which it is attached.

RARP server Process on a computer that provides mappings of hardware addresses to IP addresses.

RAS *Remote Access Service.* Service that enables a remote client to access a network and its shared resources.

Redirector Module in a client software environment that intercepts application program requests for service and directs them either to the local operating system or to a protocol stack that provides access to a remote operation system.

Relay process Mapping process for translating information in a frame in order to forward it to a network of a different type.

Remote bridge Used to connect two LANs by way of a WAN rather than directly.

Renewal interval Time between the registration of an entry in a WINS database and the point at which it will be marked for deletion.

Repeater Device that regenerates the data signal in order to extend the transmission distance.

Replication (domains) Provides automatic export or import of subdirectories from a PDC or workstation.

Replication (WINS) Action that produces replicas of the local WINS database on other WINS servers on a network.

Replication interval (WINS) Time interval after which a pull partner of a WINS server will ask for an updated replica of the database on that server.

Reverse lookup files Files that contain IP address-to-host-name mappings; accessed when a host knows the IP address of another host but does not know its name.

Routers Multiport devices that connect networks and, when necessary, isolate networks and subnets, by using the Internet layer of a protocol stack.

Routing Information Protocol (RIP) IGP protocol that periodically transmits a routing table to routers on directly attached networks.

Routing table Provides a mapping of destination network IP addresses to the IP address of the router interface that should be used to forward a packet based on the "cost" to use that interface.

S

SAM *Security Account Manager.* Process that maintains the user and group accounts database.

SCSI *Small Computer Systems Interface*

Seconds threshold Time at which the DHCP Relay will time out and send a message to the client advising that no DHCP server has replied.

Secure communication channel Session between an authenticated workstation and the domain controller.

Session layer Layer of the OSI protocol stack that provides the mechanisms necessary to establish and close multiple logical connections between processes on different PCs.

Shielded twisted pair cable Twisted pair cable that is covered with a metallic layer that shields against electromagnetic pickup.

Shortest path first (SPF) Precursor of the OSPF algorithm.

SID *Security ID.* Index to the record of user credentials used to authenticate access to resources.

Simple Network Management Protocol (SNMP) TCP/IP protocol used to obtain statistical information about a network device.

SMTP *Simple Mail Transfer Protocol.* TCP/IP protocol whose implementation sends e-mail to mail servers.

Socket Address pair consisting of an IP address and a port.

Spanning-tree algorithm Used to manage connectivity of networks connected by bridges, to eliminate loops.

SRAM *Static Random Access Memory.* RAM that is not refreshed and provides faster service that DRAM.

SSL *Secure Sockets Layer.* Presentation layer protocol that uses RSA encryption of packets to provide the WWW service.

Standalone (member) server Server that does not maintain a copy of the domain's database of domain computer and user accounts.

Subnet mask Four bytes, in IP address format, to which an IP destination address is compared to obtain the destination network address.

Switch Multiport bridge, which can operate on more than one packet at the same time.

Synchronization Transmission of the entire contents of the master domain directory on the primary domain controllor to a backup domain controller.

System call Request for service of the operating system on which an application program is running.

T

TCP/IP *Transmission Control Protocol/Internet Protocol.* Suite of protocols.

TCP/IP Printing Provides the line printer (LPR) protocol that enables a client to send a print job to a print spooler running the service line-printer daemon (LPD) on another computer.

Telnet TCP/IP application layer protocol. The server process on the local computer enables the client process on the remote computer to emulate a terminal of the local computer.

Thicknet Term for 0.50-inch-diameter, relatively inflexible coaxial cable used as an interconnecting medium in a LAN.

Thinnet Term for 0.25-inch-diameter, relatively flexible coaxial cable used as an interconnecting medium in a LAN.

Token (security) Contains user ID and user rights; created when a user logs on to a Windows NT domain and used to validate all future actions taken by the user.

TOS *Type of Service.* Field in an OSPF router link state advertisement specifying a type of service that the router provides.

Transfer syntax Format that the layers below the Presentation layer in a protocol stack to create packets.

Translational bridge Connects dissimilar networks and translates the MAC header used on one network into the MAC header used on the other network.

Translational bridging Translating a frame in the process of forwarding it; occurs when a bridge connects two networks of different types.

Transparent bridge Filters and forwards frames between segments and networks that are using the same media access control protocol.

Transparent bridging Forwarding a frame "as is"; occurs when the bridge connects two networks of the same type.

Transport Control Protocol (TCP) Protocol in the TCP/IP stack that provides error detection and recovery in the transmission of data between the application program in a source computer and the application program in a destination computer.

Transport layer Layer of the OSI protocol stack that provides both reliable and unreliable mechanisms for transporting information among computers on a network.

Trusted Computers on this type of domain have access to resources on the trusting domain because they have been authenticated in the Windows NT security process.

Trusting Computers on this type of domain will trust users authenticated on the trusted domain to access their resources.

Twisted pair cable Cable in which each circuit in the cable consists of two copper wires that are twisted around one another; sometimes covered with insulating material in order to help eliminate electromagnetic pickup from other equipment in the area.

U

UI Frame that carries information but is not numbered or tracked.

Unique name NetBIOS name claimed by only one entity on a Windows NT domain.

Unnumbered information (UI) frame HDIC-type frame that carries information; these frames are not numbered or tracked.

Unshielded Twisted Pair (UTP) cable Twisted pair cable that is not covered with a protective metallic layer.

Update Count Number of changes to the local WINS server database that, when made, will cause the local WINS server to send a message to the push partner requesting it to request an update of the local server's database.

User Datagram Protocol (UDP) Unreliable transport protocol in the TCP/IP stack that allows best-effort delivery of data between the application program in a source computer and the application program in a destination computer.

V

Verify interval Time interval from the point when the local WINS server registers a mapping obtained from a partner server to the point when the local WINS server must verify that the mapping is still active.

Version ID Hexidecimal number that is an index of the time when a mapping was registered with a WINS server relative to the other mappings on the list.

Virtual directory Identified in an http address by an alias that maps to the path to a real directory.

Virtual link (OSPF) Under OSPF protocol, a link that is not part of the backbone area, but provides a link between areas.

Virtual Terminal Protocol Protocol in the Presentation layer of a protocol stack that allows a PC to emulate a terminal of a remote computer.

VLM *Virtual Loadable Module.* In NetWare, software modules that implement Redirector functions.

W

Well-known port ID ID of a process that is used so often that it has been assigned a unique ID.

Wide area network (WAN) Network of unlimited size that is composed of a network of switches that route messages between computers or other networks attached to the switches.

Wildcard mask Four bytes, in IP address format, to which an IP address is compared, to determine the OSPF area in which an interface lies.

Window (sliding) Number of frames that can be transmitted from the source computer to the destination computer before an acknowledgment frame must be received by the source computer. The term "sliding window" is used because the window "slides" along a scale on which the frames sent by the source are numbered; the window size being used is shown in the window field of the TCP header.

Windows NT domain A group of servers, computers, and users, connected by LANs, WANs, and the Internet that share resources protected by common security and user account information.

WINS TCP/IP application layer protocol. The server process maintains a database of NetBIOS names to IP address mappings that is queried by the client process.

Wiring closet "Location" where hubs, and other network devices such as bridges and routers, are placed for centralized access and maintenance.

INDEX

concepts, 273–276

DNS Manager, 276–278

zones. *See* DNS zone(s)

domain suffixes, 285

dot (.), domain names, 273

DRAM (dynamic random access memory), 5

drive mapping, sharing on domains, 237–238

drivers, 32

Dynamic Host Configuration Protocol (DHCP), 92, 94, 181–199, 323

  client installation and configuration, 183–188

  functions, 182

  IP addressing, 182

  Relay service, 196–198

  server installation and configuration, 188–196

dynamic random access memory (DRAM), 5

E

Edit Phonebook Entry screen, Dial-Up Networking, 308

EGPs (Exterior Gateway Protocols), 156

Electronic Industries Association/Telecommunications Industries Association (EIA/TIA) standard 8802-3, 8

e-mail protocols, 302–306

  POP, 305–306

PPP, 302–303

SMTP, 303–305

emergency repair disk, 43

encapsulation, 20

Encapsulation ARPA statement, 150–151

End of text command, SMTP, 305

Enhanced Small Device Interface/Integrated Drive Electronics (ESDI/IDE), 37

enterprise networks, 22

Ethernet is up statement, 150

Ethernet LANs

  media, 15–16

  types, 14

Exclusion Range, DHCP server scope, 191

Exterior Gateway Protocols (EGPs), 156

extinction interval, 270

extinction timeout, 270

F

FCS (frame check sequence), 303

fields

  ARP, 131

  ICMP, 101

  IP, 98–100

  OSPF, 168–169, 170

  RIP, 159

  TCP, 96

  UDP, 97

File menu, Microsoft Internet Explorer home page, 340

file system servers, 13

File Transfer Protocol (FTP), 11, 53, 91, 94, 330–332

filtering, 145

Find tab, Help utility, 64

Find utility, 65

Flag field, PPP, 303

Flags field, IP, 98

flat names, 272

format

  IP addresses, 125–130

  OSPF messages, 166–172

  PPP frames, 302–303

formatting partitions, 39

forwarding, 145

forwarding frames, 147

forward parameter, bridges, 151

FQDNs (fully qualified domain names), 273–274

Fragment Offset field, IP, 98

frame(s), 18–22

  forwarding, 147

  PPP format, 302–303

frame check sequence (FCS), 303

From: command, SMTP, 304

FTP (File Transfer Protocol), 11, 53, 91, 94, 330–332

FTP Service Properties screen, 330–331

full synchronization, 217

fully qualified domain names (FQDNs), 273–274

CORIOLIS TECHNOLOGY PRESS©

The Magnificent 7

Presented by
Creative PROFESSIONALS PRESS™

Creative Professional Press:

- Leading-edge guides geared toward art & design professionals
- Superb books that combine the creative aesthetics and technical expertise needed by graphic designers, Web publishers, and multimedia developers
- Elegant, colorful books presented on high-quality paper designed with white space and page balancing to display impressive images
- Magnificently visual and interactive books that "show while telling"—including tips and information not found elsewhere
- A must for your graphics design library

Digital Camera Design Guide
1-57610-184-3, $45.00

Softimage 3D Design Guide
1-57610-147-9, $39.99

Looking Good in Print, 4e
1-56604-856-7, $29.99

Looking Good in Presentations, 3e
1-56604-854-0, 29.99

Character Animation Enhanced
1-56604-771-4, $59.99

3D Studio MAX R2 f/x
1-56604-770-6, $49.99

Bryce 3D f/x
1-56604-855-9, $49.99

CORIOLIS
VENTANA
An International Thomson Publishing Company I T P

SATISFACTION SURVEY
We'd like to hear from you!

First Name: _____ Last Name: _____

Street Address: _____

City: _____ State: _____ Zip: _____

Email Address: _____

Daytime Telephone: (_____) _____

Book title: _____

Date product was purchased: Month _____ Day _____ Year _____ Your Occupation: _____

Overall, how would you rate this book?
- ❏ Excellent
- ❏ Very Good
- ❏ Good
- ❏ Fair
- ❏ Below Average
- ❏ Poor

What did you like MOST about this book?

What did you like LEAST about this book?

Did you use the CD-ROM? If so, how did you use it to prepare for the exam?

Are you planning to take, or have you taken, the certification exam?

Did you use this book in conjunction with an Exam Cram book?

Would you use another Exam Prep or Exam Cram book to prepare for a Certification Exam?

Is there any subject or program you would like to see an Exam Prep or Exam Cram book for?

What is your level of computer expertise?
- ❏ Beginner
- ❏ Intermediate
- ❏ Advanced

Please describe your computer hardware:
Computer _____
Hard disk _____
3.5" disk drives _____
Video card _____
Monitor _____
Printer _____
Peripherals _____
Sound Board _____
CD-ROM _____

Where did you buy this book?
- ❏ Bookstore (name): _____
- ❏ Discount Store (name): _____
- ❏ Computer Store (name): _____
- ❏ Catalog (name): _____
- ❏ Other _____

What price did you pay for this book?

What influenced your purchase of this book
- ❏ Recommendation
- ❏ Advertisement
- ❏ Magazine review
- ❏ Store Display
- ❏ Mailing
- ❏ Book's format
- ❏ Other _____

How many computer books do you buy each year?

Please send to:

Certification Insider Press   14455 N. Hayden Rd., Ste. 220, Scottsdale, AZ 85260

Certification Insider™ Press

To order any Certification Insider Press title, complete this order form and mail or fax it to us, with payment, for quick shipment.

TITLE	ISBN #	QTY	PRICE	TOTAL

Shipping

For orders shipping within the United States, please add $4.00 per book,

For 2-day air add $10.00 for the first book,

$2.50 for each additional book.

e-mail: order@coriolis.com

Note: AZ residents please add 7.15% sales tax.

Subtotal = $

Shipping = $

Tax   = $

Total   = $

Mail To: **The Coriolis Group** 14455 N. Hayden Road, Suite 220 Scottsdale, AZ 85260

Orders: **800/410-0192** or **602/483-0192**

Fax: **602/483-0193**

Name _____

Email_____ _____Daytime phone _____

Company _____

Address (No PO Box) _____

City_____State _____Zip _____

Payment enclosed _____ ❏ VISA ❏ MC Acc't # _____Exp Date _____

Signature_____Exact name on card _____

Check your local bookstore or software retailer for these and other bestselling titles, or call toll free:

800/410-0192

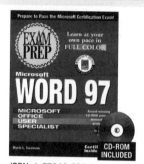

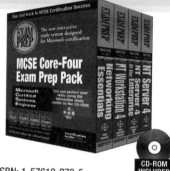

ABOUT THE CD-ROM

To become a Microsoft Certified Professional, you must pass rigorous certification exams that provide a valid and reliable measure of technical proficiency and expertise. The CD-ROM that comes with this book can be used in conjunction with the book to help you assess your progress in the event you choose to pursue Microsoft Professional Certification. The CD-ROM contains specially designed test simulation software that features two 58-question practice exams. The questions were expertly prepared to test your readiness for the official Microsoft certification examination on TCP/IP (Exam #70-059). The practice exam questions simulate the interface and format of the actual certification exams.

Practice Exam Features:

- ◆ 58 questions, just like the actual exam
- ◆ 90-minute timed test to ensure exam readiness
- ◆ Questions can be marked and answered later
- ◆ Graphical representation of your test grade

Solutions to End-of-Chapter Questions and Projects

For further help in making sure you are prepared for the TCP/IP certification exam, we have included solutions for the end-of-chapter Review Questions, Hands-on Projects, and Case Projects on the CD.